"The king of the Alley"

William Duer

Politician, Entrepreneur, and Speculator

1768–1799

"The king of the Alley"

William Duer

Politician, Entrepreneur, and Speculator

1768–1799

Robert F. Jones
Fordham University

American Philosophical Society
Independence Square   Philadelphia

Mᴇᴍᴏɪʀs ᴏꜰ ᴛʜᴇ
AMERICAN PHILOSOPHICAL SOCIETY
Held at Philadelphia
For Promoting Useful Knowledge
Volume 202

Copyright 1992 by the American Philosophical Society. Publication of this
work was subsidized in part by the Henry LaBarre Jayne Fund of the
American Philosophical Society.

Library of Congress Catalog Card Number: 92-70401
International Standard Book Number: 0-87169-202-3
ISSN: 0065-9738

Jacket illustration: A sketch of William Duer in the New York State Library,
Albany, map of New York State from collections in the Library of the
American Philosophical Society.

To the Memory of
Thomas T. McAvoy, C.S.C., 1903–1969
and
Marshall Smelser, 1912–1978
of the University of Notre Dame
Friends and Teachers

Abbreviations
Used for Manuscript Depositories

AAS	American Antiquarian Society, Worcester, Massachusetts
CHS	Connecticut Historical Society, Hartford, Connecticut
CUL	Columbia University Library, New York, New York
HSP	Historical Society of Pennsylvania, Philadelphia, Pennsylvania
LC	Library of Congress, Washington, DC
MHS	Massachusetts Historical Society, Boston, Massachusetts
NA	National Archives, Washington, DC
NYHS	New-York Historical Society, New York, New York
NYPL	New York Public Library, New York, New York
NYSL	New York State Library, Albany, New York
PCHS	Passaic County Historical Society, Paterson, New Jersey

PREFACE

William Duer belonged to the middle ranks of those who led America to success in her struggle for independence, standing just behind such men as John Jay and Robert R. Livingston. Both Jay and Livingston have had their biographers; few of those on Duer's level have. When it is remembered that the same generation of leaders fought the War for American Independence, helped to keep the United States together under the Articles of Confederation, and established a national government under the Constitution, it is obvious that a study of any important member of that generation will be helpful in understanding this most important period in American history. Duer, as a member of the New York State Convention and the Continental Congress, as Secretary to the Board of Treasury under the Confederation and Assistant to the Secretary of the Treasury when the federal government was organized, had a role in all the significant changes which occurred during the revolutionary period.

However, Duer's career in public service is not the only justification for studying him. Interspersed with his public career, and too often depending on it, was his career as a stock speculator, land promoter, army contractor, and merchant. For William Duer never tired of combining, or trying to combine, public office with private profit. While he was Secretary to the Board of Treasury, he floated the Scioto Land Company, one of the biggest speculations ever attempted in the United States. The origin of the company and its purchase of land from Congress depended on Duer's official position. While Assistant to the Secretary of the Treasury in 1789-90, Duer continuously and heavily speculated in government securities although the statute organizing the Treasury Department forbade such speculation. Even when he was not in office, he used his friends in office. When Robert Morris, Superintendent of Finance for the Continental Congress, began feeding the Army through contracts with private individuals, Duer received one of the first contracts and became one of the most frequent recipients of them. Morris and Duer had become friends and business associates while both were members of the Continental Congress. Other examples of Duer's mixing of business and public service will also be found. Although he was not alone in his use of public office for personal profit, there were few, if any, in his time who managed to feed for so long and in such quantities at the public trough.

Finally, Duer's career as an entrepreneur and stock speculator deserves study, if only for the size and variety of his financial projects. It is this area which has already received some scrutiny. Joseph S. Davis's essay, "William Duer, Entrepreneur, 1744 – 1799," examines Duer's financial career, but very little else. His life up to 1786 is covered in twelve pages by Davis and he ignores Duer's political activity in that year when he served in the New York State Assembly, as well as his later work during the ratification controversy over the federal constitution in New York. Also, Davis covers Duer only within the narrow scope of the "business" historian while I have taken a more inclusive view here. Within his self-imposed limits, Davis handled Duer in a masterly fashion and I am much indebted to him. All historians stand on the shoulders of those who have gone before them, and my task in writing this study would have been much more difficult without Davis's study; I gratefully acknowledge the assistance. However, I have chosen to cover Duer's career in all the various areas in which he worked because I think that its widest significance is in his blending of public and private life to his personal enrichment.

While this is the first full scale study of Duer's entire career, it is not intended, nor should it be taken, as a biography. Duer, the entrepreneur, Duer, the legislator, Duer, the speculator, can be described and perhaps even explained. But Duer, the man, cannot. The first obstacle to such a study is the lack of material. Although there are nine boxes and three volumes labeled "Duer Papers" in the collections of the New-York Historical Society, few of the letters and documents were written by Duer. He seems seldom to have kept copies of his correspondence; even if he had followed that practice, it may not have been of much value, as Duer commonly neglected to answer letters, even important letters.

Fortunately, he had several garrulous associates, among them William Constable, Andrew Craigie, and Walter Livingston, and from their papers, one can find out much about his operations and something about the man. Also, Duer was essentially a lone wolf. While he was almost always associated with others in his financial operations, it was usually because he lacked the capital to carry on the project by himself or he needed his partner's influence or office. Those of his letters which do survive are entirely conventional in their subject matter and expression and reveal little about the man.

Joseph Davis is not the only person I must gratefully acknowledge for assisting me during the preparation of this study. My first debt, one which I have tried to satisfy in the dedication of this work, is to Professor Marshall Smelser of the University of Notre Dame. He originally suggested the topic to me and then, when the opportunity to work on it presented itself, guided my original research and writing through to the completion of the doctoral dissertation which is the core of the study. My only regret is that he has not lived to see it finally published in book form. The debt is great and the means of satisfaction very small. Throughout the years the staff of the New-York Historical Society has been uniformly gracious and competent in assisting me and guiding me to material I might otherwise have overlooked. Arthur Breton, now at the Archives of American Art, and Thomas Dunnings have been especially helpful. The staff of Duane Library, Fordham University, were patient and efficient in securing rare materials and inter-library loans for me; Joseph LoSchiavo was especially helpful in obtaining loans quickly. The staffs of the following libraries also gave practical demonstrations of why the word "service" figures prominently in the job descriptions of librarians and archivists: the Manuscript and Rare Book Divisions of the New York Public Library, Special Collections at Columbia University Library, the Manuscript Division of the New York State Library, Albany, Massachusetts Historical Society, the National Archives, the Manuscript Division of the Library of Congress, Connecticut Historical Society, the Pennsylvania Historical Society, the William L. Clements Library, and the American Antiquarian Society. By a pleasant coincidence (and a timely relocation), William Joyce was very helpful to me at the last two libraries named. I must also acknowledge with gratitude the assistance of Fordham University in providing me with the free time indispensable to research and writing. It is especially gratifying that this study is being published by the American Philosophical Society, for that ancient and worthy institution twice aided me with research travel grants during its preparation. As a small token of my gratitude, I went to the writings of the Society's (and the United States') third president for the title for this book; it was Thomas Jefferson who styled Duer as "the king of the Alley" in writing to Thomas Mann Randolph, March 16, 1792 (*Writings*, Ford ed., V, 455). One seldom errs in taking a cue (or a title) from Mr. Jefferson. Finally, my lovely and serene wife, Rita, and our children have been with me throughout the research and writing of this book; their presence has always been much more of an encouragement than a distraction and I thank them for their love and support.

Robert F. Jones

TABLE OF CONTENTS

Chapter I

Early Career, 1768-1776

It has become a penetrating glimpse of the obvious to say that most of those who emigrated to Britain's North American colonies came "to do better." Without doubting the sincerity of the various individuals and groups with more idealistic goals, it is nevertheless true that the desire to move ahead in one's chosen field, to own land, to be free of obligations to others, figured prominently in the motives of those moving to the colonies. As the colonial economy developed in the eighteenth century, it became more and more attractive to the ambitious young men of Britain, especially those fortunate enough to come over with either capital or access to capital. William Duer is certainly one of those who came "to do better." Throughout his career, he seldom hesitated when confronted with a choice between his own fortune and the selfless performance of whatever public duty he was charged with at the time; indeed, he became quite adept at turning the public posts he filled—and he filled many—to his own profit. It is not my intention to present Duer as typical of the generation who carried on the American Revolution, but rather to use his career as a demonstration of the way in which the Revolution and its accompanying War for Independence presented opportunities for self-advancement and self-enrichment to those enterprising enough to see them and not too scrupulous in taking advantage of them.

Duer came from the squirearchy of eighteenth-century England, from a family which had already emigrated once before. During the Civil Wars of the seventeenth century, they had fled to the West Indies to escape the anger of the Lord Protector. By the early eighteenth century, they had returned to Devonshire where William was born on 18 March 1743. John, his father, retained estates on Antigua and Dominica. William was graduated from Eton and received an appointment as an aide-de-camp to Lord Clive whom he accompanied to India when the latter was appointed Governor-General of the East India Company. His stay cut short by illness, he returned to Britain to learn that his father had died. He and his brother, John, received the property on Dominica and money. As soon as he recovered from his illness, William went to Dominica.[1] In 1768, he came to New York to contract for a supply of lumber for his own and, possibly, other plantations in the Islands. While there, he was introduced to Philip Schuyler, who had extensive lands on the Hudson River above Albany; probably acting on Schuyler's advice, Duer decided to stay in the colony and purchased land at Fort Miller, thirty-five miles above Albany in an area only then being opened for settlement.[2]

New York's social and political structure closely resembled that of Great Britain; it possessed a landed aristocracy of considerable importance in the colony's political life, a rigidly stratified—for America—set of class lines, and an Anglican Church established in the most populous counties. The provincial capital, New York City, clustered on the lower tip of Manhattan Island, was still surpassed in population and importance by Philadelphia and Boston, but signs of its future dominance were already burgeoning. It enjoyed a thriving trade with the British sugar islands, sending lumber and provisions and receiving molasses, the raw material for the most popular liquor of the time, rum. Twenty-one thousand of the colony's 168,000 people lived in the capital with the next largest town, Albany, having only 3,000 inhabitants. Albany was also the county seat for a county of the same name, taking in all of the colony north and west of its site; the county's population was 35,000 and it was presently to be divided.

New York's affairs were directed by a royal governor—since 1770, Sir William Tryon, late of North Carolina—and an elected assembly. Prominently represented in the assembly was the colony's ruling class, a small group of closely related families enjoying the possession of large tracts of land which they either rented to tenants or held for future development. One of these, the Rensselaer manor, was originally granted by the Dutch when they had held the colony; the others had been granted by the British. Three of the manors were large enough to send representatives to the assembly in their own name, the Rensselaer mentioned above and the Cortlandt and Livingston manors. Those farmers who held long-term leases (usually defined in terms of a number of lives) were considered to be freeholders and, if their farms were large enough, were admitted to the suffrage; the political conduct of these tenants has long been debated by historians. Most recent writers believe they acted generally like freeholders and certainly did not constitute a captive vote for the large landowners to wield. Their presence is another complicating factor in assessing the life of one of the most politically active colonies in British North America. Although New York's landholding families intermarried among each other and produced a bewildering network of cousins and in-laws, these relationships counted for little in the politics of the colony which instead turned about an array of rivalries concerning land, trade, office, and other matters. The two major parties or groupings in New York politics can be described in a variety of dichotomies, the most inclusive of which would be popular Whigs and moderate Whigs. When he allied himself with Schuyler, Duer in effect was joining the moderate group. But the work involved in developing his lands apparently kept him from mixing heavily in provincial politics until the acceleration in the quarrel between Britain and the colonies which came as a result of the passage of the Intolerable Acts and the meeting of the First Continental Congress in 1774.[3]

Soon after buying his land at Fort Miller, Duer borrowed £1400 from his sister, Henrietta Duer Rose, secured by a mortgage on "lands in America," a debt still outstanding when Duer died in 1799. Some of this went to construct a house at Fort Miller which, from its description, was more suited to life in Devonshire than in the near wilderness in which it was located; its owner obviously did not intend to lead a spartan existence. A saw mill, warehouses, and a store were also built. Schuyler may have advised Duer as to the construction of these buildings and he was also lending him money at this time. The practical benefits of Duer's relationship with the influential landowner did not end at advice and loans; in connecting himself with Schuyler, Duer had gained the friendship of the most influential figure in New York's northern reaches and a major figure in the colony's politics. While this would be more important in the future than it was in the early 1770s, even then it had its benefits. In 1772 a man named O'Hara talked of setting up a store at Fort Miller; all Duer's sometime partner, Robert Snell, had to do to deal with the threatened competition was to let O'Hara know that the existing store and a proposed one at Saratoga were "supported by Two of the Principal Gentlemen of the County. [H]e immediately apprehended" that it was Duer and Schuyler and, if that was the case, "he would not stay there in opposition to Coll. Schuyler." Duer was advised to get Schuyler to support the story if O'Hara inquired, but Snell's bluff was never called.[4]

For the next few years, while brother John looked after the Dominica plantation, Duer built up his mercantile business, operating through the Canadian firm of Phynn, Ellice and Company. In 1771-72, he proposed to Alexander Ellice that they join in a contract to supply the British Army posts in the Great Lakes area. Phynn, Ellice had done well supplying the army during the French and Indian War, and Duer was understandably interested in a contract with the largest consumer of the time, the government. Besides his desire to earn a profit, the offer also shows that he felt himself to be in a relatively strong economic position, considering the high start-up costs of an army supply contract. Despite a trip to London, the effort failed. He also sent the lumber he had originally come for down to Antigua and Dominica, receiving island produce in return. In addition to attempts at large-scale efforts such as the army contract and inter-colonial trade, Duer's store supplied the daily needs of the area settlers, down to two and one-half yards of calico or a pen knife or two "pair flannel trowsers & whip thong." While he may have felt himself strong enough to risk supplying army posts, he was not going to pass up the smaller profits found in such homely transactions.[5]

It was not all business, however. In 1771 Duer poured out the sad story of his unrequited love for an unnamed young lady to Robert R. Livingston. Livingston was the eldest son of a judge of the province and the head of the Clermont branch of an especially numerous and wealthy family which controlled thousands of acres on both banks of the Hudson below Albany. Their land was farmed by slaves, hired hands, and tenants. In the tangled politics of the Provincial Assembly, they helped to represent the landowning interests and usually allied themselves with landowners further upstream such as Schuyler. The familiar tone of the letter shows how easily the young Englishman was fitting into the upper reaches of provincial society, even if "the Dear

Cause of my Sufferings" did not appreciate it. This should not be surprising as the move from Antigua to Fort Miller had been essentially a horizontal one, for Duer had come to New York blessed with capital and position.[6] Having entered easily into the provincial aristocracy, Duer started to take up some of the civil duties expected of persons in his position. In 1772 he became a member of the road commission of Charlotte County, a new county formed from the northern and eastern reaches of Albany County, and named for King George III's consort. The road commission was the first governmental body formed for the new county.[7]

The appointment may have been made *in absentia*, for Duer was in Britain for at least part of 1772; he made the trip to lobby for the previously mentioned army contract as well as a lumber contract with the Royal Navy. His New York lands were producing more lumber than could be sent to the Islands, and he probably needed additional income. Robert Snell, his partner at the Fort Miller store, reported that the refusal of several of Duer's notes had made him unable to pay some pressing obligations. The amount, £60, seems small to have created such a situation, however, and perhaps Snell himself was to blame. He was reported to be allowing workmen who were hired to build a new store house to spend their days drinking and playing cards, certainly more pleasant than working out of doors in winter weather, but not what they were being paid for. While Snell was failing to keep things under control at Fort Miller (the rumors proved all too true), Duer was also failing in London, both with the army contract and the effort to sell lumber to the Navy. What he had proposed shows either an excessive faith in the influence of his London associates or naivete on Duer's part, for he asked the Admiralty to establish four new yards to receive his masts and spars when they were receiving more than enough of each through the Surveyor General of the King's Woods in North America. Undaunted, Duer tried again two years later and succeeded in having the Admiralty receive a small cargo of plank to check their quality. Whatever the verdict, the fast-breaking crisis in British-American relations brought the second effort to an unsuccessful end.[8] By June 1773, he had returned to New York and discovered for himself how poor Snell's stewardship had been. He was appalled at the "negligence" of his affairs and had to ask the American Stephen Sayre, then heading a London banking house, to extend him a further credit of £100 so he could get free of someone he did not "trust," probably the negligent Snell. He promised Sayre a good bill before his became due, being ungraceful enough to comment that "I speak this with the good faith of an Englishman, not as an American."[9]

While bringing his private affairs into order, he took on another public duty. The courts of Charlotte County were being organized and as a large landowner, Duer was expected to serve. Also, because of the role the courts played in validating titles and other aspects of law dear to the interests of landowners, Duer would want to be involved. As expected, Philip Schuyler was named first judge with Duer and Oliver DeLancey, a representative of a large and well-endowed political family, following in order. The first court was held at Fort Edward on 19 October 1773 with Duer presiding because Schuyler was ill.[10] The position was no sinecure, especially in Charlotte County. For years the governors of New Hampshire and New York had been giving land grants in the border area between the two colonies, each claiming exclusive jurisdiction over the entire area. To add to this confusion, a third group of settlers had taken advantage of the situation and squatted. Ethan Allen, holder of a New Hampshire grant, once gave a Charlotte County justice of the peace, the Reverend Benjamin Hough, 200 lashes and threatened, according to the minister, to be even rougher with "damned Yorkers . . . and whip them within an Inch of their Lives" in the future. Another New Yorker reported Allen as following up on the threat by burning six houses, a mill, and some grain. The violence peaked just before 1776 and, as the records show, presented the county's judges with quite a bit of work.[11]

The origins of the conflict between Great Britain and her North American colonies are not easy to explain in the case of any one of the colonies, and they are especially complicated in the case of New York. Certainly, some of the more common issues were at work in the colony, for example, the annoyance of the New York City mercantile community at the attempts of Parliament to restrict more severely the trade of the colony, the anger of many more at the refusal of the Privy Council to allow a bill emitting paper money. But New York politics were also riven by a number of internal divisions: upper Hudson v. the seaboard counties, landed v. the mercantile interest, Anglican v. the dissenting churches. In the early 1770s, the contest was more or less between popular and moderate Whigs, who agreed on the necessity of resisting Crown policy but disagreed on how far and by what means, with the old issues of provincial contention always just in back of this new issue.[12] Duer, whose surviving letters are empty of political content at this time, may fairly be placed with his friend and patron, Philip Schuyler, as a member of the upriver, landed, moderate Whigs whose resistance to Crown policy was tempered by the fears aroused by the popular group, centered in Manhattan and enjoying the support of the city mechanics as well as small farmers in the southern counties. Because of his residence in Charlotte, however, Duer may not have been too involved in the earliest stages of colonial resistance. Often the particular conflicts at this time turned about the organization and control of this or that extra-legal committee formed to protest the Crown's latest misdeed. Charlotte frequently did not participate. When provincial delegates to the First Continental Congress were chosen in 1774, Charlotte and other upriver counties did not send delegates to the meeting which named New York's delegation. The counties may have been indifferent to the congress or they may have been too loyalist, but by the time delegates for the Second Congress were chosen, Charlotte was aroused and sent several representatives to the selection meeting, Duer among them. However, he did not attend the April 1775 meeting in New York City, giving no reason.[13]

During this time, the Whigs were trying to reorganize the government of the colony so they would firmly control it. The legal provincial assembly was in a kind of limbo from which it would be recalled for a brief, ineffective session early in 1776. The Whigs hoped to control the province through the Provincial Congress, an extra-legal body chosen by the county committees formed to enforce the Continental Association of the First Continental Congress, or else by vaguely described meetings of the "principal freeholders" or "respectable characters" of a particular area. Four of these congresses were chosen from May 1775 to July 1776. No one of them was especially successful in carrying on the usual tasks of government, in addition to the unusual task of preparing for possible armed resistance to the British Army. At the time of the first Provincial Congress, few New Yorkers expected the quarrel with the Crown to end in an effort to estab-

lish American independence. By the time of the last Provincial
Congress, the overwhelming issue and the one which broke up
the meeting was whether or not to approve the Continental
Congress's resolution of independence. Each of the congresses
dealt with the difficult task of maintaining an adequate representation of New York's counties by using such expedients as
recognizing an individual as the deputy for several counties, but
nothing succeeded in keeping the quorum needed to operate as
an executive. When this problem first appeared, the delegates
used a device suggested by the Continental Congress, the Committee of Safety. First used from July 8th to the 25th, 1775, this
preserved the appearance of legality as its acts were subsequently
approved by the congress when it reconvened. It was especially
useful after active hostilities began, for it kept the direction of
New York's affairs in a small body instead of the unwieldy constitutional convention cum legislature established in June 1776.
But the absence of a quorum plagued even the small Committee
of Safety.[14]

While the congresses were preoccupied with the various and
difficult tasks presented by a colony moving half-heartedly and
hesitantly from resistance to independence, William Duer was
preoccupied with the single but also difficult task of keeping the
Charlotte County courts open. A party from the Hampshire
Grants had taken advantage of the uncertain status of government
to try and close the court; these "persons of desperate fortune
and bad character" had been dispersed only by the timely arrival
of a Captain Motte's militia unit. The Hampshire people had
objected to Duer's court ostensibly because it was held in the
name of the king, but the judge believed they were simply trying
to block writs of eviction sought by a New York title holder. He
was probably correct. Despite the obvious self-interest of the
Hampshire men, Duer feared much more than legal inconvenience to the New York claimant should the court be closed; as
many other moderate Whigs of his time, he thought that once
the courts went: "it will not be an easy matter to restore order
among a people of so turbulent a spirit. Our country will then
be reduced to a worse dilemma than any other. We shall not only
have to oppose the incursions of the enemy on the frontiers, but
shall be torn to pieces with injustice, anarchy and confusion."
Duer thus disclosed the fear of many like himself, conservative

socially and politically, but ready to be quite radical in resisting Crown policy, that the people would not be content simply to follow their lead, but would instead try and carry the resistance through to other matters. For the moment, Duer believed the difficulty could be handled by a clear statement from the Provincial Congress on the necessity of keeping the courts open. Before the congress could reply to his request, events took over and his court ceased operation as a royal court on 20 June 1775.[15]

The unruly Hampshire men were not the only problem Duer saw as confronting the Whig cause in Charlotte County; someone was trying to deprive it of his services. He complained to the President of the Provincial Congress, Peter Livingston, that anonymous characters were spreading doubts about his attachment to the liberties of America. Feeling the "warmth of an innocent, injured man," he asked for an immediate, private hearing before a committee of the congress. Whatever the allegations were, Duer obviously took them seriously as he traveled to New York City to lay his case before the congress. That body also took him seriously and quickly examined his complaint, deciding that the charges were baseless and that he merited the "public countenance and protection of this congress."[16] The substance of the charges was not noted. What is interesting about the episode is Duer's obvious anxiety about his status with the Whigs. No one can argue that he had committed himself to independence at this point—June 1775—but he had certainly aided and abetted as strong a resistance to British policy as possible. Located where he was, it would probably not have been difficult to lay low and avoid conspicuous activity on either side of the issue. Since Duer did not leave behind very much by way of personal record, it is difficult to say exactly what persuaded him to adhere to the American cause. His American land holdings, mercantile and lumbering interests did not make him a patriot, for many in similar circumstances chose to remain loyal to the king and sacrificed their property. His English birth and education, his family's plantations in the West Indies, and his recent arrival in America fit the pattern of a typical American Loyalist, so much as any group so diverse could be said to have a type. Perhaps the most important influence pushing William Duer toward attachment to the American cause—if he had to be pushed—was the example of the important men in his section of New York. Philip Schuyler, the Livingstons, James Duane, and others went to the American side. From the time he had first bought land at Fort Miller, Duer had conformed to the manner and ideals of the society in which he had placed himself. During the rest of his career, he would conform to the society around him, differing only in the audacity with which he was willing to push his later financial projects. It would not be surprising if this attachment to the patriotic cause of American liberty was one of the first examples of that conformity.

The closing of his court, coincidental with the first stages of the War for Independence, did not mean that Duer had nothing to do in Charlotte County. In June 1775, Benedict Arnold brought some men serving under him to Fort Ticonderoga at the lower end of Lake Champlain. There he received orders from the Massachusetts Congress, which had commissioned him, to give way to a Connecticut colonel, Benjamin Hinman. Annoyed that neither his expenses nor pay for his men had yet been settled by Massachusetts, Arnold refused and threatened to return several captured lake craft back to the British.[17] The threats were taken seriously by the Massachusetts agents sent with the orders and they were accordingly grateful for the "influence and well-timed exertions of Judge Duer" in preventing "fatal consequences" coming from a "dangerous meeting set on foot" by some of Arnold's men "who appeared to have their own interest more at heart than the public good." After being promised pay for his men, Arnold left and the crisis, if it was a crisis, was over. The Massachusetts group's leader, Walter Spooner, valued Duer's efforts so much he wrote the Provincial Congress, reporting the incident and praising Duer's "zealous efforts for the public good."[18] The affair did not end there for Duer. When he heard in July of the possible appointment of Arnold as Adjutant-General of the New York militia, he complained as pointedly as possible to the new Major-General of militia, Philip Schuyler, that his experience with Arnold led him to predict that Arnold's "Unaccountable Pride" could lead him "to sacrifice the True Interest of the Country." More immediate but less prophetic was Duer's assertion that the nomination was a "tacit Reproach of my Conduct, who [exerted] myself to the utmost in defeating his Designs." Schuyler had been considering Arnold but, probably owing in part to Duer's comments, he was not appointed.[19]

Then the tables turned, at least partially. The Provincial Congress nominated Duer to be Deputy Adjutant General with the rank of colonel and notified John Hancock, President of the Continental Congress, of their choice, stressing that it did not mean they disapproved the province delegation's nomination of Lewis Morris. But this did not sit well with the delegation and Gouverneur Morris complained from Philadelphia that Duer had no military experience and that "He is volatile. He is communicative, unstable." Morris could have saved himself the bother for Duer declined the commission. He had already pointed out to Schuyler the "peculiar Delicacy of my Situation" and assured him that if he could take the commission without losing "the Character of an Honest Man," he would do so. As in the previous episode, when his loyalty had been questioned, Duer felt the matter serious enough to warrant a trip to New York City in mid-August to lay his case directly before the congress. As before, the details of his problem do not survive, but there is a mention of risking the property of his brother in Dominica; perhaps he feared that acceptance of a militia commission might mean the seizure of the jointly-owned Dominica plantation. A congress committee considered the case privately and concluded on 23 August that Duer should be allowed to decline the appointment, but that he should be given a copy of the report "as a testimony that his so declining proceeds not from any motive unfriendly to this country, but from a necessity that results from the particular state of his affairs." The congress accepted the report and nominated one of the ubiquitous Livingstons, Robert G., Jr., instead. Although he never accepted the commission, this episode was apparently the justification for the title "colonel" awarded him by many of his friends and business associates in later life.[20]

The winter of 1775-76 passed quietly in America. The only royal force of any size in the insurgent colonies was besieged in Boston by a combination of short-term enlisted men and militia under the official command of George Washington. Although the thirteen colonies, acting as the Continental Congress, sponsored the army around Boston and sent an abortive expedition against the British forces in Canada, they had not formally declared their independence of Great Britain and their exact status was armed resistance to British encroachments on American rights. Many colonists had not yet chosen one side or another and, if they were lucky—and many were—they would not have to choose. But William Duer had obviously, albeit unofficially, chosen the locally identified side of the angels, of the patriots bent on upholding their conception of the scope and content of American liberty. The quiet which New York enjoyed then preceded one of the most trying times any colony faced during the struggle for American independence. New York's central position between the New England colonies and the South, plus the exposed condition of its capital and principal sea port, made it a prime target for the British once they moved out of New England. But without the goad of a direct and immediate threat and distracted by the presence of many potential loyalists, the Whig party in the Provincial Congress could do little to prepare the colony for defense. The winter passed with a good bit of political maneuvering when the congress was in session and ineffective letter writing by its Committee of Public Safety when it was not. But throughout the first four months of 1776, the moderate Whigs moved closer to the radicals on the question of independence and increasingly the question came to turn about "when" and not "whether."

Duer spent the winter at Fort Miller, tending to his own affairs and doing several errands for Schuyler, now in command of the forces defending New York's northern frontier against an invasion from Canada. One of the most delicate tasks he was given by Schuyler concerned Sir John Johnson, son of Sir William Johnson, the "Mohawk Baronet," and heir to both his father's lands and influence with the Iroquois tribes of the New York frontier. Sir John had recently settled a large number of Scottish Highlanders on his lands. Schuyler had good reason to suspect that they would be more loyal to Johnson than to the American cause; organized under the direction of their clan chiefs, they could also be much more effective than the usual run of tenant farmers. The general had tried to get Sir John's permission to send militia onto his lands, but finally had to send him an ultimatum in January 1776. Schuyler asked Duer to deliver the letter, waiting two days for any reply the landlord might want to make. On this occasion, force was not needed. Sir John gave his word neither to leave his lands nor to engage in anything harmful to the American cause. Schuyler's discretion was not foolish; when the Highlanders surrendered their weapons according to the terms of Sir John's parole, more than six hundred muskets and nine cannon were collected. The Highlanders were probably less of a worry to Schuyler than Johnson's influence with the Indians; as he explained to the congress: "Sir John, to oblige our friend [*sic*] Indians was released on his bond and hostages." However, Schuyler (and Duer) were not finished with Johnson, or rather Johnson was not finished with them.[21]

The confused position the colonists occupied at this time was neatly illustrated when Duer requested a speedy payment from Schuyler for some plank he had sold the army, explaining "I should not be so urgent were I not under a Necessity of making up a sum of Money to remit to Canada." Six months later when the gage of formal war had been finally thrown down to the British, this would be treason to the American cause, but in February 1776, after almost a year of undeclared war between the colonies and the Crown, it was but one more example of the halfway house the Americans occupied.[22]

Until May 1776, Duer's residence in that house was unofficial. He had not attended the meeting choosing New York's delegates to the Second Continental Congress, nor had he accepted the military commission offered the summer before. But he now protested strongly to the Provincial Congress that, although he had been selected to represent Charlotte County at the previous month's elections, the county committee had excluded him from the delegation. Others had asked him to accept election so that he could save the county from the "anarchy and oppression" which threatened it, but now men who were "strangers to integrity and the true Principles of Civil liberty" were opposing him. Conscious of his "zealous attachment to the Grand Cause," he asked the congress to seat no one from Charlotte until he arrived to prove the truth of his contentions. Before Duer could get to New York City, however, he was again conscripted by Schuyler to treat with Sir John Johnson.[23]

Rumors had come to Schuyler that not all the weapons at Johnson Hall had been handed over and that Sir John was planning mischief with his Scots and some Mohawks. Duer was first sent to the Albany Committee, acting as a kind of regional government with information against Johnson. If they approved, he was to take Colonel Elias Dayton and his New Jersey militia to arrest Sir John and the Scots. But before Duer and Dayton could reach Johnson Hall, Sir John and his Highlanders had fled to Canada. Duer stayed there taking depositions, arranging a parole for Lady Johnson, and the like until early June, despite his professed desire to leave for New York City. By then, he was suffering from an "Indisposition of body" which kept him at the Hall some time further.[24]

When Duer recovered, the third Provincial Congress of which he had wanted so much to be a member, was ending. When it had been elected in April 1776, a decision on independence was clearly in the offing. Since the beginning of the year, when it was learned that Parliament had prohibited trade with the colonies, Congress had been cutting the ties between them and the mother country, ordering all loyalists—defined as those who refused to accept the Continental Association—disarmed (14 March), issuing letters of marque and reprisal against British shipping (25 March), opening American ports to foreign shipping (early April), and advising the colonists to devise new forms of government based on the will of the people (10 and 15 May). These events naturally affected the third Congress and in the elections by which it was chosen, the question of when independence was to be declared was frequently debated. But the leaders of the Whig majority, in their half-hearted desire to avoid the final break, succeeded temporarily in pushing that question back and instead focused on whether or not a new frame of government should now be drafted to replace the defunct colonial charter and its successor, the ad-hoc congresses and committees. The congress also debated whether or not it had the power to draft such a frame of government. But the Whigs were not convinced that they had the people behind them and James Duane, viewing the April elections from Philadelphia where he represented the colony in the Continental Congress, captured their mood perfectly, when he advised delay until the people's opinion was crystal clear; they must be followed, not driven.[25] This advice so obviously suited the congress's mood that, whether it was generally known to them or not, it was followed. They resolved that the former colonial government had ceased to exist and that a new government should be formed to exclude "all foreign and external power," but they then went on to doubt they had the power to form such a government. Accordingly, they called for yet another set of elections in early June; in these, the voters would be asked either to confirm their present representatives or choose new ones, giving them the power to form a new government "suited to the present critical emergency." This was as close to a referendum on independence as the people of New York would ever have, nor would it be dealt with any more forthrightly by their new representatives. The third Congress adjourned on 30 June; despite a resolve to meet again three days later, it never reconvened.[26]

Just as Britain's former colonies in North America found themselves at a watershed in July 1776, so also did William Duer. For the people of the colonies, the decision to cut themselves off from the Crown, to strike out on an independent course marked a decision from which there could be no turning back without being subjected to colonial regulations far more severe than those which they were then protesting, and that was the least that could happen. For Duer, the step was just as momentous. Using his status as a West Indian landowner and English gentleman, he had moved easily into the upper levels of New York society, into the group which held most of the colony's wealth and political power. Until now, Duer had, relatively speaking, stayed in the background. But, as his protest regarding his presumed election to the third Congress shows, he now wanted to push himself into the forefront. He was sufficiently known to the leaders of the conservative bloc of the patriotic party, the moderate Whigs, to be considered reliable by them and to be tapped for service when the new Provincial Congress met. His service there, in many diverse assignments, would further demonstrate his loyalty, energy, and ability to New York's leaders and result in his selection as a member of the state's delegation to the Continental Congress.

References

1. "Colonel William Duer," *The Knickerbocker Magazine*, 40, no. 2 (August 1852): 95-96.
2. Ibid., 96; Don R. Gerlach, *Philip Schuyler and the American Revolution* (Lincoln, NE, 1964), 54-56, hereafter cited as Gerlach, *Schuyler*; Certificate of Sale, Wm. & Catherine Bayard to Wm. Duer, July 24, 1768, NYSL, 10828 (5); by this, 1300 acres on the east bank of the Hudson River were exchanged for £2455 (lawful money).
3. Patricia U. Bonomi, *A Factious People: Politics and Society in Colonial New York* (New York, 1971), Chaps. VI, VII, hereafter cited as Bonomi, *Factious People*; Gerlach, *Schuyler*, App. C, "Outline of New York Real Property Law and Electoral Rights."
4. Wm. Duer to Henrietta Duer, Feb. 14, 1769, William Duer Papers, NYHS, hereafter

cited as Duer Papers; William H. Hill, *History of Washington County, New York* (Fort Edward, 1932), 187; Gerlach, *Schuyler*, 54-55; R. Snell to Wm. Duer, Jan. 26, 1772, Duer Papers, NYHS.

5. Accounts with Phynn, Ellice and Company, Thomas Shipley and Company, Duer Papers, NYHS; R. H. Fleming, "Phynn, Ellice and Company," *Toronto University Contributions to Canadian Economics*, 4 (1932): 20-21; "Account from Duer's Store, November 1775," John Williams Papers, vol. I, 59a (HY 12382), NYSL.

6. Wm. Duer to Robert R. Livingston, Oct. 11, 1771, Gratz Coll., HSP; for the Livingstons' place within the colony, see George Dangerfield, *Chancellor Robert R. Livingston* (New York, 1960), Part I, *passim*.

7. *Calendar of Land Papers* (Albany, 1864), 554; *History of Washington County* (Phila., 1878), 38; with the outbreak of the War for Independence, the county was renamed after the American commander-in-chief.

8. R. Snell to Wm. Duer, Oct. 28, 1772, Patt. Smyth to Wm. Duer, Dec. 1, 1772; Duer's connection with Snell was dissolved at Duer's initiative at the end of the year, see Wm. Duer to R. Snell, Dec. 1, 1773, R. Snell to Wm. Duer, Dec. 8, 1773 and the Snell folder, also Letter Book and Timber Contracts, Duer Papers, NYHS; see also Navy Board to Admiralty, Oct. 30, 1772, ADM/B/l87, National Maritime Museum, Greenwich, London, England.

9. Wm. Duer to Stephen Sayre, Jun. 24, 1773, Duer Papers, NYHS; the balance was apparently not paid, despite Duer's English good faith; see Ralph Izard to Wm. Duer, Oct. 8, 1777, Anne I. Deas, ed., *Correspondence of Mr. Ralph Izard* (New York, 1844), 356-59.

10. Gerlach, *Schuyler*, 229-30; Edgar A. Werner, *Civil List and Constitutional History of the State of New York* (Albany, 1888), 387; Duer succeeded Schuyler when the latter resigned in 1777, but he never presided as first judge because of his own service in the Continental Congress, 392; Hill, *Washington County*, 178; see "Washington [Charlotte] Co., Records of the Court of Common Pleas," 3763, vol. I, NYSL for the record of Duer's judicial activity.

11. "Deposition of the Reverend Benjamin Hough . . .," in E. B. O'Callaghan, ed., *The Documentary History of the State of New York* (Albany, 1851), IV, 527-28; see Dixon Ryan Fox, *Yankees and Yorkers* (New York, 1940), for a reasonably complete history of the boundary controversy.

12. Bonomi, *Factious People*, Chaps. VII, VIII.

13. Bernard Mason, *The Road to Independence: The Revolutionary Movement in New York, 1773-1777* (Lexington, KY, 1966), Chap. 1, hereafter cited as Mason, *Road to Independence*; Thomas Jones, *History of New York During the Revolutionary War*, ed. E. F. DeLancey (New York, 1879), I, 39; Peter Force, comp., *American Archives* (Washington, 1839), 4 s., II, 351-58, hereafter cited as *Am. Arch.*

14. Mason, *Road to Independence*, Chap. 6.

15. Wm. Duer to Peter VanBrugh Livingston, Jun. 5, 1775, *Journals of the Provincial Congress* (Albany, 1842), II, 29, hereafter cited as *Journals*; see also the report of the Charlotte County Committee of Public Safety to Peter VanBrugh Livingston, Jun. 28, 1775 in *Am. Arch.*, 4 s., II, 1124-25; the Provincial Congress's Committee of Safety congratulated Duer for keeping his court open, Henry Williams to Wm. Duer, Jul. 11, 1775, *Journals*, II, 71-72.

16. Wm. Duer to Peter VanBrugh Livingston, Jun. 14, 1775, ibid.., 42, see also 43, 44.

17. James T. Flexner, *The Benedict Arnold Case* (New York, 1962) thinks it was only an empty threat.

18. Walter Spooner to president and members of the congress of the Colony of New York, Jul. 3, 1775, *Journals*, I, 76-77; see also Edward Mott to Gov. Jonathan Trumbull, Connecticut, Jul. 6, 1775, *Am. Arch.*, 4 s., VI, 1592-93.

19. Wm. Duer to Philip Schuyler, Jul. 19, 1775, Silas Deane to Philip Schuyler, Aug. 20, 1775, Philip Schuyler Papers, NYPL, thereafter cited as Schuyler Papers.

20. *Journals*, I, 91; Gouverneur Morris to Robert R. Livingston, Jun. 2, 1775, Robert R. Livingston Papers, Ac. 1931, LC; Wm. Duer to Philip Schuyler, Aug. 11, 1775,

Schuyler Papers, NYPL; Wm. Duer to Peter VanBrugh Livingston, Aug. 15, 1775, *Journals*, II, 37-38; ibid.., I, 117; see also Ms. # 21321, RG 93, War Dept. Coll., NA, a return of arms received at Springfield, Mass., Aug. 2, 1777, originally issued to "Coll. Duer, Militia"; no extant list of Charlotte County militia has Duer's name on it.

21. Philip Schuyler to Sir John Johnson, Jan. 18, 1776, Schuyler Papers, NYPL; *The New York Journal*, Feb. 6, 1776, see the issues of Feb. 15, 22, 29 for Schuyler's reports on his dealings with Johnson; Philip VanCortlandt had a sarcastic view of the expedition, see Philip VanCortlandt Memorandum Book, [Jan. 16, 1776], Historic Hudson Valley, Tarrytown, NY.

22. Wm. Duer to Philip Schuyler, Feb. 1, 1776, Schuyler Papers, NYPL.

23. *Calendar of Historical Manuscripts in Albany, Revolutionary War* (Albany, 1868), I, 305-06, hereafter cited as *Calendar*; *Journals*, I, 453; Wm. Duer to John Williams, May 2, 1776, John Williams Papers, vol. I, 63b (HY 12382), NYSL; see also "rough draft of minutes of Charlotte Co. Committee, [prior to Jun. 27, 1776]." Loc. cit., vol. I, 65a, for evidence of Duer's activity on the local scene.

24. Philip Schuyler to the Committee of Albany, to General [John] Sullivan, to Volkert P. Douw, May 14, 1776, Schuyler Papers, NYPL; Philip Schuyler to Col. Elias Dayton, May 14, 1776, *Am. Arch.*, 4 s., VI, 447-48; Wm. Duer to Philip Schuyler, May 22, 1776, Elias Dayton to Philip Schuyler, Jun. 4, 1776, Schuyler Papers, NYPL.

25. Mason, *Road to Independence*, Chap. 5, espec. 167, 177; James Duane to John Jay, May 18, 1776, John Jay Papers, CUL.

26. Alexander C. Flick, "The Provincial Congresses and the Declaration of Independence," 267-68, in Alexander C. Flick, ed., *History of the State of New York* (New York, 1933), III; hereafter cited as Flick, *History*.

Chapter II

The New York State Convention

July 1776–April 1777

As the Third Provincial Congress was coming to an end, the Continental Congress in Philadelphia, after its own vacillating, was confronting squarely the question of independence. On 2 July, every state except New York approved the resolution of independence submitted a month earlier by Richard Henry Lee of Virginia. Lacking the authority to vote for independence, New York's delegates could only sit impotently while their colleagues moved on. Thus, by the time the Fourth Congress met, the most important issue confronting the Americans had been settled and New York's role reduced to one of *ex post facto* consent or protest. Recognizing what the next Provincial Congress would have to do, New York conservatives made certain it would be filled with congenial spirits, or, at least, did all they could to make certain. As the elections were being held, Schuyler informed some Charlotte County notables of his faith in Duer's attachment to the American cause—apparently some still believed he might be a loyalist—and asked that his statement be made public, "that the Justice I have done him may become equally public." The general reminded his audience of the difficult work confronting this congress and the necessity of choosing "the most sensible men" available. It was a mark of how much Duer had been accepted by the conservative group that he was thought reliable and effective enough to be pushed for the congress. Schuyler's politicking succeeded, and Duer was chosen for the congress where one of his first assignments would be to the committee charged with drafting New York's state constitution.[1]

The spring of 1776 saw the war move to New York. The

British had ended their occupation of Boston in March, removing
their troops to Halifax, Nova Scotia. From there and other points,
a British military and naval force converged on New York where
troops were landed on an undefended Staten Island on 2 July.
By early August, General Sir William Howe had gathered a force
of 34,000 soldiers, supported by a large fleet of war vessels and
auxiliaries. Washington had anticipated the enemy move and
gathered a force of about 20,000 to defend the city. Unfortunately for the patriots, Howe clearly had the advantage, not only
in numbers and equipment, but also in the setting of the encounter; defending a city located on an island surrounded by navigable
waters against an enemy with unchallengeable naval superiority
was just about hopeless. However, the Continental Congress had
ordered Washington to defend the city and, despite the difficulty
of the task, it is hard to disagree with their mandate. The psychological implications of abandoning the city without a fight
could have been disastrous to the fragile patriot cause.

On 15 July, Duer took his seat in the Convention of the State
of New York, the title the Provincial Congress had taken after
its retrospective ratification of the Continental Congress's resolution of independence. He was immediately appointed to a committee and, on the next day, made his first motion, that the
Hudson River be obstructed so that British ships could not use
it. The motion was adopted and a committee appointed to implement it; although Duer was not on it, he seems to have acted as
a kind of gadfly to it as well as a liaison for it with General
Washington. He also brought himself to Washington's attention
in other ways.[2] Having taken a message to Washington's headquarters in Manhattan, immediately on his return to White Plains
in central Westchester County where the Convention was sitting,
he got in touch with Robert R. Livingston and John Jay, both
of the Committee on Obstructing the Hudson and told them of
the general's anxiety that the channel be blocked, arguing, with
a penetrating glimpse of the obvious, that if it was accomplished,"the Designs of the Enemy in this Campaign are effec-
tually baffled, if we fail we cannot be in a more lamentable situation than we are." He urged that at least one of them go to
headquarters to correct the "Languor and Procrastination" he
saw there. As if this was not enough, they were also to talk with
an incendiary, Mr. Hazlewood of the Pennsylvania Committee

of Safety; he was "peculiarly clever—the Fireships charged in his Manner must I am confident prove destructive to any vessel they fix upon."[3] Duer was correct, of course, in urging extraordinary urgency and activity for, as events showed, the American situation was indeed critical, but he was also showing a tendency to suggest a good many more projects than he, or anyone else, had the time to carry through properly. Administration would never be one of his strong points, nor prudence one of his more notable qualities.

Thus, within two weeks, Duer had become an active member of the Convention, on tap for committee assignments, conspicuously eager to work. The times were so out of joint that it is not surprising that the usual custom of a freshman legislator staying decently out of sight did not apply, especially if the new man had talent and energy. And Duer had shown himself to have both. He also had the advantage of being a member of the conservatives who were able to control much of the Convention's proceedings, thus pushing their own people forward.

Moving back to Manhattan Island, the Convention began work on the constitution on 1 August at Harlem, then a small village about ten miles north of the city. The usual step would be to appoint a committee to bring in a preliminary draft, but the conservative-radical split in the Convention, brought on by the entry of popular political figures during the Revolutionary Era disturbances, immediately surfaced. A radical member moved to bring in a draft bill of rights before any constitution, arguing that such a bill was the foundation for truly free government. Duer played the role of conciliator in the debate that followed and moved that drafts of both a constitution and a bill of rights be brought in simultaneously by the same committee; his motion passed by a large majority. The Convention then appointed a thirteen man committee, including John Jay, Robert R. Livingston, Gouverneur Morris and Duer. Despite the obvious urgency of their task, the committee would not report out a draft until March 1777, with the constitution going into operation the following month. The delay is partially explained by the military operations of August—October 1776 which saw the fall of Manhattan to the British and the eventual evacuation of Continental forces from the entire lower Hudson Valley. But the conservatives may also have obstructed the work of drafting because they feared that radicals might stampede the Convention. Just as important as defending New York against the British was the effort to keep New York's affairs under the direction of its pre-war leaders; those who had run the colony now expected to run the state.[4]

The Convention thus not only had to form a constitution but also to carry on the ordinary and extraordinary tasks of government in the midst—literally—of a war. It fell to them to marshal the limited resources of New York to aid Washington to whatever extent possible. Although Duer was not on any of the committees directly involved in the war effort at this time, he may have either taken or been given informal charge of the attempt to obstruct the Hudson. On 12 August, he was marked as "on duty" and absent from the Convention and when the obstruction committee sent two sloops down to assist in the task, they were to be delivered to Duer. One week later, the Committee of Safety ordered Duer to cooperate directly with Washington in the task. Before he could act on the order, the Continental forces lost the Battle of Long Island and Washington evacuated all his troops to Manhattan Island during the night of 28-29 August. Reacting to this, Duer moved that the Convention leave Manhattan before the enemy cut them off. On the 29th, the legislators adjourned for one week, designating the "English Church" in Fishkill as their meeting place. Fishkill was a small trading village on the east bank of the Hudson, about fifty miles north of New York City. Duer was placed on the Committee of Safety charged with administering the state's affairs until the Convention met again.[5]

The legislators met on schedule, but the "English Church" proved to be "very foul with dung of doves and fowls, without any benches, seats or other conveniences whatever" and they moved to the Dutch Church which had a cleaner, if not a more godly, congregation. Almost immediately, Duer was given a short leave to attend to unspecified "private affairs," but a week later, after summoning Duer and Robert R. Livingston back by messenger, the Convention resolved that, because of the critical situation the state faced, all members were required to attend constantly. The lack of a quorum was not going to stop the Convention if passing resolutions could prevent it. Thereafter, whether from pique at being sent for or from a conviction that the Convention had been correct, Duer consistently voted against leaves of absence for fellow members, even if he was the only one opposed.[6]

The success of British arms in the fighting on and around Manhattan had emboldened New York's loyalists and led to Duer's most significant piece of work to date. Impelled by "the great laws of self-preservation . . . to provide that no means in their power be left unessayed to defeat the barbarous machinations of these domestic as well as external enemies," the Convention charged some of its members, Duer among them, to devise a method for "preventing the dangers which may arise from the disaffected in the State." On 21 September, the committee recommended a standing committee "for the express purpose of enquiring into, detecting, and defeating all conspiracies . . . against the liberties of America." Its original members included Duer, Jay and others. It sat almost constantly for four months until it was replaced in February 1777 by a commission staffed from outside the Convention. The Committee on Conspiracies had the power to subpoena witnesses and had the assistance of several messengers and a troop of soldiers. The amount of work it handled—500 cases in less than 130 days—was impressive, especially considering that all of its members had other assignments. Until 10 January, Duer attended regularly, serving as chairman at almost half the meetings.[7] The committee's vigor made an immediate and, if one picturesque source can be trusted, strong impression on the loyalists of Westchester County. In early October, an American militiaman, Enoch Crosby, was traveling through the county to rejoin his unit when he fell in with a stranger. His new companion took him for a loyalist and confided that many in the area felt the same way. "Though the vigilance of Jay, Duer, Platt, Sackett, and their deluded instruments compel my friends to be very circumspect in their movements," he hoped to move through the lines with some friends and join the king's forces. Crosby got away on a pretext and went to the committee, telling them where the loyalists were to rendezvous for the attempt to get through the lines. American troops were able to capture them and the committee, elated by this success, hired Crosby. He was to travel about Westchester and Orange Counties, posing as a loyalist, in the hope of uncovering similar attempts to join the enemy. The committee, with the help of Crosby and others, as well as the efforts of subordinate local committees, worked diligently at suppressing loyalism.[8]

On top of the Committee on Conspiracies with its heavy work

load, Duer was also appointed, along with Robert R. Livingston, to be a liaison with General Washington; all requests for aid, whether from or to the Convention, were to go through Duer and Livingston, who were also to receive whatever reports of operations the general might wish to send. Tench Tilghman, of the general's staff, was deputed to handle the correspondence from headquarters, with Duer usually writing for the Convention. This task was added to Duer's other work until the Continental forces retreated from the Hudson Valley in November. At the end of September, the Clerk of the Convention, John McKesson, noted that all coordination between Washington and the State rested on Duer and "a certain Tench Tilghman, a Clerk to the general's Clerk." While the letters usually dealt with supplies and troop movements and the like, the writers also indulged themselves by dealing with other matters, a sprained ankle of Duer's, for example, or philosophical considerations on a rumored outbreak of war in Europe. If McKesson was correct in supposing Duer to be the only link between the Continental Army and New York State, then Duer should be congratulated for a faithful performance of his task and the Convention reproved for giving such a duty to only one or two men, each of whom had too much else to do.[9]

The letters reflected the ups and downs of American fortunes, at this point—October 1776—mainly downs, as there had been a steady retreat by the Americans to a shaky line just above Harlem on Manhattan Island. Duer implicitly criticized—as did many other patriots—Washington's generalship when he asked Tilghman if Major-General Nathanael Greene could not be spared from his command in New Jersey as his presence in New York would be "of great consequence.—I am much mistaken, if he is not possessed of that Heaven-born genius wh[ich] is necessary to constitute a great General." In reply, Tilghman gently and obliquely rebuked Duer by agreeing with him; Greene was a "first Rate military Genius . . . in whose Opinions [Washington] reposes the utmost confidence," thus leaving no doubt as to who commanded the American forces. Sometimes a letter seemed to be a form of therapy for Duer as when, on 11 October, he began with a gloomy (and largely accurate) assessment of American fortunes, but, in a phrase which must have been hackneyed even then, affirmed it the duty of all patriots "to struggle against the

Tides of adversity" for Americans "are not to expect to purchase our Liberties at a cheaper Rate than other nations have done" and concluded with his faith in an eventual American victory. Redeeming his promise to Tilghman to fight with all the "Vigour" he could, the next day he suggested to the Convention that "the Members furnish themselves with Arms and Ammunition," lest they be surprised by the British. His motion was fortunately buried; the difficulties of keeping a quorum were considerable enough without being increased by accidental gunshot wounds. However, the gesture was certainly in line with someone who could straightfacedly struggle against the "Tides of adversity."[10]

As the British steadily improved their position, moving troops into southern Westchester County on 13 October, Duer was given more work. Enlistments for 1777 were being considered and two committees visited the various New York units to receive recommendations for new battalions being formed. When their work was completed, the committees were to meet together, with Duer as chairman, and fill the commissions. As the load increased, even his energy began to flag and he asked to be relieved from the duty of selecting a site for barracks to be built near Peekskill. He apologized to Tilghman for taking on the additional duty, but he was too "immers'd in the Business of an Inquisitor General."[11]

While Duer's complaints of overwork were well founded, not all the work was official. He had recently contracted with Quartermaster General Thomas Mifflin to purchase all the grain needed by the Continental forces in New York, receiving a 2 1/2 percent commission for his labors. In October, he spent $45,000 for Mifflin, receiving $1,125 for himself. As the Continental forces soon left Westchester, this incident serves chiefly as an example of the tendency mentioned before to spread himself thin, taking on more than he could possibly handle. And he did not really cut his work for the Convention for, by the end of October, barracks at Peekskill (and Fishkill) were being built under his supervision. After completion, they served as military hospitals until the British burnt them in a raid in March 1777.[12] It could hardly be expected that Duer's super-active style would not irritate some of his associates, but John McKesson had a more substantive criticism than too much energy; he suspected Duer of inflating his own role at the expense of other equally worthy patriots. The clerk described him coming in one evening, looking for information on the militia, so he could write an "important Letter to head Quarters," and then, because of his own impatience, misunderstanding clearly phrased information. McKesson suspected that Duer was passing himself off as the savior of the state in his letters to Tilghman (he was not). He assessed Duer's work on the barracks as consisting of a great deal of "bustle" and not too much accomplishment. Although it is obvious that McKesson disliked Duer personally, his criticisms could have reflected the resentment of some in the Convention at what McKesson thought of as Duer's brashness and take-charge attitude, especially when combined with what was seen as ineffectual energy.[13]

McKesson's anxiety was understandable; the American cause badly needed some success. After the British move onto the mainland, Washington moved almost all of his men into Westchester before Howe could outflank him, leaving 3,000 men behind at Fort Washington, near Manhattan's northern tip. An indecisive battle on 28 October at White Plains covered a subsequent American retreat to North Castle, about fifteen miles farther north. Howe drew back to Dobbs Ferry on the Hudson and, as he so often did during his American campaigns, bided his time. Tilghman interpreted the pause as a good omen: "All Matters are as quiet as if the Enemy were 100 miles distant."[14] This was wishful thinking.

The pause in the fighting and maneuvering did not mean any pause in Duer's work. In early November, he was arranging with General James Clinton for assistance for the Committee on Conspiracies. Its own troop was going to attempt the capture of loyalists at a rendezvous and Clinton was asked to provide patrols in the area to bring in any stragglers. Duer was especially anxious about the success of the ambush as an enemy officer was supposed to be with the group. His caution was advisable for it was one of Clinton's patrols which captured the officer who was sent onto Washington's headquarters after questioning by the committee. Duer also pushed ahead with the barracks, even to the point of securing conscripted militia when workmen could not be found.[15]

The pause in operations ended abruptly in mid-November. Washington had already divided his forces, leaving some at North Castle, some at Peekskill, and sending the rest to Fort Lee, New

Jersey, across the Hudson from Fort Washington. On the fifteenth Howe suddenly moved against that post, capturing it with its entire garrison and much materiel. Five days later, Washington was surprised at Fort Lee by a sudden British move across the Hudson; only the soldiers escaped, leaving behind all their stores, tents, and the like. Washington now began to retreat across New Jersey, a retreat which would not end until the sudden success at Trenton on 26 December. All of this left New York pretty much on its own. The troops at North Castle were not expected to remain there much longer and since no one expected Howe to go into winter quarters just yet, Westchester County could see more action. By way of clearing the field, the Committee on Conspiracies ordered "all persons of influence & of equivocal characters" to be sent out of the state; Duer was charged with executing the order.[16] He also went onto a committee to confer with General George Clinton, state militia commander, and make what arrangement of the state's forces seemed best. By the time the committee met with Clinton, early December, General Charles Lee had obeyed Washington's order to send the North Castle units to him; this left the state with only the men at Peekskill under General William Heath and its own militia. The committee, on the 9th called out the militia of Ulster and Orange Counties and placed them where they could either defend the Highlands to the west of the Hudson or cooperate with any Continental forces which might come into northern New Jersey. At the time both Lee and General Horatio Gates, with another Continental force were moving through the area on their way to Washington. Other than the defense of the Highlands, Clinton was to use the militia as he saw fit, going out of the state if necessary. Duer informed Gates of the arrangement of New York's forces in the hope that some kind of a counterattack might be mounted. He asked Gates to send the information on to Washington and Lee "in order that they may pursue such measures as they judge best calculated for the general good." The letter had an almost plaintive tone, as if Duer saw a chance to inflict a defeat on the enemy, a chance which was fast fading.[17]

His anxiety was certainly justified by the sad state of Westchester County, now divided between British and American sympathizers, with the farms of Whig, loyalist and those truly neutral being raided indiscriminately. The forces under Heath, at Peeks-

kill in the northern end of the county could not give any protection against British and loyalist incursions, especially as the
former had moved their outposts across the Harlem River into
the present day Bronx. The Convention, impressed by the suffering of an area "exposed to the Ravages of a Cruel & Merciless
enemy," appointed a committee to plan an expedition into the
county. They could use any means in order to strike at the enemy,
protect the property of the "good Subjects of this State," and
confiscate loyalist property. More than just Westchester was thought
of as the resolution also mentioned "the Island of New York" as
an objective, provided a raid could be conducted with "secrecy,
vigor and Dispatch." Generals Clinton and John Morin Scott
were on the committee, with Gouverneur Morris, John Langdon,
and Duer representing the Convention. It was usually referred
to as the "Secret Committee," with Westchester (and Manhattan)
as its unspoken objective. Duer was released from the Committee
on Conspiracies because the new committee required his "indispensable attendance." The Secret Committee was given £600
and empowered to draw upon the state's militia and directly
request Continental forces.[18]

New York had done about all it could to bolster any disposition
by Heath to move aggressively in Westchester. Now Washington
added to the pressure on him by informing him of his successes
at Trenton and Princeton and ordering him to feint towards New
York City in the hope that it would bring back some of the
British forces in New Jersey. Heath's response was a move against
Fort Independence, an old American fort in southern Westchester
on 18 January 1777. Despite a verbally impressive demand for
their surrender, the well-armed, well-provisioned British force
saw no need to comply with Heath's request and easily sat out
an ineffective ten-day siege. Now the weakness of the American
forces was painfully evident. Even before it ended, Duer anticipated the failure of the siege and complained to Washington: "It
is obvious to every discerning Person that we have been insulted
by a handful of traitorous Banditti, and that we run the risque
of either being routed or cut off br a Night Surprise, or of
abandoning this Part of the Country with Disgrace." The discouraged militia would probably go home and the lack of a local
success cause Whigs to despair and loyalists to exult. Duer ended

by wondering out loud if another general—ingenuously, he named three he thought qualified—might do better. He repeated much the same message to Clinton the next day, concluding with the acid comment that the mountain had labored and brought forth a ridiculous mouse.[19] He was so heartsick over the whole thing he could say no more, except to note that the militia was under "such bad Regulation and so ill officered that nothing heroic can be expected from them." Perhaps a new draft and new officers could do better.[20]

Washington reacted to the news from Fort Independence as Duer had: "I attribute our ill success in the neighborhood of Kingsbridge to the same Cause that you do." The general especially regretted that there had been no follow-up on the surrender demand. Duer's suggested changes in general officers could easily be made, but Heath as major-general would still take precedence. To Heath, Washington wrote two letters. He publicly regretted the Fort Independence fiasco and urged him to continue consulting Duer and others "who best know the Country." But privately, the commander-in-chief censured Heath for his conduct of the whole affair and described the army as not only defeated, but also disgraced.[21] Thus Washington's reply to Duer's criticism was not just an act of politic deference to an influential state politician, for he agreed with him and reprimanded Heath strongly.

Not everyone viewed the events at Fort Independence as gloomily as Duer. The usually somber James Duane looked forward to seeing Schuyler, as he had several stories about the incident involving Duer "which will divert us over a Pipe." And Duane hoped that there might be more to follow as there were rumors that Duer was planning something on his own with some volunteers.[22] He was exploiting, or at least suspected of exploiting, his roving commission to the fullest.

In mid-February the situation changed again, as usual for the worse. Some of the New York militia went home at the end of their terms of service. General Heath then decided that the Connecticut militia should defend their home state only in their home state, and he pulled them back over the border. Now Westchester was defended by fewer that one thousand New York militia. These Duer contemptuously dismissed as worth less than half their number of Continentals, their officers as little better than "miserable animals." His needlessly harsh comments were more

an indication of his anger and frustration than reality. But, despite
the loss of Heath's men, he was not giving up and asked that, if
troops could not be sent, several Convention delegates come to
assist Jonathan Tompkins and himself, the only committee members left in the county. But the Convention decided that, among
the various difficulties which confronted them, Westchester County
was not that important. Not only would more soldiers not be
sent, but the committee members would be replaced by commissioners chosen from outside its ranks. As a final blow, Duer
was ordered to return to the Convention for the "completion of
the important affairs for which they were elected."[23]

Duer held out against the order to return as long as he decently
could. Just as he received it, General David Wooster withdrew
his New York militia to the northern part of the county, leaving
the south completely unprotected except for a force of about 160
men posted in an exposed position on Long Island Sound. Duer
protested to the Convention against the injustice of requiring a
loyalty oath of the inhabitants, then not even trying to protect
those who took it. Further, the Convention should appreciate
the possible effect of their abandonment of Westchester's Whigs.
If the scene of battle now shifted to Westchester's northern neigh-
bor, Dutchess County, how much support could be expected
there? Almost as if he hoped single-handedly to rescue the Convention from its mistakes, Duer promised to stay where he was,
"however exposed we may be, and not withstanding the threats
of the enemy against us for the active part we have taken in the
public concerns," unless forced or ordered to retreat. And stay
he did, at least into early March, planning the enlistment of a
troop of mounted rangers to replace the troops the Convention
refused to send. Apparently, the rangers were never enlisted,
which was just as well, for the Secret Committee had no authority
to sign anyone up, although Duer made certain that his good
intentions came to the notice of General Washington.[24]

He could postpone his return to the Convention no longer.
After an absence of more than two months, he returned to Fishkill
and resumed his seat. Westchester was hardly worse off because
of his departure. Even while the Secret Committee had been at
work, the property of patriots as well as loyalists had been looted
under the cover of foraging. By mid-March, the 160 militiamen
on the Sound had been routed by the enemy, whose control of

southern Westchester was unchallenged. About the only significant effect of the Secret Committee's work was the removal of
substantial quantities of forage to Peekskill and beyond, safely
out of the reach of the British for the time being. The ineffec-
tiveness of the committee cannot fairly be blamed on Duer or
any other of its members. At no point did they have the whole-
hearted cooperation of the local commanders, two of whom
retreated suddenly, leaving the remaining troops in exposed positions. With conditions as they were, the committee did well to
remove forage. More could not be expected.

Duer had been called back and the committee replaced by
commissioners because a draft constitution was finally ready for
the Convention's consideration. The draft was a much more conservative document than one would normally expect in the midst
of a revolution. The conservatism showed clearly in the office of
the governor. Its occupant was to be elected directly by the voters
for a three-year term and was indefinitely re-eligible for election.
He shared in the duties of appointment and legislative review
with councils drawn from the legislature and judiciary. The suffrage was also quite restricted and there was no separate bill of
rights, although certain rights were guaranteed by specific provisions of the constitution. Most other state constitutions, already
in effect, had weak governors, selected by the legislatures for
short terms and with limited re-eligibility. Neither did these governors generally share in the areas of appointment and legislative
review. For unexplained reasons, the radicals in the Convention
did not strongly protest the failure to report a bill of rights
simultaneously with a constitution, as provided in the committee's original charge. Also unexplained was how the conservatives
managed to get such a draft out of committee and, with relatively
few changes, accepted by the Convention. As noted, delay, conscious delay by the conservatives helped. Later, Jay attributed the
conservative victory to "well timed delay, indefatigable industry,
and a minute attention to every favorable circumstance." Most
of the drafting seems to have been done in the last three months
of 1776 when Duer could have attended the committee's meetings. After 1 January, when he was absent in Westchester, the
committee concerned itself mainly with revisions. Aside from
this rudimentary observation, it is difficult to say more about any
influence he might have had on the document. Also, his generally

conservative ideas would simply complement those of Jay and Gouverneur Morris and Robert R. Livingston, also active members of the committee. He certainly approved of the new frame of government, later calling it "the best system which has yet been adopted."[25]

Before the "best system" had begun to work, Duer had left the Convention and was representing New York in the Continental Congress in Philadelphia. Philip Schuyler had been removed from his command in northern New York in March because of various disputes, most stemming from his patrician disdain for the democratic sensibilities of the New England units in his forces. His successor was Major-General Horatio Gates. New York had insisted that Schuyler have a chance to explain his side of the complex situation and Congress had agreed. In preparing what might be called his defense, he had requested that some friends be sent to Congress to "say more than would perhaps be proper for me to say" and that the members "may receive the fullest Conviction of the unjust and Injurious treatment I have sustained." On 29 March, Duer was appointed, presently to be joined by Jay, Duane, and Gouverneur Morris.[26]

Thus Duer left the Convention a little more than eight months after joining it. From the day he was sworn in, he had taken an active, even conspicuous part in its proceedings. During the crucial period, August-September 1776, when the Battle for Manhattan was taking place, he had served on all but one of the Committees of Safety. For a little more than half of the ad-hoc committees on which he had served, he had written the reports. His service on the Committee on Conspiracies had been arduous, especially when joined with his supervision of the Peekskill and Fishkill barracks construction. Finally, his work on the Secret Committee had been a thankless, frustrating attempt to perform a task for which the essential tools were lacking. None of this is meant to imply that Duer did more than many other members of the Convention, but he did work hard, and usually effectively for New York. What may be the most telling compliment about his work in the Convention was recorded by the loyalist, William Smith, then living on parole at Manor Livingston: "Mr. Paterson tells me that it is said in New York that all would be peace in this Colony but for Ph. Livingston, Robt. R. L[ivingston] Jay Duane Scott and Duer and that ag[ain]st the last they uttered the severest Execrations."[27] If you are going to be a rebel, you might as well be a notorious rebel. Duer seems to have succeeded.

References

1. Philip Schuyler to Rev. Dr. [Jonas] Clark, et al., Jun. 18, 1776, Schuyler Papers, NYPL.
2. *Journals*, I, 524; *Am. Arch.*, 5 s., I, 1409; R. R. Livingston, et al., to George Washington, Jul. 17, 1776, ibid., 392; Convention of the State of New York to George Washington, Jul. 16, 1776, ibid., 1409; George Washington to President, Continental Congress, Jul. 19, 1776, ibid., 445-46; George Washington to Jonathan Trumbull, Jul. 19, 1776, ibid., 450.
3. Wm. Duer to John Jay and Robert R. Livingston, Jul. 21, 1776, Robert R. Livingston Papers, Ac. 1931, LC; on July 26th, the Convention hired Hazlewood to charge several fire ships and referred him to Jay or Livingston, *Am. Arch.*, 5 s., I, 1454.
4. Ibid., 5 s., I, 1465-66; Mason, *Road to Independence*, 214-19; see Mason's Chap. 7 for a full treatment of the drafting of the constitution.
5. The Secret Committee on Obstructing the Hudson to the Provincial Convention, Aug. 16, 1776, *Am. Arch.*, 5 s., I, 1498, see also 1522, 1555-56.
6. Ibid., II, 662, 665, 673, 690; see also 711, 714, 717, 723.
7. *Journals*, I, 633-638; Dorothy C. Barck, ed., *Minutes of the Committee and of the First Commission for Detecting and Defeating Conspiracies in the State of New York, December 11, 1776—September 23, 1778* (New York, 1924); hereafter cited as Barck, *Minutes*; in the text the short title will be the Committee on Conspiracies.
8. H. L. Barnum, *The Spy Unmasked; or, Memoirs of Enoch Crosby, the Hero of Mr. Cooper's Tale of the Neutral Ground* (New York, 1828), 54-61; contrary to Barnum's title, James Fenimore Cooper always denied that the adventures of any one individual inspired *The Spy*. A conversation with John Jay furnished both the inspiration and the background for the tale, originally published in 1821. Despite the melodramatic dialogue, Barnum accurately depicts Crosby's adventures while in the committee's employ. The anonymous author of *The Knickerbocker* article on Duer claims for him the credit of having hired Crosby; Jay Monaghan in *John Jay: Defender of Liberty* (New York, 1935), 91, gives the credit to Jay. There is nothing in the Minutes of the Committee to support or deny either claim; both Jay and Duer were present when Crosby was hired. Crosby's story is conveniently found in John C. Dann, ed., *The Revolution Remembered* (Chicago, 1980), 339-47, which reprints his 1832 pension application.
9. Wm. Duer to George Washington, Sep. 21, 1776, *Am. Arch.*, 5 s., II, 453; Wm. Duer to Tench Tilghman, Sep. 21, 1776, Duer Papers, NYHS; a transcript of the correspondence is in the Duer Papers; John McKesson to George Clinton, Sep. 29, 1776, *The Public Papers of George Clinton* (New York, 1899), I, 367; hereafter cited as *Clinton Papers*.
10. Wm. Duer to Tench Tilghman, Oct. 2, 1776, Tench Tilghman to Wm. Duer, Oct. 4, 1776, Wm. Duer to Tench Tilghman, Oct. 11, 1776, Duer Papers, NYHS; *Am. Arch.*, 5 s., III, 242.
11. Ibid., III, 248, 252; Tench Tilghman to Wm. Duer, Oct. 8, 1776, Wm. Duer to Tench Tilghman, Oct. 18, 1776, Duer Papers, NYHS.
12. Thomas Mifflin to Wm. Duer, Oct. 26, 1776, *Am. Arch.*, 5 s., II, 1254; Account Book, 1776-1778, Cash Payments of Q.M.G. Department to Various Persons, Vol. # 98, RG 93, War Dept. Coll., NA.
13. John McKesson to George Clinton, Oct. 31, 1776, *Clinton Papers*, I, 387, 419.
14. Tench Tilghman to Wm. Duer, Nov. 2, 1776, BV I, Duer Papers, NYHS.
15. Wm. Duer to James Clinton, Nov. 6, 1776, Emmett Coll., # 4188, NYPL; *Am. Arch.*, 5 s., III, 302-303; Duer was sending as far as Albany to get plank for the barracks; *Minutes of the Albany Committee of Correspondence* (Albany, 1923), I, 614.

16. Barck, *Minutes*, 12.
17. Committee of Safety, Convention of the State of New York, *Am. Arch.*, 5 s., III, 362; *Journals*, I, 746; Wm. Duer to Horatio Gates, Dec. 9, 1776, ibid., II, 337.
18. Resolution of the Convention of the State of New York, Dec. 19, 1776, ibid., III, 301; Barck, *Minutes*, 32; Resolution of the Convention of the State of New York, Dec. 30, 1776, *Calendar of Historical Mss*, I, 578; the membership of the committee changed several times; only Duer remained throughout its life. Since he appears to have dominated the committee and to have done most of the work, the changes have not been given.
19. "Paturiunt [*sic*] Montes, nasceter [*sic*] ridiculus mus."
20. George Washington to William Heath, Jan. 5, 1777, John C. Fitzpatrick, ed., *The Writings of George Washington* (Washington, 1932), VI, 472; hereafter cited as *Washington Writings*; Wm. Duer to George Washington, Jan. 28, 1777, George Washington Papers, LC; hereafter cited as Washington Papers; Wm. Duer to George Clinton, Jan. 29, 1777, Clinton Papers, I, 565-66; see Graham Philip Dolan, "Major General William Heath and the First Years of the American Revolution," unpub. Ph.D. diss., Boston Univ., 1966, 275-306, for a defense of Heath's generalship on this occasion.
21. George Washington to Wm. Duer, Feb. 3, 1777, Washington Papers, LC; George Washington to William Heath, Feb. 3, 4, 1777, *Washington Writings*, VII, 94-96, 99-100. On Feb. 6, Heath answered Washington's order to consult Duer by stating he would comply only because he was ordered—"otherwise I should not do it in Military affairs, altho' I much esteem him for his good sense and Judgement in other affairs"; ibid., VII, 96, n. 76.
22. James Duane to Philip Schuyler, Feb. 15, 1777, Schuyler Papers, NYPL.
23. Wm. Duer to the President of the Convention of the State of New York, Feb. 17, 1777, *Journals*, II, 366-67; Convention to Wm. Duer and Committee, Feb. 22, 1777, ibid., II, 375; see also Wm. Duer to Maj. Gen. [David] Wooster, Feb. 13, 1777, 11662, and Feb. 18, 1777, 3427, NYSL, for more of the committee's activities.
24. Col. VanRensselaer to Wm. Duer, Wm. Duer to Col. VanRensselaer, Feb. 24, 1777; there are almost as many VanRensselaers in New York history as Livingstons, but this colonel is otherwise unknown; Wm. Duer to the President of the Convention of the State of New York, Feb. 25, 1777, ibid., II, 375-77; "Resolves of Committee . . . March 4, 1777," Duer Papers, BV I, NYHS; George Washington to Wm. Duer, Mar. 6, 1777, Washington Papers, LC.
25. Mason, *Road to Independence*, 231, 225 and Chap. 7 generally; Duer quoted in E. Wilder Spaulding, "The State Government Under the First Constitution," 165 in Flick, *History*, IV. Charles C. Thach, Jr., *The Creation of the Presidency, 1775-1789: A Study in Constitutional History* (Baltimore, 1923), Chap. II contrasts the differing treatment of the executive in the revolutionary state constitutions; see 34-45 for comments on the office of governor in New York. Jackson Turner Main compares and contrasts the various state constitutions briefly and clearly in Chap. 5 of *The Sovereign States* (New York, 1973).
26. Philip Schuyler to R. R. Livingston, Mar. 17, 1777, Robert R. Livingston Papers, NYHS; *Journals*, I, 855, 931.
27. Mar. 30, 1777, William H. W. Sabine, ed., *Historical Memoirs of William Smith, 12 July 1776 to 25 July 1778* (New York, 1958), 99, hereafter cited as *Historical Memoirs of William Smith*.

Chapter III

The Continental Congress

April 1777–January 1779

William Duer's move to the Continental Congress was not simply from one legislature to another; the congress and the New York State Convention resembled each other only superficially. In the congress, New York was only one of thirteen professedly sovereign states, each of which had an equal vote, states whose conflicting interests and desires had to be reconciled and balances struck. There had been local interests in the Convention, to be sure, but they could be, and often enough were, overridden. States, however, especially when combined into sectional alliances, were too strong for that. Even Duer's first task, the reinstatement of Philip Schuyler to his command in northern New York, was a sign that no state could have its undisputed way in Congress. Thus Duer was no longer a member of a self-assured aristocracy striving to retain its former position within the new arena of state politics. Now he had to cajole and convince others to support New York, a task calling for gifts not so necessary at home. Also, while Duer always had the support of his fellow delegates in the Convention, on several occasions he found himself the only New York representative at Congress. However, along with the increased responsibility went increased freedom of action. He was guided only by the loose instructions issued by the Convention and its successor and represented New York much as he saw fit. His presumed independence did not dismay some who thought him only a puppet of Schuyler's; William Smith was pleased to see him going to Philadelphia as he believed that the general favored peace and "He has influence upon Duer."[1] Now Duer would have the chance to show he was more than a puppet.

New York's newest delegate was sworn in on 7 April and began to work immediately on his most essential task: making friends for his state. He made an excellent start on this when he impressed peppery John Adams of Massachusetts—hardly one of New York's friends—as "a very fine fellow, a man of sense, spirit, and activity . . . exceeded by no man in his zeal." Adams would not always think so highly of Duer, but he had made a good start and the point about his zeal was well taken. He was no sooner settled in than he looked up Roger Sherman of Connecticut and told him of the New York Commission on Conspiracies' discovery that William Franklin, former royal governor of New Jersey, then living on parole in New Haven, was handing out protections to the good people there, all the while boasting that no one could stop him. There may have been some malice in disclosing this as the Yankee was one of the most fervent supporters of Major-General Horatio Gates, Schuyler's replacement in his command.[2]

As in the Convention, Duer found himself immediately loaded up with a variety of committee assignments, no less than four within his first week in Congress. This was not at all unusual in a body which had to be executive as well as legislative; most of the executive work was accomplished by committees, both standing and ad hoc. One of his early assignments placed him in the middle of Pennsylvania's complicated state politics. General Sir William Howe was feinting toward Philadelphia in an effort to draw Washington away from the cover of the Ramapo Mountains of northern New Jersey where his troops had wintered. The movements drew Congress's attention to protecting provisions stored in the city from British seizure, and a committee was appointed to study their possible removal. Ordinarily, the Pennsylvania government would have seen to the safety of the stores, but the plural executive provided for in its controversial state constitution lacked a quorum and could not act. Duer wrote the committee report which suggested that Congress step in and order the state authorities to allow the stores to be removed by the local commander of the Continental forces. Since Duer's reputation as a member of New York's conservative bloc had preceded him to Philadelphia, in the highly politicized atmosphere of the capital, the Constitutionalists (those who supported the constitution) saw the committee's report as an attempt to embarrass the state authorities and directed their attention to the new man in town as the one responsible. Although the situation was not the work of any political group, the Republicans (conservatives who opposed the constitution) did take advantage of it to try to discredit the state government.[3]

The Constitutionalists were correct to suspect Duer. In describing the incident, he hoped the committee's suggestions would help to "save a powerful State, which must have fallen a sacrifice to a speculative system of politics." He also contrasted the "languor" of Philadelphia with the vigor and activity of New York: "Would to Heaven that the spirit and activity which has of late animated the Councils of the State of New York would diffuse itself throughout the other States. A portion of their electrical fire is certainly wanting." Even if the struggle for independence ended in failure, New York could console itself with the realization that she had fought the good fight; Duer felt that Pennsylvania's "speculative" politics would deny the state that small consolation.[4]

On 18 April, James Duane and Philip Livingston arrived to fill out the New York delegation. Their first task was to secure a formal examination of Schuyler's conduct, since some of those who opposed him pretended there had been no criticism, hence no need for an inquiry, hence no opportunity to correct the wrong done the general and the State. "This subtle bargain did not pass," reported James Duane; instead a committee consisting of one member from each state was appointed to examine the conduct of General Schuyler "since he has held a command in the army of the United States." Duer represented New York. Now the state had a chance to vindicate its hero.[5]

Schuyler's merit would not have to speak for itself. Duane had commented that New York's reputation seemed to stand high, but the delegates did not know many of their colleagues, save by name, so they rented a house and presently began to have their fellow congressmen in for dinner as often as possible. Also, they would not concentrate on Schuyler alone; the only place to influence national policy and correct state grievances was in the congress and the only way to do it was to set an example of activity and intelligence in prosecuting the national war effort. At a time when state regional loyalties usually overrode any attachment to the still dimly seen entity, the "United States," such nationalist energy was seldom found. And Duer set a pace which his colleagues seldom matched. In the week of 23 April alone, he served on four temporary committees, ranging from the reinforcement of Washington's forces to the prevention of "ill consequences" as a result of an enemy raid on Danbury, Connecticut. He wrote two of the reports, including the most difficult one, that of enlarging Washington's army. These committees were in addition to those to which he had already been appointed. The Convention, preparing to put the new state constitution into effect, gave the delegation a vote of confidence by reappointing it in mid-May and adding General Schuyler and the able, albeit cynical Gouverneur Morris, to its ranks, although neither took his seat that year.[6]

Schuyler was reinstated in his command by a favorable vote in late May, but only after much "address and great attention" had been given the problem by the New Yorkers. This was in spite of New England's general dominance in Congress during this time. While Gates was their hero, the haughty Schuyler made no effort to conceal his disdain for Yankee militia officers and the Yankees returned the compliment. They did not trust him. Duer attributed the congressional victory to "Time, and great Temper and Address," presumably more legitimate parliamentary tools than the "Arts and Influence" the Yankees had exercised on Gates's behalf. "Truth assisted with Management" had brought about a six (New York, Pennsylvania, Maryland, North Carolina, South Carolina, and Virginia) to three (Massachusetts, Connecticut, and New Hampshire) vote for Schuyler. But Duer was honest enough to note that Virginia's yea was a miracle and New Jersey was divided and could not vote only because two of its delegates, men with definite New England sympathies, were absent. Now, with Schuyler reinstated, he felt that New York had recovered its "full weight" and could pay attention to other issues important to the state. Duer could also pay attention to things important to him. He felt his work in Philadelphia was now finished and asked Robert R. Livingston to obtain a leave for him to attend to personal matters; "Ruin may result otherwise." He had not been to Fort Miller since he left it for the Convention in June 1776 and the property badly needed attention. His request was both understandable and common. It was understandable because the British had reached half-way down Lake Champlain in 1776 when they chased the Americans from Canada; would they repeat the effort in 1777's campaigning season and could they be stopped again? Duer had every right to be anxious about his property at Fort Miller. It was common because many delegates quickly tired of life in Philadelphia and either requested replacement or simply went home; Duane had done this in 1775 and early in 1778 he would take advantage of an official trip to Albany to go home and stay there for the rest of the winter.[7]

While Duer waited for an answer from Kingston where the Convention was sitting, he continued his many duties, one of which was on a three-man committee to devise "ways and means for defraying the expenses of the present year." His colleagues were Robert Morris, a Philadelphia merchant and future Superintendent of Finance for the congress, in which post he would be very important to Duer's career, and John Witherspoon of New Jersey, president of the college which became Princeton University. Duer had also asked Livingston's advice on this vexing question, and when the answer came, it was conventional and predictable. Conservatives felt that the congress had to secure the power to levy taxes and end its dependence on state requisitions, which were honored or not as the states saw fit. This is just what Livingston advised Duer to push for, but the congress never screwed itself up to attempt such a tax on its own and when it did ask the states—all of which had to agree to amend the Articles of Confederation—at least one always refused. Duer was probably more interested in the response to his leave request than in any intelligent but unrealistic advice about taxes. As he may well have feared, the reply was a gracious no; New York needed three men in Philadelphia and Gouverneur Morris could not be spared from Kingston. Neither could Duer be spared from Philadelphia. If he did not stay, "C[ongress] will sink into their old lethargy . . . now stay until you have things in a proper train." If he followed that advice, Duer's stay would be a long one indeed.[8]

As summer began, affairs neither in the congress nor back in New York gave Duer any peace of mind. In mid-June, as if to shake Congress out of its lethargy, Horatio Gates appeared at its door, attempting to justify his conduct in the recent quarrel with Schuyler. By a subterfuge, Roger Sherman gained the floor for Gates where he indulged himself with a long, rambling, and incoherent defense, or at least Duer described it so to Schuyler; he was removed only with some difficulty. Duer was disturbed by this threatened renewal of a fight he thought New York had won. He was also upset by news of sharply contested elections in New York for positions under its new constitution. While he lamented sincerely enough the "Spirit of Electioneering" which would cause that "Sourness of Mind which is the Natural Result of Contested Elections," a complaint reminiscent of his fears when the same spirit of dissension had surfaced in Charlotte County in 1776, what he was also concerned about was the victory of the more democratic group in New York. He saw the opposition to Schuyler's candidacy for governor and other conservatives for seats in the Senate and Assembly as a plot to take the government away from those who should run it. Witness his expectation that John Morin Scott, one of those running against Schuyler, would "make use of every Act however gross or wicked which he thinks will serve to make himself popular." To be popular was apparently an unwholesome thing. There was no hope that the new government could be as powerful as the old, if it had to contend with the malevolent opposition of Scott and his kind. It is obvious that Duer, along with many of his contemporaries, first, had no idea that an opposition could be loyal and, while agreeing on the basic framework of the government, honestly differ on its execution; second, that he believed government to be an extraordinarily fragile thing, resting on the implicit consent of the people to be governed by the local aristocracy, however chosen. Challenges to those who considered themselves to be that aristocracy were not easily to be borne. Paradoxically, while Duer feared that things were falling apart in New York, Pennsylvania seemed to be getting things together nicely. Mainly because of the apparent threat from Howe, the Philadelphia militia had been mustered; before this, political divisions had prevented a call. But time would soon show that while New York was not so badly off as Duer believed, neither was Pennsylvania quite so well off.[9]

Now that Schuyler seemed safely beyond the reach of the malevolent Yankees, it remained to deal with other threats from the Eastern states; a New Yorker had to be appointed Commissary-General of Supplies in the state to stop its looting by New Englanders and Congress had to approve New York's claim to the Hampshire Grants, which was now calling itself Vermont. While these were difficult, Duane felt that neither was impossible.

They would simply concentrate on one thing at a time rather than belabor Congress with too many complaints. And they must continue entertaining, "for it was no time to consult parsimony" in making friends for New York.[10]

While final decisions might be difficult to come by, a state could at least safeguard its position. On 30 June, Congress resolved that Vermont could not claim independence on the basis of either the Declaration of Independence or a May 1776 congressional resolution urging the states to form new governments. The resolution noted that Congress's purpose was to protect the colonies as they stood in 1775; how could any of those actions undermine the integrity of any of the colonies now that they were states? Both New York's argument and the June 30th resolution were in Duer's handwriting. Thus he had been able to cap his earlier success in getting action on Vermont postponed with congressional disapproval of its claims insofar as they were based on congressional resolutions. And he seemed to take an undue pleasure in reporting that one of the Yankees supporting Vermont, Roger Sherman of Connecticut, was "quite thrown off his Bias, and betrayed a Warmth not usually learnt within the Walls of Yale College," by New York's victory.[11]

Neither New York's nor Congress's problems were all official ones to be dealt with by resolutions and the like. Duer also helped with non-legislative problems. The Marquis Phillippe duCoudray presented himself to Congress in June 1777 with a commission injudiciously granted him by Silas Deane, an American agent in France. It made the marquis a major-general and chief of artillery and engineers, thus at once sending him over the heads of several American officers who had already served two long, arduous years. Because of their and other officers' objections, the commission could not be honored, but neither could the marquis be sent back to France, for he was much too influential at court. The congress did what any reasonable assembly would do, they stalled and hoped that something else might happen. The marquis was assigned to study and report on the defenses of Philadelphia with Duer assisting, primarily as a translator, as the Frenchman spoke no English. By the marquis's own testimony, Duer helped very much over the summer. This was all that was needed, for, in September, duCoudray showed the wisdom of Congress's procrastination by drowning in an accident. The relieved legislators ordered a full military funeral; to use Duane's apt phrase again, "it was no time to consult parsimony." Duer may have drawn duty as duCoudray's guide because he spoke some French and was also a member of the Board of War, on which he had been placed on 2 July. He served on it throughout the eventful winter of 1777-78. At this time, the Board was assigned most of the duties of a War Department and general staff, including the planning of campaigns and the review of plans from headquarters. Naturally, this came on top of Duer's other assignments.[12]

The renewal of fighting in northern New York in the summer of 1777 renewed Duer's anxiety about his property and he repeated his request for a leave of absence, this time basing it on the necessity of complying with contracts. Although he did not know it, he had little reason to go to Fort Miller; Schuyler had removed to Albany whatever could be moved and assigned seventy men to guard the house. Indeed, Schuyler was more successful in helping Duer than in stopping the British and their Hessian mercenaries, all under the command of General John Burgoyne. Ticonderoga and several other forts had already fallen when Schuyler was relieved a second time, confirming Duer's worst fears. Gates again replaced him. While Duer prepared to present New York's case for its general yet again, he also had to help deal with the invasion and served on a committee which recommended that Washington send 500 men to reinforce Gates.[13]

Washington complied with the recommendation by sending Daniel Morgan's corps of Virginia riflemen to Gates, but he did not do so willingly for he had his own British general to worry about. Howe and most of his force had spent the earlier part of the summer feinting with Washington in northern New Jersey; they had then returned to New York City and embarked on transports, destination unknown, on 23 July. The fleet was sighted at the Capes of the Delaware on the 30th obviously heading for Philadelphia. But then they pulled back out to sea while Washington hovered in central New Jersey, anxiously waiting for another sighting, news of which finally came on 10 August. The enemy were sailing south along the Maryland-Virginia coast. Anticipating their landing near the head of the Chesapeake Bay, Washington moved into position and met the enemy along the Brandywine Creek, about twenty-five miles southwest of Philadelphia, on 11 September. Although the Americans were outflanked and fled the field in disorder, they quickly reformed and kept themselves between the enemy and Philadelphia, fighting several indecisive actions.

News of the battle distracted Congress from its customary concerns. The legislators were debating a formal frame of union to tie the thirteen states together into a confederation. Although they had been fighting Britain for more than two years, they were still united only by the unofficial congress with its undefined powers and responsibilities. The threat to the capital gave yet another reason to put aside the topic which had been considered intermittently since July 1776. Instead, Congress turned to an ill-considered effort to deal with internal enemies. A committee was appointed to look into Major-General James Sullivan's allegation that several "persons of considerable wealth [living in Philadelphia] commonly called Quakers . . . are with much rancor and bitterness disaffected to the American cause." Duer, John Adams, and Richard Henry Lee of Virginia had their report ready on 31 August, only three days after the committee was formed. They recommended that the Pennsylvania authorities arrest the eleven persons accused by Sullivan and anyone else suspected of "gross disaffection," with no one being spared simply because he was a Quaker. The severity of the recommendation was doubtless owing to nothing more substantial than congressional suspicions of Quaker pacifism, exacerbated by the enemy threat. The state authorities complied with the request, but not before twice engaging in the charade of requesting instructions, so as to make it crystal clear that they were acting under congressional direction. Thus, for a second time, Duer incurred the anger of the Pennsylvania Constitutionalists, probably with less justification than in the initial clash.[14]

While the threat of the Quakers was being considered, Howe neatly drew Washington away from Philadelphia in mid-September, exposing it to enemy capture. Congress adjourned on the 19th, agreeing to re-convene at Lancaster, about eighty miles west of the city. Duer probably left that day, for he was in Bethlehem, thirty-five miles north of the city, the next day. Before leaving, he and fifteen other congressmen testified to the kindness shown them by the Moravian Brethren, a German pietistic sect which had settled the town. The Brethren were also caring for some

wounded and sick Continental soldiers, and the legislators asked
the Army not to disturb them or their property in spite of their
pacifism. Duer and his colleagues eventually rejoined what was
left of the congress in York, on the far side of the Susquehanna
River, a bit safer from enemy action than Lancaster. York would
be the Continental capital until the spring of 1778, as the British
had taken Philadelphia on 26 September.[15]

As the congress was retreating, New York renewed its delegation. On 23 September, the State Assembly (having succeeded
the Convention when the new constitution was put into effect
in April) appointed a five-man delegation: Duer and Duane, who
were then attending, Philip Livingston, who had gone home
during the summer, Gouverneur Morris, who had never taken
his seat, and Francis Lewis. Any three of them were to be in
Congress at one time, while any two of them could cast the state's
vote. By this, it was hoped that New York's voice would be
strong and constant and never again have to depend on only two
representatives, one of them sick.[16]

Once settled in at York, the congress turned again to the proposed frame of union and concentrated on it long enough to
complete it. On 15 November, the Articles of Confederation
were sent to the states for their consideration and ratification.
Temporarily recovered from an illness which had bothered him
for much of the summer, Duer attended regularly and cast New
York's vote with Duane. On several amendments designed to do
away with equal voting and introduce voting proportional either
to a state's population or wealth, New York voted for equality.
At this time Virginia, with a population almost double that of
its nearest rival, was the only one to favor proportional voting.
But, on an amendment to proportion a state's financial contribution to its assessed wealth, Duer voted yea and Duane nay and
the state's vote was lost. Local concerns also surfaced. On a
motion to allow the states to describe their own boundaries to
Congress, New York, Pennsylvania, and Maryland voted yea, the
first because of its quarrel over Vermont. Pennsylvania approved
because of its quarrel over a Connecticut claim based on the
latter's sea-to-sea charter as well as its fixed western boundary,
the principal factor with Maryland. This was defeated, but so
was one which would have given Congress sole power to fix
western boundaries (no vote was given on this). New York appar-

ently wanted to get its controversy into Congress where its luck had so far been good. They succeeded when a motion giving Congress power to act as a court in settling inter-state disputes was put into the Articles.[17]

Presently, Duer was placed on a committee to translate the Articles into French and see to their distribution in Canada, which Congress still hoped to coax into the rebellion. Duer, James Lovell of Massachusetts, and Francis Lightfoot Lee of Virginia formed the committee. Their report (as distinct from the translation) went far beyond Congress's apparent intent when it recommended a post on Lake Champlain above Fort Ticonderoga and the recruiting there of a "French Legion" made up of Canadian prisoners, other Canadians, and Frenchmen living in the United States. The Legion would be used to foment a revolution in Canada "whenever the U. S. shall deem such a measure expedient." The report, in Duer's hand, was submitted on 2 December and put over for consideration, but never again surfaced. Later in the month, he again put his idea before Congress through the device of a Board of War report; again, it was ignored. His desire to see Canada either join the rebellion or at least be disturbed was understandable as New York had suffered the most by incursions from Canada. Burgoyne had been defeated at Saratoga in October while Gates was in command, but only after he had come a third of the way down the Hudson. No one knew when another attempt might be made by the enemy. Also, New York was complaining that Gates neglected the defense of the state, hence the anxiety about a post above Ticonderoga. But expressing this understandable concern by the grand but unrealistic scheme of enlisting a French Legion showed Duer's imagination again running away from him; in Westchester, it had been a company of rangers, but Congress was a larger stage, so it was now a legion of French Canadians. That few paid any attention apparently did not concern Duer too much; a variation would appear later.[18]

Still, one must admire him. His companion since he came to Congress, James Duane, had taken advantage of a congressional assignment in the Lake Champlain area to go to Albany—and no farther—where he spent the winter with his ill wife. Duer's leave had to be postponed yet again as Francis Lewis, a new member, and he both had to attend or the state could not vote.

But the postponement of his leave and the prospect of a winter in the crowded, uncomfortable quarters which the small village of York provided did not dispirit him. He could write confidently of a "bold stroke" against the enemy and be encouraged by British withdrawals in Westchester and on Lake Champlain. Certainly, he could not have been encouraged by the atmosphere in Congress where too many other members had followed Duane's example. In early December, it was necessary to ask five states to send more representatives—New York was one—and two states to send somebody as they were completely unrepresented. It had become difficult to staff even the most essential committees. The problem of the Continental currency, the loss of Philadelphia, blamed on Washington's generalship, the ragged, starving condition of the few men left under the general's command in winter quarters at Valley Forge, the supply system that caused all that misery, all this and more dispirited other patriots, but Duer held on to at least a measure of his optimism.[19]

In such a context, it was only natural that some began to fasten on a new commander-in-chief as the panacea for the manifold ills besetting the American cause. Naturally also, some looked favorably on Horatio Gates, the victor of Saratoga, whose star still shone brightly, as the potential savior of his country. One does not have to see in this understandable desire of some congressmen to infuse fresh blood into the American high command, a plot or cabal to unseat Washington and replace him with a man whom retrospection has shown to be inferior in most respects. But the Conway Cabal, as it was called, was seen by some contemporaries as an insidious plot to unseat the virtuous and all-competent Washington by a covey of dissident congressmen and incompetent foreign adventurers. Some historians have continued this view in a more sophisticated form. Others see it as a natural result of the tension and rivalry between the New England States and Virginia, the Yankees adopting Gates as an antidote to the aristocratic commander-in-chief. And at least one historian of the revolutionary period sees the "plot" as nothing more than a myth conjured up by an overly suspicious Washington.[20] It is not necessary to adopt any of these viewpoints to explain Duer's role in the confusing events of December 1777–March 1778 which have been thrown together as the Conway Cabal, but, of the three basic views, the last seems most likely. That there was widespread discontent with Washington's command is evident; that there was sectional friction in the congress and that Horatio Gates was widely admired for his victory cannot be doubted. But these coincidental sentiments, even when refracted through the inexperienced eyes of Marquis de Lafayette and the apparently suspicious eyes of Washington, cannot be taken to add up to an organized plot or even active hostility to the commander. Duer's part in the opaque chain of events was probably coincidental. From the beginning, he was suspected of being dishonest by Lafayette, so the French volunteer was more than ready to believe the worst of him. When the supposed fomenter of the plot, Brigadier-General Thomas Conway, a French volunteer of Irish birth, first irritated Washington in November, the commander's anger caused Conway to think of resigning. He was kept in York for a while with nothing to do until Gates, who arrived there on 19 January, revived plans for a Canadian expedition. On the 23rd, the Board of War with Gates as its new president, formally suggested and the congress adopted a proposal to invade Canada and capture Montreal. Lafayette was placed in charge with Conway as his second-in-command. After some detail changes by the Board, Lafayette returned to Valley Forge where he learned that Duer was to accompany the expedition as congressional representative. Although he was very angry, there was nothing he could do about it and he left for Albany, the expedition's embarkation point on 7 February, several days after Duer and Conway. Despite prior arrangements, he did not meet either of them en route. When he arrived at Albany, he found neither preparations nor enthusiasm for the expedition. Philip Schuyler had already told Conway, on the scene three days before Lafayette, that, although he had proposed such an attempt in November, at this time it was quite unfeasible. After speaking with Schuyler and others at Albany, Lafayette agreed that the venture was impossible and busied himself trying to improve the situation there. He returned to Valley Forge in April, by which time Conway had resigned from the Army and the Canadian project had been given up formally by the congress. For his own part, Duer had never shown up in Albany and had probably never gone any farther than Reading, about thirty miles from Valley Forge. He had been absent from Congress for about a week in January because of illness and probably did not feel up to the trip to

Albany. Why he accepted the charge from Congress is not clear, but he may have wanted to force the state authorities to grant him leave by presenting them with a *fait accompli*, his presence in Albany. Robert R. Livingston had already indirectly urged him to come home and help prevent what Livingston saw as the maladministration of Governor George Clinton.[21] With the collapse of the Canadian venture and Conway's resignation, the rumors and suspicions of a plot against Washington's command disappeared. As already stated, Duer's part in all this was probably coincidental. He was a member of the Board of War which had given Conway a position as Inspector-General and which had proposed the Canadian invasion without first consulting Washington, but these actions can be explained without recourse to any plot or cabal. Even if they could not be explained, Duer's role in either was not large enough to make him a principal. His trip to Albany was the most important part he could have taken and his failure to go shows him as a rather lackadaisical conspirator, if conspirator he was.[22]

As the spring of 1778 approached, Duer was completing a full year in Congress and a review of his role there is in order. As in the Convention, he had managed to make himself conspicuous, but there was always a shortage of willing, competent people and Congress readily appointed anyone who seemed to possess either trait to as many committees as he would accept. Duer served on at least sixty temporary committees, many dealing with supply problems or the constant search for money. His most important standing committee was the Board of War; it often met daily and membership on it often involved sub-committees drawing up instructions for commanders and others. He also served on the commerce and foreign affairs committees before he left Congress. His membership on the temporary committee dealing with the defense of Philadelphia probably caused the most grief as it involved him in Pennsylvania state politics in a dispute which outlasted his congressional term. He was probably an effective worker on his temporary committees as he seems often to have written the reports, an activity which also involved him in controversy. When General Washington objected to congressional conditions on a proposed prisoner exchange with the British, the reply which Duer drafted was so acerbic it had to be toned down before it could be sent to His Excellency. Duer very much resented the tampering with his literary efforts.[23]

We can only surmise about his work on the floor of Congress. He himself told of his activity on behalf of Schuyler shortly after arriving in Philadelphia and since Duane confirmed most of what he said, his self-testimony can be accepted as evidence he was not backward in debate. He seems often to have required the roll to be called on a vote—votes which he frequently lost—so he was adept enough at using parliamentary procedure to stave off, possibly prevent a defeat. Elias Boudinot of New Jersey testified to his effectiveness in debate; as Commissary of Prisoners, Boudinot had borrowed in enemy-occupied New York to feed the prisoners there. When Congress balked at giving him specie to pay back the loan, Boudinot stopped his purchases and the prisoners suffered more than usual. Pulling out all the stops, he appealed to Congress a second time and read from a captive's letter, telling of the privations they suffered. Hearing this, "Mr. Duer (a man of much Feeling) . . . declaimed so severely ag[ains]t. the ungrateful Conduct of the House" that £10,000 in specie from Burgoyne's war chest was sent to New York. Any one who could talk the Continental Congress out of that much money in a half-hour was an effective speaker, as well as a man of some compassion. Duer knew it took more than eloquence to get things done, votes were needed, and he often worked hard at getting absentees back for critical votes. Practical politicking as well as conventional legislative duties must have taken up a good bit of his time and there is evidence that Duer, like most congressmen, had little free time. Even a friend as important as Robert R. Livingston complained that he found Duer "of late too much a Man of business to answer my letters." Henry Laurens, as President of Congress, in a position to know, noted the "multiplicity and hurry of business in which that Gentleman is engaged." However, these same complaints of unanswered correspondence continued into Duer's later career, when there was much less justification for them.[24]

Duer also gained the respect of some outside Congress as well as the notice of the enemy. Colonel Alexander Hamilton, then on Washington's staff, rejoiced that his adopted state did not follow the practice of most states in sending their second raters to Congress, for New York had Gouverneur Morris "and may I not add a Duer?" Morris himself, not an easy man to impress, assured Governor Clinton that Duer contributed importantly not just to New York, "but to the united States of which Congress are fully sensible." Although the enemy did not assess Duer's contributions, he had gone far enough up the ladder of rebellion to come to their notice; Paul Wentworth, secretary of the British peace delegation of 1778, described him somewhat unkindly, but not entirely inaccurately, as a "violent, superficial but popular Zealot created by the times." Of course, what Wentworth called zealotry, Americans called zeal. The Maryland loyalist and Anglican clergyman, Jonathan Boucher, characterized Duer in his epic verse, "The American Times," as "The spritely genius" and asked if he could control "The flow of wit, the follies of the soul,/ Abandon every muse, and every grace,/For eminence among a savage race?" The parson mourned both Duer and Duane, "amiable in the former part of their lives, now alas how changed!" especially their fall from political, if not theological grace.[25]

But the "flow of wit" to which Boucher referred could overflow with disagreeable results. Some of those present during an incident in Reading in January 1778, at which Duer commented sarcastically on British reports of their victories, believed he took advantage of the unfortunate situation of an enemy officer who was on parole there. A hot argument was avoided only by the officer's discretion. Several thought Duer should have apologized for his sarcasm, but instead he "triumphed in his success." The New Yorker seemed the type to "play the bashaw in time of prosperity," but his critic could not admire him; "it was no mark of game to crow upon a dunghill."[26] Thus Duer was attractive and talented enough to win the notice of both friend and foe, but possessed of a wit and turn of phrase which could overflow into malicious sarcasm. Confident of his own ability, talent, and correctness, he probably did not credit the sincerity of those with whom he disagreed. And he was obviously happier running his own show—or practically his own show—in Philadelphia and York than he had been under the tutelage of Schuyler, Robert R. Livingston, Duane, and other New York notables.

Duer spent much of the winter away from a congress which seemed to him both unable and unwilling to tackle seriously its array of difficulties. From Reading, he reminded General Washington of his zeal for the cause by reporting a rather improbable plot on the part of a deserter to surround the American camp at Valley Forge and capture the troops there. He also traveled to Basking Ridge, New Jersey, the country seat of Major-General William Alexander, who called himself Lord Stirling (and was so addressed by the "rebel" generals), to pay court to his daughter, "Lady Kitty," a quest which had begun in 1776. While relaxing there, Duer took advantage of his physical detachment from Congress to take a hard look at it and gave his reaction to Robert R. Livingston. The sad state of American affairs was traced to "the Parties prevailing in our Army, and the Want of foresight, and Attention to business in Congress." While the army was inactive during the winter, public business could more easily be done, yet too many congressmen had gone home and left too few "Men of Business, and real Patriotism to Struggle against Men activated by contracted State Politicks, and rendered impenetrable to all the Effects of Reason by the Superlative Dint of Stupidity." He was confident of the correctness of his judgment; however, he was also confident that the parties in the Army which had produced "an Inactive Campaign, a Relaxation of Discipline and all its Concomitant Evils" could be turned to advantage in future campaigns. Just how this particular miracle was to be accomplished was not specified, but he was certain that with Robert Morris "and other men of Business and Integrity [in Congress]. . . . Something may perhaps be done to alter the present Sickly State of public Affairs."[27] Obviously Duer was on the side of the nationalists here, of those who would fight the War for Independence without any fine regard for the prerogatives of the States, but he may also have been reflecting the concern of many Middle State representatives as to the conduct of the war by the largely Yankee dominated congress. The currency was in disarray, the supply system had just barely managed to keep the few men at Valley Forge alive, the officer corps had been divided by the sort of ill-tempered reactions seen in the Conway Cabal; in brief the war needed to be put on a more businesslike basis. The congress alone could not handle both policy making and execution. Its efforts would have to be assisted by outside agents of some kind.

Duer returned to Congress before the end of March where he found a good many of his colleagues present. This led to a burst of activity which permitted the disposal of several items which had long hung fire. A half-pay measure for Army officers, which had been strongly supported by Duer against the opposition of those who feared it would lead to the creation of a professional army, was passed, along with a revamping of the quartermaster and commissary departments. Not all the activity, however, was welcome; Duer had to work hard to delay a committee report on the abandonment of Fort Ticonderoga the previous September, while Schuyler was still in command there. The general was expected to take his seat in Congress soon and he could undertake his own defense.[28]

These encouraging signs of Congress's active concern with essential business were eclipsed by even more welcome news of an alliance with France. The news was not entirely unexpected; copies of a Parliamentary plan of reconciliation far more generous than anything seen before had already been received and many Americans suspected that such generosity could be inspired only by British knowledge of a Franco-American alliance, news not yet received in America. Their suspicions were confirmed by the receipt on 2 May of copies of two treaties with the French, one of amity and commerce, one of alliance, which had been concluded the previous February. The semi-secret, limited aid previously given by the French would now be replaced by open aid and, possibly, direct participation. Congress's joy was mixed in some cases with fear and suspicion, fear of the traditional enemy of Britain and her former colonies, suspicion that a corrupt Old World monarch could not possibly have pure motives in helping a republican revolution against a brother monarch. But the fears and suspicions were pushed aside by necessity and Congress ratified the treaties unanimously on 4 May with only slight modifications. Resolutions of eternal friendship accompanied the treaties back to France. As if heartened by the news, as it certainly was, Congress resumed its active pace and quickly reorganized the Army and made some further changes—improvements, it was hoped—in the supply system.[29] International alliances were not the only ones contemplated by Duer that spring and the French agreement inadvertently gave his campaign for Lady Kitty's hand a boost. She joined her father at Valley Forge and attended several celebrations in honor of the alliance. Although Duer was not mentioned as attending, the trip to Valley Forge from York was much easier than to Basking Ridge. Not that he would have had much time for romancing. The spring had also brought a flood of business for the Board of War, troublesome French volunteers and the like and it found Duer still "fairly worn down" from the previous fall's illness. Also, formal duties, as usual, were not everything. Congress had just created the post of Inspector-General of the Army and appointed to it a Prussian volunteer whose ability was real, but whose title of nobility was not, "Baron" Frederich von Steuben. The exact duties of the office were not yet settled and Washington had some trouble parrying Steuben's understandable efforts to expand his authority beyond the Commander-in-Chief's understanding of it. After reaching what he hoped was an agreement with Steuben, Washington gave him permission to visit a friend in York. To forestall any further attempts by Steuben, Washington (through Hamilton) warned Duer not to approve any changes in the formal organization of the Army which Steuben might urge. The commander-in-chief had what he hoped was a rough, workable compromise and it was not to be changed. Thus forewarned, the Board was able to turn Steuben away gently when he lobbied it for additional authority.[30]

More than the French alliance cheered Congress. The British had found that their occupation of Philadelphia produced relatively little inconvenience for the Americans, much too little to justify its continued occupation. On 19 June, Washington was able to inform Congress that the city was free of enemy troops. A resolution was passed to convene on 2 July in the capital, there to prepare for a formal celebration of the new alliance and the nation's second anniversary of independence. The return to Philadelphia not only meant the end of an uncomfortable exile in York, but was a tangible sign of the reviving fortunes of the American cause. Thus was the winter of their discontent turned into high summer, although the change did not come until high summer had actually arrived. Congress had barely settled back in when news of the impending arrival of a minister from France came. They were not yet accustomed to having an ally and had given little thought to the accompanying problems, the significant as well as the trivial. Duer and several others were charged with finding suitable accommodations for the minister and escorting him to his rooms. It was not quite so easy to puzzle out the correct procedure by which a republic might receive a minister of a monarchy. Although Conrad Alexandre Gérard arrived in early July (along with a French naval squadron), it was 6 August before he was formally received, with appropriate but republican pomp and ceremony, by Congress.[31]

Through all this Duer continued, as he had for more than a year, to represent New York, a task he had performed almost without respite, despite his repeated requests for a leave of absence. Now almost every letter home from the New York delegates—Duer's partners were Francis Lewis and Gouverneur Morris—contained references to his impending departure. In late July, while informing Governor Clinton of a congressional loan to New York, he assured him he would not leave until he was certain the state would continue to be represented. Morris referred to Duer's momentary departure on three separate occasions. The congressman himself took at least one trip to Basking Ridge, there to pay court to Lady Kitty rather than recalcitrant colleagues. He did not use his imminent departure as an excuse to slacken his activity in Congress, continuing on his standing committees as well as the almost daily addition of temporary committees for specific purposes. Thus he twice deliberated on the defense of Philadelphia and also had to determine the possible loyalism of David Franks, a Philadelphia merchant and commissary to the British prisoners in the city. Individuals sent him plans for military campaigns which they wanted the Board of War to consider. And he continued to attend Congress's daily sessions, speaking on, among other things, price-fixing laws which several states, New York among them, had passed. He and his colleague, Francis Lewis, contended that restrictions usually increased prices because of the illicit trading they inspired.[32] Such opinions were commonplace among conservatives bent on removing or opposing the laws, usually put on the books by radicals attempting to cut down what they perceived as blatant profiteering by merchants. Thus, whatever his wishes (and expectations), Duer was still very much a member of Congress.

But, with the fall, he became much less patient about his long-promised relief. The most likely candidates were the two absent members, Schuyler and Duane, but neither showed any inclination to come to Philadelphia. Finally, on 16 October, the New York Assembly elected a new delegation; Schuyler, Duane, Lewis, and Morris were returned, Duer was dropped, and William Floyd was added. The Assembly also urged those not already in Philadelphia to take up their seats so the state's representation would not be interrupted.[33]

Despite the arrival of Duane early in November, Duer lingered in the city until January 1779. The reason for his delay was in the quarrel then going on with much verbal violence in Congress and the newspapers between the supporters of Silas Deane and those of Arthur Lee. Both were members of the American delegation in France, Lee being the first American to arrive there as an authorized agent of Congress. The dispute ostensibly centered about supplies sent to America through a dummy trading company, a device meant to cover their transfer from the French government to the rebels before the alliance. Deane asserted that the goods had to be paid for, Lee that they were a gift of the French crown and that Deane was trying to bilk the United States into paying him a percentage-commission on their value. The dispute over these contentions masked several subquarrels, one between the predominantly Yankee supporters of Lee and a New York-Pennsylvania group supporting Deane, a second quarrel turned about Pennsylvania's controversial constitution with its radical supporters also backing Lee and the conservatives who attacked it taking up Deane's cause; finally, Gallican nationalists and anti-French provincialists used the topic to square off against each other. Whatever the real issues were supposed to be, they were soon obscured by "prolix articles of political flapdoodle." Yet another theme in the quarrels was the suspicion by some radicals that congressmen were mixing public concerns and private profits in their commercial dealings. The mixing of public and private business, which the commercial ethics of the day largely tolerated, was not understood or condoned by the Adamses, Samuel or John, or the Lees, Richard Henry, Francis Lightfoot and Arthur, but it was the custom of the Morrises, Robert and Gouverneur, James Wilson of Pennsylvania, and Duer.[34]

The quarrel had intensified since Deane's return home from France in July for a brief visit. Duer, while not openly espousing his cause, had become identified with Deane. They had corresponded, while Deane was still in France, about private matters. Now, just as Duer was about to leave Philadelphia, Deane wearied of the delay in obtaining a congressional hearing and made a public appeal for support in December. He was attacked almost immediately by Tom Paine, now Secretary to the Committee for

Foreign Affairs, but still writing as "Common Sense." Duer's contribution to the "political flapdoodle" came a week later. It was a long, exhaustive, and exhausting apologia for Deane which did much to substantiate the "flapdoodle" tag. Writing as "Plain Truth," Duer contradicted just about every one of Paine's assertions and presented Deane as a loyal and competent patriot being maligned for unknown but certainly unworthy reasons.[35] The contents of the piece are not as interesting as the possible reasons for it. The part of polemicist is very different from that of sympathizer and Deane had not lacked for the former, so why had Duer joined the fray? One clue lies in a British intelligence report sent out of New York City in February 1779; in it Duer was identified as "Plain Truth" and linked with a commercial house to be opened in Nantes, France. Among the partners were Deane, Duer, and Robert Morris. Duane explained Duer's lingering in Philadelphia as owing to his writing for Deane and "to settle a Mercantile Connection which promises much advantage." Paine had already alleged that the Deane-Lee quarrel was just a "bubble ... to answer both a mercantile end and a private pique."[36] "Plain Truth" 's effort may have been a token of Duer's loyalty to Deane at a time when commercial relations involved not only fair dealing, but personal loyalty as well. Also, if Congress became convinced that Deane had acted wrongly, he would not be sent back to France and any ventures depending on his residence there as a privileged diplomatic agent would die aborning. Thus Deane's integrity was a commercial as well as a political issue. For three years, Duer had been claiming that his public service was damaging his private affairs and if he did not resume private life, he would be ruined. Apparently his mending efforts had already begun. In addition to the mercantile house, he and Deane were also partners in a contract to supply masts and spars to the Spanish navy.[37]

By now Duer had cut his official links with Congress, attending for the last time on 16 November. He left the city to the praise of some, Robert Morris styling him a "worthy Honest fellow ... his only fault is an over-zeal & anxiety" in public affairs. That "over-zeal" may have been what James Duane was referring to when he commented that Duer would have to be "content with his Continental Character which notwithstanding he has some enemies is very respectable."[38] "Some enemies" was not an understatement. Shortly after he left Philadelphia, Duer was attacked in *The Pennsylvania Packet* by "T[iberius]. G[racchus]." "T. G." condemned him for an officious interference in Pennsylvania's politics which had "brought him to the hatred and contempt" of many in the state. Duer's activities and their repercussions were held up to Gouverneur Morris, to whom the polemic was ostensibly addressed, as an example not to follow. "T. G." then linked Morris, Duer, and Benedict Arnold, military commandant of the city, in crimes too heinous and too well known to print. This mild reproof, by eighteenth-century standards, brought a reply from Duer which was intemperate both in length, more than 3,500 words, and in language. He explained every possible action which might have offended Pennsylvanians of good judgment and integrity and excused them on the grounds of either sound policy or necessity. For example, the commandeering of wagons which, as a member of the Board of War, he ordered in February 1778 was absolutely essential—"if there is any Crisis in the Affairs of a Nation in which Laws must sleep . . . that which has been mentioned was one." Opposition to a loan from Congress to Pennsylvania was justified by a consistent opposition on his part to such loans until accounts between Congress and the states were adjusted. He noted that it was impossible to serve conscientiously in Congress without offending someone, and he only hoped he had avoided giving "just Grounds" for offense. "T. G." 's charges were probably a smokescreen for partisan activities in Pennsylvania. After his work in writing such an extensive rejoinder, it may never have been printed.[39] Why he had written at all is not that clear. "T. G." may have caught him off guard and he wrote without reflection. On thinking it over, he could have decided that renewing his commercial career under the cloud of a new controversy was not wise and his silence might help to put the whole thing down. Since the scribbling of an anonymous and partisan Grub Streeter like "T. G." could not have convinced any but the already convinced, Duer's decision to let well enough alone was untypical but wise.

With this, Duer's congressional career was closed. It had lasted much longer than he had either expected or wanted it to last. Although he had asked for a leave as early as May 1777, he had stayed on almost without interruption until November 1778. At any point in between, he could have followed the example of

James Duane who did not return from a trip to Albany for almost
a year. That he did stay on, serving both his state and country
until New York had a full delegation entitles him to special mention in a body as plagued by absenteeism as Congress was. While
in the congress, he was a diligent and active worker, serving on
two important permanent committees, the Board of War, and
Commerce and Finance at one time, as well as the Committee
on Foreign Affairs. In addition, he served on innumerable temporary committees, for many of which he wrote the report. Now
he was going to turn that diligence and activity to his own account
as he exploited the friendships with influential figures in and out
of Congress which he had also developed in Philadelphia.

References

1. *Historical Memoirs of William Smith*, 105.
2. Worthington C. Ford, ed., *Journals of the Continental Congress, 1774-1789* (Washington, 1907), VII, 230, hereafter cited as JCC; John Adams to Abigail Adams,
   Apr. 19, 1777 in C. F. Adams, ed., *Familiar Letters of John Adams and His Wife
   Abigail Adams During the Revolution* (New York, 1876), 260; Roger Sherman to
   Jonathan Trumbull, Apr. 7, 1777, Emmett Coll., Ms. # 1564, NYPL.
3. JCC, VII, 254, 260, 271, 274, 275; Robert L. Brunhouse, *The Counter-Revolution
   in Pennsylvania, 1776-1790* (Harrisburg, 1942), 29-30, and *passim* for details of the
   very tangled situation in Pennsylvania at this time, hereafter cited as Brunhouse,
   Counter-Revolution.
4. Wm. Duer to Abner Ten Broeck, Apr. 17, 1777, *Journals*, II, 418.
5. James Duane to Robert R. Livingston, et al., Apr. 19, 1777, John Jay Papers, CUL.
6. JCC, VII, 293-94, 296, 300, 314; *Journals*, I, 917, 931.
7. Philip Livingston and James Duane to the New York State Convention, May 23,
   1777, James Duane Papers, NYHS; "Mr. Duer is stept out . . . which prevents his
   signing this letter," Wm. Duer to Robert R. Livingston, May 28, 1777, Livingston
   Collection, NYHS; H. James Henderson, *Party Politics in the Continental Congress*
   (New York, 1974), 105, 112-17, an excellent treatment, hereafter cited as Henderson, *Politics*; Jonathan Gregory Rossie, *The Politics of Command in the American
   Revolution* (Syracuse, NY, 1974), 150-51, hereafter cited as Rossie, *Command*; E.
   P. Alexander, *A Revolutionary Conservative: James Duane of New York* (New York,
   1938), 130-33; see below, 45.
8. JCC, VII, 362; Robert R. Livingston to Wm. Duer, Jun. 12, 1777, Livingston
   Coll., NYHS.
9. Wm. Duer to Philip Schuyler, Jun. 19, 1777, Schuyler Papers, NYPL.
10. James Duane to Robert R. Livingston, Jun. 24, Jul. 2, 1777, Livingston Coll.,
    NYHS.
11. JCC, VIII, 508-13; the resolution is in *Journals*, II, 509-10; see Wm. Duer to Abner
    Ten Broeck, Apr. 17, 1777, *Journals*, II, 418 for Duer's first success in the Vermont
    affair; Wm. Duer to Robert R. Livingston, Jul. 9, 1777, Livingston Coll., NYHS;
    Sherman never learned anything formally within the walls of Yale College; he had
    only a common school education. But he did serve for several years as treasurer of
    the college corporation and was given an A. M., *honoris causa*, in 1768, *Dict. of Am.
    Biog.*, XVII, 89; see Peter S. Onuf, *The Origins of the Federal Republic: Jurisdictional
    Controversies in the United States, 1775-1787* (Phila., 1983), Chap. 5 for an exhaustive
    treatment of the controversy.
12. Marquis Phillipe duCoudray, "Observations on the Delaware Forts," *Pennsylvania*

Magazine of History & Biography, 14 (1900): 347; Edmund C. Burnett, *The Continental Congress* (New York, 1941), 243-44, hereafter cited as Burnett, *Congress*; JCC, VII, 525.

13. Wm. Duer to Robert R. Livingston, Jul. 9, 1777, Livingston Coll., NYHS; Henry Brockholst Livingston to Philip Schuyler, Jul. 29, 1777 (this letter is marked "missing," see the precis, Index. Vol., # 576), Schuyler Papers, NYPL; JCC, VIII, 648-49.

14. JCC, VIII, 704; ibid., VII, 688, 694-95; Brunhouse, *Counter-Revolution*, 42-43; Duer wrote the committee report.

15. James Duane to George Clinton, Sep. 15, 1777, Emmett Coll., Ms. # 664, NYPL; Clinton had been elected governor in the New York elections that spring; Burnett, *Congress*, 246-47; John W. Jordan, "The Military Hospitals at Bethlehem and Lititz During the Revolution," *Pennsylvania Magazine of History & Biography*, 20 (1896): 146.

16. "Resolution of the New York State Assembly," copy, Duane Papers, NYHS; on Oct. 3rd, the Senate agreed with the Assembly and Gov. Clinton approved.

17. JCC, IX, 779-80, 801, 806-807, 841, 927-27; on the handwritten copy of the final draft, several of the amendments in the procedures for settling boundary disputes were in either Duane or Duer's handwriting, a clear sign of their concern over this area; see Henderson, *Politics*, 146-49, for a quantitative analysis of several of the votes on the Articles; his comments on Duer as a states' righter should be considered carefully; New Yorkers, and especially an upstater like Duer took the Vermont issue very seriously and, in this area, voted a narrow conception of the state's interest.

18. JCC, IX, 985-87, 1037; although nothing came of the proposal for the French Legion, it had some influence at the time of the Conway Cabal, see below, 47; Robert R. Livingston to Gouverneur Morris, Jan. 29, 1778, Livingston Coll., NYHS.

19. JCC, IX, 994, 1004, 1013, the call was sent out on Dec. 9th, 1777; Wm. Duer to [James] Wilson, Nov. 30, 1777, Gratz Coll., HSP.

20. A representative of the plot theory is Louis Gottschalk, *Lafayette Joins the American Army* (Chicago, 1937), Chaps. VI-IX, who, by adopting Lafayette's viewpoint, sees a complicated conspiracy centered about the proposed expedition to Canada, commanded by Lafayette, which turned into a wild goose chase, hereafter cited as Gottschalk, *Lafayette Joins*; Washington's editor, John C. Fitzpatrick, *George Washington Himself* (Indianapolis, 1933), sees a plot directed against Washington growing out of the sectional tension between Virginia and New England. Douglass Southall Freeman, *George Washington, Leader of the Revolution, 1776-1778* (New York, 1951), Chaps. 20-25, especially pages 586-612, straightforwardly describes the events which are lumped together as the Conway Cabal and, without saying so directly, suggests there was a conspiracy against the Commander-in-Chief. Bernhard Knollenberg, *George Washington and the American Revolution* (New York, 1940), Chaps. V-VIII, thinks Washington overreacted to criticism in a private letter which Conway had written to Gates and concocted the plot largely out of his indignation. He sees the Cabal as a myth. Henderson, *Politics*, 118-20 and Rossie, *Command*, Chap. XIII, agree with Knollenberg, hereafter cited as Knollenberg, *Washington*; I also agree with Knollenberg. For my own statement, see my *George Washington: A Biography* (Boston, 1979, repr., 1986), 63-64.

21. Marquis de Lafayette to George Washington, Oct. 14, 1777, Lafayette Corr., Vol. I, Pierpont Morgan Library, NYC; Gottschalk, *Lafayette Joins*, 56, 110-31, 134-68; Marquis de Lafayette to Henry Laurens, Jan. 27, 1778, *South Carolina Historical and Genealogical Magazine*, 7 (1906): 182; JCC, X, 87; Marquis de Lafayette to Henry Laurens, Feb. 9, 1778, to George Washington, Feb. 19, 1778, William A. Duer, ed., *Memoirs of . . . General LaFayette* (New York, 1837), I, 153, 154; Phillip Schuyler to Thomas Conway, Feb. 17, 1778, Schuyler Papers, NYPL; see also Schuyler to Robert R. Livingston, Mar. 28, 1778, Livingston Coll., NYHS; JCC, X, 217, 253-54; Wm. Duer to George Washington, Feb. 16, 1778, Washington Papers, LC; Francis Lewis to Pierre Van Cortlandt, Jan. 5, 1778, Edmund C. Burnett, ed., *Letters of Members of the Continental Congress* (Washington, 1926), III, 15-16, hereafter cited as Burnett, *Letters*; Robert R. Livingston to Gouverneur Morris, [Jan. 5-7, 1778], Livingston Coll., NYHS.

22. Knollenberg, *Washington*, 50-59, 80-84, 188, 206-208; William A. Duer, *Life of William Alexander, Earl of Stirling* (New York, 1847), 183-84 for a story told by Duer's son of his readiness to risk his life to save Washington's position during the Cabal. It rests on no contemporary evidence, but see Morgan Lewis to William A. Duer, Apr. 10, 1837, Autograph Letters, Vol. I, #45, NYHS; see also Rupert Hughes, *George Washington* (New York, 1930), III, 256; for the confused character of the events historians have called the Conway Cabal, see Gouverneur Morris to Robert R. Livingston, Mar. 10, 1778, Livingston Coll., NYHS for Morris's suspicion that Duer and Major-General Thomas Mifflin, Pennsylvania, were at the head of the anti-Washington effort.

23. JCC, VII, 363, XI, 776-77, X, 337, XI, 559; see above, 36, and below, 56-57, for the Pennsylvania incidents; for Duer's reply to Washington, see JCC, X, 294-95 and Thomas Burke to Richard Coswell, Apr. 29, 1778, Burnett, *Letters*, III, 204.

24. Elias Boudinot, Jul. 31, 1778, Burnett, *Letters*, III, 356-58; Wm. Duer to Robert Morris, Apr. 12, 1778, ibid., 164; Wm. Duer & Gouverneur Morris to Robert Morris, May 11, 1778, ibid., 230-31; Robert R. Livingston to Gouverneur Morris, Jan. ?, 1778, Livingston Coll., NYHS; Henry Laurens to Chevalier de Luneville, Aug. 23, [1778], Burnett, *Letters*, III, 381.

25. Alexander Hamilton to George Clinton, Feb. 13, 1778, Harold C. Syrett, ed., *The Papers of Alexander Hamilton* (New York, 1961), I, 425, hereafter cited as Syrett, *Hamilton Papers*; Gouverneur Morris to George Clinton, Jun. 23, 1778, Emmett Coll., Ms. # 9478, NYPL; [Paul Wentworth], "Minutes respecting political Parties in America and Sketches of the leading Persons in each Province [1778]," B. F. Stevens, comp., *Facsimiles of Manuscripts in European Archives Relating to America, 1773-1783* (London, 1895), XXV, # 487; Camillo Querno [Jonathan Boucher], "The American Times . . .," [New York, 1778, Evans # 16697], 36-37.

26. Alexander Graydon, *Memoirs of His Own Time . . .*, J. S. Littell, ed. (Phila., 1846), 302-303.

27. Wm. Duer to George Washington, Feb. 16, 1778, George Washington to Wm. Duer, Feb. 21, 1778, Washington Papers, LC; Gouverneur Morris to Robert R. Livingston, Mar. 10, 1778, Livingston Coll., NYHS; for an explanation of the Stirling title, see Paul D. Nelson, *William Alexander, Lord Stirling* (University, AL, 1987), Chap. III, hereafter cited as Nelson, *Alexander*; Wm. Duer to Robert R. Livingston, Mar. 10, 1778, Livingston Coll., NYHS.

28. Wm. Duer to Robert Morris, Apr. 12, 1778, Burnett, *Letters*, III, 164; Wm. Duer & Gouverneur Morris to Robert Morris, May 11, 1778, ibid., 230-31; Henry Laurens to George Washington, Apr. 4, 1778, ibid., 150-51.

29. JCC, XI, 538-43, 545-46, 548.

30. *New York Journal and General Advertiser* (Poughkeepsie), Jun. 15, 1778; John Jay to Gouverneur Morris, Jun. 3, 1778, Jay Papers, CUL; Alexander Hamilton to Wm. Duer, Jun. 18, 1778, Syrett, *Hamilton Papers*, I, 497-501; John M. Palmer, *General Von Steuben* (New Haven, 1937), 170-76; Broadus Mitchell, *Alexander Hamilton* (New York, 1957), I, 157-58.

31. JCC, XI, 685.

32. Wm. Duer and Gouverneur Morris to George Clinton, Jul. 21, 1778, *Clinton Papers*, III, 567-69; Gouverneur Morris to Robert R. Livingston, Aug. 17, Aug. 28, Sep. 22, 1778, Livingston Coll., NYHS; Wm. Duer to George Clinton, Aug. 18, 1778, *Clinton Papers*, III, 660-61; JCC, XI, 825, XII, 981, 990-91, 1032-33; Edward Hand to Wm. Duer, Sep. 20, 1778, Duer Papers, BV I, NYHS; for the radical economic thought of the time, see Eric Foner, *Tom Paine and Revolutionary America* (New York, 1976), esp. Chaps. 4 and 5.

33. Walter Livingston to Philip Schuyler, Oct. 16, 1778, Schuyler Papers, NYPL.

34. The quotation is from Brunhouse, *Counter-Revolution*, 60-61; see Burnett, *Congress*, 360-69, and Jack N. Rakove, *The Beginnings of National Politics: An Interpretive History of the Continental Congress* (New York, 1979), 249-55, and Henderson, *Politics*, 187-96, for full discussions of the affair; Richard Henry Lee to Francis Lightfoot Lee, Jul. 21, 1778, Burnett, *Letters*, III, 352.

35. Robert A. East, *Business Enterprise in the American Revolutionary Era* (Gloucester, MA, 1964, repr.), 197-98, hereafter cited as East, *Business Enterprise*; see Thomas P. Abernethy, "The Commercial Activities of Silas Deane in France," *American Historical Review*, 39 (1934): 477-85; Julian P. Boyd, "Silas Deane: Death by a Kindly Teacher of Treason?" *William and Mary Quarterly*, 3 s., 16 (1959): 165-87, 319-42, 515-50, for corroboration of some of the charges of Lee's supporters; Silas Deane to President, Continental Congress, Nov. 1, 1778; Charles Isham, ed., *The Deane Papers* (New York, 1888), III, 43-45; "Strictures on the Address of Common Sense to Mr. Deane . . . by Plain Truth," *The Pennsylvania Packet*, Dec. 21, 1778. Although Duer did not acknowledge authorship, Duane mentioned that he had "taken up the Pen for Mr. Deane against Common Sense," James Duane to Robert R. Livingston, Jan. 3, 1779, Livingston Coll., NYHS; also, on Dec. 8, Edward Langworthy promised Duer the letters he had asked for, Edward Langworthy to Wm. Duer, Dec. 8, 1778, Burnett, *Letters*, III, 540, and "Plain Truth" used several letters; finally, Andrew Elliott, a loyalist living in New York City, mentioned that Duer was spoken of as "Plain Truth," "Paper of Intelligence No. 2, Transmitted by Andrew Elliott, New York, to the Earl of Carlisle," Stevens, *Facsimilies*, I, # 115.
36. *Loc. cit.*; James Duane to Robert R. Livingston, Jan. 3, 1779, Livingston Coll., NYHS; *The Pennsylvania Packet*, Dec. 14, 1778.
37. See below, 65-69.
38. JCC, XII, 1134-35; Robert Morris to James Duane, Sep. 8, 1778, Duane Papers, NYHS; James Duane to Robert R. Livingston, Jan. 3, 1779, Livingston Coll., NYHS.
39. *The Pennsylvania Packet*, Mar. 2, 1779; Duer and Deane lived with Arnold for a time, James T. Flexner, *The Traitor and the Spy* (New York, 1953), 228; Wm. Duer, "Camp on Raritan . . .," Mar. 9, 1779, Emmett Coll., Ms. # 669, NYPL; extracts are in Burnett, *Letters*, IV, 97-103; Duer's essay may have been printed in the *Packet*, but copies for the time of likely publication do not survive. I have assumed that it was not printed.

Chapter IV

Commercial Life after the Congress

January 1779–December 1783

After the delay in leaving Philadelphia, Duer wasted little further time in starting to mend his "damaged fortunes." In mid-March, he was at Fishkill, an important Continental supply center. From there he was trying to sell his Charlotte County lands to Philip Schuyler in order to obtain the necessary funds for a quick financial coup. An obliging Silas Deane had sent rumors of a peace from Paris, rumors seconded by a member of Congress. Duer's plan was to secure the largest possible quantity of Continental currency, which he believed would rapidly appreciate at the news of a peace treaty. He also wanted to go to Staten Island (within British lines) for an unspecified purpose. Fortunately for Duer, he could not go through with either of his plans. Schuyler was not interested in the land, and thus he was not caught with a large sum of depreciating Continental currency when the peace rumors proved false. General Washington refused to exempt Duer from the general rule of securing Governor Clinton's permission before giving him the Staten Island pass. Duer decided not to pursue the matter further, especially as it might "give to the Enemy an Opportunity of assigning Reasons for it, injurious to the Interests of America, and perhaps to my own character." He would find another way to accomplish his unspecified purpose.[1] While he fretted about the possible inferences some might make of a trip behind enemy lines, he showed no fear of what some might think of a meeting with William Constable at Frankford, a village near Philadelphia.

Constable, a son of the Schenectady physician who had treated Duer in 1773, had gone to Britain the same year. Having been caught there by the coming of the war, he managed to get to Philadelphia when it was held by the British, along with a cargo of scarce goods. He got some of his property out of the city, through the lines of both armies, and hid the rest in the city. All was later sold at what was likely to have been a large profit. The Pennsylvania radicals, those supporting the 1776 constitution, alleged that Benedict Arnold, who had signed Constable's pass through American lines, had shared in the profit. Arnold, now the military commandant of the city, was quickly becoming very unpopular with the radicals, the same group whose charges had already stung Duer into his wordy, although probably unpublished reply. Indeed, they had also accused Duer of sharing in the profits of Constable's dubious transaction. Associating with Constable had obvious political dangers for Duer, so it was apparent that he had, for the time, put politics behind him. Whatever the purpose of their meeting was, and it may only have been to enlist Duer's help in getting Clinton's permission for the prodigal to return to Schenectady, it was a clear signal that Duer was not concerned about any difficulties it might make for him in Philadelphia.[2] Constable was one of the business-as-usual merchants who traded wherever and however profit took them and who drove the Pennsylvania radicals and like-minded men from other states to peaks of patriotic anger.

From these two indications, it might be assumed that the rebuilding of Duer's personal finances would not be guided too much—despite his protestations of consideration for the patriot cause—by a stringent application of self-denying prohibitions of irregular or unethical conduct. No matter how innocent his desire to see a "Mr. Elliott" on Staten Island was, to consider going behind enemy lines was to open oneself and associates to the suspicion of trading with the enemy. Further, to assist Constable in getting back to Schenectady, if that was the purpose of the Frankford meeting, after the charges of illicit trading had been aired, was not demonstrating a very high standard in choosing associates. If these two incidents were prophetic, Duer's effort to regain affluence would be an interesting one.

But he was not ready to disregard all public and private ethics. While he had been in Congress, several friends in New York had reminded him of the poor impression his unsettled accounts from 1776-77 were making, in spite of the reason his congressional duties gave for postponing them. Now that that reason no longer held, he moved to settle them, advising early in May of the opening of an office in Albany to which creditors could bring vouchers, etc. for settlement. He had already taken steps to relieve some of his agents who were being pressed for monies spent at his order. Both Westchester Committee accounts and the accounts of his purchases for Quartermaster General Mifflin were still unsettled.[3] He also found time to serve as a volunteer on Governor George Clinton's staff, signing himself as "aide-de-camp." He remained with Clinton until the end of July when he was able to end one of his lengthier campaigns. He traveled to Basking Ridge where he married "Lady Kitty" Alexander on 27 July 1779. General Washington gave Alexander compassionate leave to attend the ceremony and festivities. After a wedding trip to Albany, the couple settled in at Fishkill, while Duer cast about for commercial opportunities.[4]

However, his stay in Philadelphia had prepared him for more than small-scale buying and selling in the Hudson Valley. The contacts made there had given him access to a network which spread through not only the committees of Congress, but also abroad through the French and Spanish representatives at the capital, as well as, through Deane, American representatives abroad. Before he had left Philadelphia, he had begun to exploit these connections by signing a contract, in partnership with Deane and the Pennsylvania jurist (and land speculator), James Wilson, to supply masts and spars to the Spanish navy. Don Juan deMiralles, the Spanish representative in Philadelphia, had signed the agreement, but it had to be approved in Madrid before it was valid. Don Juan's role, however, was more than official; he was to receive one-fourth of the profits, if any. (No mention was made of a corresponding share of the losses, if any.) The contract was very generous to the entrepreneurs, providing as it did for payment in specie within three days of receipt of a cargo, with an 80 percent advance if the cargoes were not convoyed to Spain, and the privilege of exporting return cargoes duty-free. Each of the American partners was to put $100,000 (Continental) into a capital fund. In March 1779, Duer and M. Jacques Rey deChaumont, styling themselves as "contractors to the Court of France," agreed with Deane, Wilson, and Mark Bird, Wilson's brother-in-law, to look for other mast contracts. Wilson and Bird, a Reading, Pennsylvania, ironmaster, also agreed to secure the masts for the Spanish contract. What seems to have happened is that these agreements—and possibly others not preserved—were proposed and tentatively accepted by Miralles and John Holker, the French naval agent in Philadelphia, with the terms being arranged and re-arranged to suit the different parties.[5] What was certainly happening was that Duer, Deane, et al., were attempting to capture what looked to be a lucrative opportunity by using Deane's presence in Paris, where he could mix public service with private profit, and by bribing Don Juan with a share of the potential profits. "Common Sense" 's assertion that the Deane-Lee squabble covered a "mercantile end" was correct enough, although possibly not the way Paine intended it. Later, when it seemed necessary, the partners tried to enlist John Jay, then Minister to Spain, to salvage the Spanish contract and thought of involving Holker more directly in the French contract. Duer's belief that public office should not prevent anyone from getting ahead, was now being given free rein. As has already been noted, he was not unique in this; any number of contemporary businessmen looked upon any chance for profit that came their way through a public office as just one of the perquisites of office.[6]

The first hopeful sign, with respect to these contracts, was a request, early in 1780, from France for two sample cargoes to be checked for quality before a formal contract was signed. Immediately Duer asked the new French minister, Chevalier Anne C. de LaLuzerne to intercede with General Washington for troops to guard mast cutters on the upper Delaware River. Duer offered to pay for the unit's rations. In addition to securing much needed masts for America's honored ally, he argued that the troops would also permit the inhabitants to return and plant a spring crop. Luzerne, as befitted his profession, dealt with the request diplomatically, relaying it to Washington with a note leaving it entirely to the general whether or not the request should be granted. The hopeful contractor also wrote to several officers whom Washington might consult, urging them to recommend it. All this was to no avail, as Washington politely turned him down, recommending he ask Pennsylvania for militia, if he felt protection was absolutely needed. Considering Duer's recent tangles with that state's authorities, that was enough to kill his interest in the Delaware and he turned to the Connecticut River valley.[7]

Affairs seemed somewhat more promising in Paris where Deane had been busy. The American agent believed he had Jay's agreement to "cautiously assist" him and he had also received formal acceptance of the French contract, pending approval of the sample cargoes. He had taken care of some protested bills of Duer's and reopened negotiations with the Spanish court about mast sales there. (Don Juan's untimely death had canceled that contract.) None of this prepared Duer for Deane's astonishing about-face in the fall of 1780 when he announced to the startled New Yorker that the contract could not possibly be executed during the war—why not wait for the peace? Not only had Deane's tone about the contract changed; he also began to show his increasing isolation from the other members of the American mission in Paris. Benjamin Franklin was a fussy old fool, John Adams's conduct could only be explained by his probable desertion to the enemy, a route which Arthur Lee would also take soon. Deane predicted that these derelictions within the American mission would probably cause the French to lose faith in the American cause and, perhaps, lose the war for the United States. Meanwhile, Duer was collecting masts at Wethersfield, Connecticut, for possible shipment. Learning that Deane had stopped working on the contract complicated an already difficult situation, as Duer was advised that the masts' quality was so poor that it would be foolish to send them.[8] Deane had also lost faith in the American cause, advising Congress to strike the best possible bargain with the British to avoid unconditional submission when the inevitable defeat occurred. Duer took several of Deane's letters to Luzerne as a token of his disapproval and told Tom Paine—who had described the New Yorker as "sometimes a sloven, and sometimes a Beau"—that Deane was a "damned artful rascal." On hearing of this, Deane angrily broke off all contact with Duer, although he did try to secure compensation from Chaumont and Wilson for advances he had made on behalf of the contract. His price was withdrawal from it, as his presence might, by 1783, be a liability. Apparently, no replies were made to his letters and thus the venture, which was to have made the partners' fortunes, effectively ended. Even in peacetime, its large scale would have made it difficult to execute; with the perils of wartime added, it became close to impossible. Fortunes were made by enterprising merchants during the war, but not in commodities as bulky and cheaply priced as masts. Also, Deane was involved in a number of commercial ventures in France, both before and after his American visit in 1778-79. The charges Lee made against him seem to have been largely true; he was using his position in Europe to increase his personal fortune. And his personal secretary, Edward Bancroft—with or without Deane's knowledge is not clear—was sending information of the American mission's activities to the British. When the whole thing collapsed, Duer was well out of it, for Deane finished the war living in London with the odor of suspected treason hanging about him. Duer's early efforts to "repair his damaged fortunes" were, to say the least, unfortunate.[9]

The mast contract was only part of those efforts. For immediate income, Duer began to buy and sell goods of all descriptions in the Hudson Valley, using the proceeds from the sale of Fort Miller lumber as his working capital.[10] He and Robert Morris thought of opening a direct trade with China, but prudently postponed this until after the war. Continuing to tap into his network of congressional acquaintances, Duer purchased several confiscated loyalist farms in New York, using money borrowed from Morris who, despite some qualms, also purchased several. Morris felt that anyone who "had an early and active part in the Revolution" would open himself to the "imputation of having had such views in the origin" of his actions by making many purchases of this sort. "It is only a delicacy of this kind and a desire to stand as fair as I deserve in the opinions of many well meaning people that disapprove this" sort of thing that gave him misgivings. (It might be pertinent to note that Duer ignored the whole question, instead urging Morris to buy still more farms. He probably did not understand Morris's point at all.) Duer also wanted to open a store near Albany in union with Morris and the French naval agent, but the latter vetoed it, saying that the risk was all his, the profits all Duer's. Thus, other than the lumber profits, Duer apparently had no capital ready to invest. Since he does not seem to have put anything into the mast venture, drawing on Deane via bills of exchange, either he started the war with nothing or his complaints of "damaged fortunes" were at least partially true. His capital, such as it was, seemed to consist mainly of the friends he had made in Philadelphia and he continued to try and unite himself with them in ventures designed to yield relatively quick returns. An example was his effort in 1780 to secure a contract to provision the one available source of hard money in the United States, the French expeditionary force. He offered to supply them with wheat at thirty shillings (NY) per bushel, taking more than one-half of that in coin as an advance. The coin would buy merchandise at a low rate, which merchandise would then be bartered for the wheat, thus realizing a double profit (it was hoped), first, on the merchandise to the farmers, second, on the wheat to the French. There was a certain profit of £20,000 (NY), according to Duer's reckoning, even after subtracting for bribes to inspectors—"for French wheels, as I am informed, require Grease, as well as English." Duer's partners were to be Holker, Morris, and Philip Schuyler, the last added to reassure the French as to the group's trustworthiness. Despite the Marquis de Lafayette's presentation of the bid, the contract went to Jeremiah Wadsworth of Connecticut and others. Duer managed to get some French gold by sub-contracting from Wadsworth. But he missed not only the primary contractor's profits, he also missed a chance to accumulate a store of specie invaluable for later operations.[11]

Trading with the French, however, promised too much to let it slip by without making another attempt. In June 1781, Duer tried again, using his father-in-law, General Alexander, still commanding in northern New York, as an intermediary. The French forces were moving south from Rhode Island and Duer wanted to feed them as they passed through New York. He realized it was "delicate to interfere in recommending a person so closely connected with you as I am, but if you can do it in such a manner as you shall deem Consistent with Propriety, you will oblige me extremely." His realization of the delicacy of the request did not stop him from adding that a word from General Washington, if it could be managed, would also help. What boost, if any, General Alexander gave his efforts cannot be determined, but this time Duer was successful. Within a month he and his partners, Daniel Parker, a Massachusetts merchant then operating in New York, and Morgan Lewis, the son of the man who served with him in Congress, were buying grain for the French. The partners shared the contract with Wadsworth so, although Daniel Parker and Company, as they called themselves, did not get all the contract, they did get their share directly, without going through a prime contractor. As with the first effort, they intended to start stores in Ulster, Dutchess, and Orange Counties where the grain was to be purchased thus securing it, they hoped, without having to spend any more of the very desirable French coin than was absolutely necessary.[12] On this contract, where Duer wanted to impress everyone with his efficiency, everything seemed to go wrong. Parker let it slip that they were buying for the French and immediately grain went up 30 percent, payable in gold at delivery. Duer seemed genuinely shocked at this proof of the attraction of French gold to others. Compounding this, agents at Fishkill were guilty of "Vanity and Indiscretion," further delaying the purchases of grain. When Wadsworth complained about the delay, Duer protested, quite untruthfully, that he had not wanted the contract because of its difficulty, but now that he had it, he would not sacrifice his mercantile reputation by losing it. Parker was responsible for what had gone wrong with this contract and some other misdeeds—unspecified—which had put all of Duer's affairs in jeopardy. If it would be helpful, Parker could be dropped. But Duer was especially insulted by the merchants Wadsworth proposed to use instead of Parker and Company. Apparently, the only competent persons concerned in the venture were Duer and Wadsworth; at any rate, they were the only ones free from blame for the mess. He finished a letter to Wadsworth with the self-serving misstatement: "It is not my Disposition or Wish to Sollicit [sic] Business—but having Engaged in it I cannot think of quitting it with any Loss of Reputation."[13] Or profit, one is tempted to add.

Actually, since leaving Congress, Duer had done little but "Sollicit" business. Now that he had it, however, and it was proving difficult, he protested that he had not really wanted it and others were to blame for whatever problems were developing. This penchant would be repeated throughout Duer's business career: the planning and offering of what promised to be a very profitable enterprise (at least according to him), its acceptance and the beginning of its execution; then, when the first difficulties appeared, Duer's generous distribution of responsibility to everyone but himself. He had the ability to relate separate transactions into a coherent pattern as, for example, in the first French contract proposal in which the advance would buy the merchandise, the merchandise the grain. This gave the partners the time they needed to sell the bills of exchange, by which the balance due was to be paid, at a profit; since the bills were taken at a 30 percent discount, only a little time was needed to make a profit on them. On paper, everything contributed to a profitable conclusion. But Duer seemed to lack the staying power needed to execute this contract, or any other mercantile endeavor, efficiently and effectively. This is in marked and puzzling contrast to the diligence with which his congressional colleagues credited him.

As if whetted by the contract with the French, Duer continued eagerly to solicit the only large-scale consumers of the time, governments, but he switched his attention to Congress. That body, reacting to the military defeats of Charleston and Camden and the treason of Benedict Arnold, all during the summer of 1780, responded to the pressure of a number of northern states and instituted several reforms designed to make more efficient and effective its execution of the war effort. Among these steps was the appointment, in the spring of 1781, of Robert Morris as Superintendent of Finance; Morris described his task as the introduction of "vigour in the laying & collecting the Continental Revenues, System and Economy in the Expenditure of them." Duer's personal friendship, illustrated by Morris and his wife's sponsoring of his first son, William Alexander, at his christening, now might pay substantial dividends. Indeed, Morris, shortly after his appointment, took Duer to task for not cooperating with him in promoting the Bank of North America, an institution chartered by Congress to assist the Superintendent. He wanted Duer to publicize it informally as a very profitable investment. This the New Yorker readily agreed to do, "in order that private Interest may Unite with public Zeal"; he believed the institution's advantages would best be presented to those who understood such matters and had the money to invest. As soon as he had the specie, Duer himself would take shares. Then, to remind Morris that this could be a two way street, that there might be a quid for the quo, he mentioned hearing of a possible flour purchase for the Army. "I flatter myself our Friendship will not delay you from employing me in this Line" as it would be more pleasing for him to supply the American rather than the French forces, providing he could do it without risking his "Fortune and Credit." Duer's patriotism had its limits.[14]

Although economy seems to have been Robert Morris's primary goal when he began his supervision of congressional finances, events soon conspired to make him, in effect, the chief provisioner of the Army. The coincidental availability of a French fleet in American waters with the British general Lord Cornwallis's retreat onto the peninsula at Yorktown in the summer of 1781 created an opportunity too tempting to be missed. If the French fleet could hold off a relief by the Royal Navy, it might create a situation where a combined Franco-American army could force Cornwallis's surrender through a siege. Timing was critical and Morris postponed plans to reform the supply system of the Army, instead devoting his considerable managerial skills to supplying the French and American forces, especially the latter, as they moved from their camps in and around New York and northern New Jersey toward the Chesapeake. Morris did not, however, forget the troops left behind to cover the British on Manhattan Island, and hired Duer to lay in 2,000 barrels of flour for the winter, a task made necessary by New York State's failure to deliver on a congressional requisition. From Philadelphia, where he had negotiated the contract, Duer instructed his agents as to the quantity needed, prices which could be paid, and the quality of Morris's bank drafts—"will answer all the Purposes of Specie in Hand." He stressed the importance of this contract as a demonstration of his ability to deliver the goods: "If I succeed in this Essay, I shall so firmly Establish myself as not to fear being Employed in Engagements which will Enable me to serve myself and Friends."[15]

Duer's expectation of future contracts was reasonable for the Army's present supply system had collapsed—witness Morris's unwilling assumption of responsibility—and an alternative system had to be devised. The men for whom Duer's flour was meant were bereft of even paper and sealing wax, almost as essential for an eighteenth-century army as flour, beef, and rum. General John Stark reported to Alexander from Saratoga that he was so short of forage, the draft horses were too weak to move the field pieces if necessary.[16] Throughout the war, supply of everything needed by the American troops had been a problem, but food had been an especially vexing one. In the beginning, army agents had purchased provisions directly from farmers. This had not supplied the Army well and it produced friction with the states when foodstuffs were moved through state embargoes. In 1779, Congress began trying to provision the Army by requisitioning foodstuffs from the states in lieu of money. The states had not paid the money requisitions and they did not now pay the requisitions in kind. Under this system, the supply of the troops fell to its lowest point in efficiency and effectiveness, with the officers frequently having to feed the men by requisitioning from area farmers. The Army was kept in the field, but the costs, political as well as monetary, were very high; under the requisition system, Congress was reduced to a kind of clerk, handling exchanges between the Army and the states.[17] After the Yorktown campaign was supplied, Morris decided to link private and public interest by employing private contractors to provision the Army. By procuring, transporting, and issuing the rations, the contractors would free the government from much of the cost of the commissariat at a price kept reasonable by sealed, competitive bidding. If the troops could be satisfactorily supplied by this system, Morris would have achieved what none of his predecessors had.

To ensure a representative selection of bids on the first contract, to begin in January 1782, Morris circularized his friends, asking them to bid. To help Duer in bidding for West Point and the posts above it, he directed him to deposit a quantity of flour and beef at the Point. If Duer won the contract, they could be used in it. If he did not, Morris would buy the provisions from him. However, even with an advantage like this, Duer's bid was too high and the contract went to Joshua and Comfort Sands. In consoling Duer, Morris told him to keep in touch as he might still be able to serve "that great Cause which every honest American is bound to Support."[18]

That opportunity was not long in coming. Jonathan Lawrence and Melancton Smith had taken a contract for the posts north of Poughkeepsie for the first three months of the year, but they chose not to continue in it and it was opened for general bidding. Duer commissioned Robert R. Livingston, then serving as Secretary for Foreign Affairs for Congress, to act for him in Philadelphia. Using the Smith and Lawrence contract as a model, Livingston drafted a proposal and entered it with a bid of nine pennies (PA) per ration. (Smith and Lawrence had not made a profit at eleven and one-half pennies.) Morris awarded the contract, but not without some reservations. He strongly suggested that Livingston's cousin, Walter, who had stood in for the Secretary at the contract signing, be associated with Duer in the contract. He was known in the area and was a "Man of patience and perseverance," who would help in securing satisfaction for the government and profit for the contractor. Apparently, Walter Livingston was expected to supply qualities Duer lacked. At the formal signing, however, Livingston acted only for Duer, not for himself. Even though he had urged Duer to bid for government business, Morris's misgivings were real, and along with the official notice of the contract, went a private word of advice. The Superintendent advised Duer to execute the contract faithfully as "your character may be much affected by any failure." He was especially concerned that the New Yorker was spreading himself too thin and again urged him to take in Walter Livingston, whose help would far outweigh any share of the profits he would take.[19]

With this rather grudging send-off, Duer's army contracting, which would continue with few interruptions until 1792, began. Morris was not the only one who had misgivings about Duer's administrative talents; Isaac Smith agreed with his brother, Melancton, of Smith and Lawrence, that Duer had bid much too low a price to make a profit. About the only one who did not seem to be worried was Duer, who wasted no time in renting the parsonage of the "Dutch Church" in Albany for two years, and settling his growing family—a daughter, Henrietta, had been born in 1781—in it. Before the end of February, he had sent an agent, Elisha Crane, north to Charlestown, New York, to trade merchandise for beef cattle. Although the contract did not begin until 1 April, he was taking no chances on missing the first distribution of rations. Before 15 March, Crane was on the scene and advising his employer as to what goods might be attractive to the area farmers.[20]

Duer's partner in the contract was Daniel Parker. Throughout the rest of the war, he would be paired with the Massachusetts man under a number of company names, and it is not always possible to tell if Daniel Parker and Company included Duer or if William Duer and Company included Parker, although usually it was the case. Parker was definitely involved in this contract, traveling to Connecticut to purchase cattle "on your and our Account" and Duer listed him as having a one-third interest in the contract in an undated letter. Nowhere in the contract is either Parker or John Holker, the holder of the other third, named. Holker's share was in return for the capital Duer needed to get moving on the contract. And move he did. He had a clerk in Saratoga, the point from which most of the issues would be made, five days before the contract began; this man advised him that the troops were seriously short of just about everything. Morris also took up Duer's offer to provide his posts with firewood and forage.[21] Whatever doubts others might have about Duer's business skills, he did not share them. Even as he was beginning issues on the north of Poughkeepsie contract, Morris was receiving bids on supplying the Moving Army, those troops not assigned to a specific garrison. When they were opened on 2 April, Daniel Parker and Company was the low bidder, but in the wrong currency; Duer's bid was eight and five-eighths pennies (PA) per ration. When Morris announced the bid, the others "were all Surprised and said he could not execute the Contract for that Sum, nor anything like it." No one will ever know who was correct, for when Morris discovered that William Trumbull, Duer's attorney, could not post the necessary security and that Duer had made several stipulations in his bid, he declared it unacceptable. He gave the contract to the next highest bidder, after explaining the situation to Congress and getting their consent to the higher price.[22]

Despite the confidence in himself he demonstrated by bidding for the Moving Army contract, Duer was already having trouble keeping the north of Poughkeepsie contract. The commander of one post, Lieutenant Nicholas Quackenbush, informed Duer's clerk at Saratoga "in his usual tone . . . the next acc[oun]t. I receive of him, he will be starved." Although Quackenbush probably survived the perils of war, the clerk, Enoch Leonard, was quite specific in his constant complaints about shortages. While the general officers had apparently made no complaints yet, Duer was having difficulty and, in early May, found it necessary to deny rumors of serious lapses which had reached Morris in Philadelphia. Undercutting the force of his denials, he also had to ask him for help in getting a loan from the Bank of North America; this was occasioned by a sharp rise in farmers' prices. Morris at first refused to help Duer because New York had refused to circulate the Bank's notes and had also failed to pay its 1781 congressional requisitions. Morris later relented and interceded for the loan, unsuccessfully. He was able to help Duer by giving him $8,200 in bank notes for April and May's issues, despite an incomplete set of vouchers. Duer was already having trouble carrying the contract from one month to another; if he had started out with adequate capital, this should not have happened. Later, Morris's remittances would be unreasonably delayed, but Duer was in trouble when the remittances were prompt and reasonably complete. He had probably diverted some of Morris's advance into other projects.[23] Enoch Leonard continued his complaints from Saratoga, where most of the men dependent on Duer were stationed; flour, whiskey, even the writing paper on which he wrote his complaints was in scarce supply. Cattle were being brought to the post, but too often were underweight. Duer's reply to these complaints was to accuse Leonard, possibly on the basis of officers' complaints, of sloppy management and dishonesty. Even if there had been shortcomings, Duer could not have been serious in his charges, for he did not discharge the clerk immediately. Rather, they were part of a recurring pattern already noted; when things began to go badly, he always shifted the blame to someone else. Leonard was the victim here. There was a simple enough explanation for Duer's difficulties; he was not offering a high enough price for the flour, beef, and other provisions, and the price he was offering was in thirty-day notes, not the cash the farmers could get from others. They had had too much difficulty in the past with Continental and state agents' promises to pay to trust Duer's promises, even if the price had been attractive. By early August, the contractor began to recognize reality and offered a bonus for grain as he was in "great Anxiety" about being able to deliver sufficient flour. Henry Livingston, Walter's brother, advised Duer early in August that cattle could be bought only for cash "as our people have been too often disappointed by the persons . . . purchasing for these few years past." A bonus would be insufficient. Only cash would do.[24]

Duer would have liked very much to offer cash, but two events conspired to make that virtually impossible: an ever increasing delay in settling accounts at the Auditor's Office in Philadelphia and a crisis in government finance, beginning in August and running through October, which affected Morris's ability to pay Duer. Beginning in July, Duer's messenger, James Geary, complained of the slowness and exactitude with which the Auditor's clerks worked. Twice, Morris sent partial payments of $5,000 against unsettled accounts when it appeared their complete settlement would take too long, thus substantiating somewhat Geary's allegation that a "Want of Capacity" in the clerks, who made "many foolish, wrong objections in direct contradiction" of the Office's rules explained the delays.[25]

Morris's partial payments did not bring thanks from Duer, but rather a stinging reproof that he could not possibly continue in the contract unless he received prompt, complete remittances. But then he went beyond the present concerns of the contract, the price of beef and the greed of farmers, to suggest that Morris shock the country out of its present lethargy and demand separate and distinct funds for the Army, something to which Duer believed the country would be driven anyway. Why not do it now, Duer asked rhetorically, before his and Morris's reputations and usefulness were sacrificed? Thus he had transferred the nationalism he had demonstrated in Congress to his current concerns, which were at once wider and narrower than those of his previous service. Wider in that a really thoroughgoing reform of congressional finances had to include giving it the power to tax, making the recently ratified Articles of Confederation the stronger frame of union for which many had been working. Duer's demand for a separate levy for the Army can be dismissed as rhetorical overkill. A steady revenue for Congress would have been spent, necessarily, on the most pressing needs, those of the Army. Thus Duer's narrower concern, that he be paid, would have been eased by any congressional tax, not the separate fund he had proposed. Drastic or moderate, any demand for payment was catching Morris at a very bad time. British attacks on American commerce increased to a peak in the summer of 1782 and dried up his usual sources of money. This came at the same time several loans from the Bank of North America had to be at least partially redeemed. Morris was facing increased demands with decreased revenue.[26]

The superintendent's inability to pay caught Duer with no ready money on hand. The contract had required payment in specie, but Morris had paid in notes, receivable either for state taxes ("Morris notes") or payable by private traders who had purchased bills of exchange from Morris; since the interruption of trade with Europe had deprived him of the latter source,

Morris had to send more of the former, but cautiously, since the states were receiving little in taxes. Thus Morris could only lamely counter Duer's impertinence; "Your Complaints are I believe in some measure well founded but your Vivacity gives them more Weight" than they merit. He promised Duer a combination of Morris notes and a draft on General Washington for specie for his next payment. All Duer had to do was submit careful accounts and Morris might, he hoped, even be able to keep him in advance of his actual expenditures.[27]

Morris was a bit too hopeful. When the draft was presented to the general, he was unable to honor it. Duer then demanded from Morris enough specie to meet his creditors' demands or he would stop supplying the men on 1 October. (A copy of this letter was carefully sent to General Washington, perhaps in hope he would increase the pressure on Morris.) His major fear seemed to be that a failure to pay his debts would hurt his reputation and hinder him in conducting business in the area after the war. There was no regret, real or feigned, that he might have to stop serving his country or even a recital of his prior public service, with the implication that he had done all that could be expected. Rather, his creditors had gathered in Albany to be paid and, because of Morris, he could not pay them. Minor considerations of patriotism and the just demands of the cause on its adherents were not to cloud the issue.[28]

Although Duer was continuously protesting his imminent ruin to Morris, and the contractors' agents were continuously complaining they lacked this or that part of the daily ration, somehow or other the soldiers were being fed adequately (which, in itself, was a welcome contrast to what had been the case). Alexander Hamilton, then serving as collector of Continental taxes in New York (that is, those funds the state paid on its requisition), told Morris that the contract was being executed "generously to the satisfaction of the officers and soldiers," all the more remarkable because Duer would probably lose by it. These remarks were appended to a report on New York's economy which Morris had requested. For the report, Duer had estimated that he would spend $52,000 to $57,000 from April to December 1782, or an average of about $6,100 per month, making Morris's partial remittances of $5,000 not very much below what Duer's actual expenditures should have been.[29] Thus, Duer's problem really was not so much with the quantity of Morris's payments as with their quality.

The exchange between the two men over August's issues illustrates the problem. Morris had advanced Duer $7,000, more than the value of the rations delivered. But Duer argued that he was actually owed money, since he refused to regard the Morris notes as payment until he had been able to redeem them for specie at a state tax office. (This in spite of an earlier assertion by Duer that Morris notes "will answer all the Purposes of Specie in Hand," but that was said to an agent purchasing flour who was also ordered not to part with them for a "farthing less" than their specie value.)[30] Morris replied that the notes when accepted as cash were surely a "payment of money" and pointed to the obvious fact that if the government's contractors did not accept its promises to pay, any attempt to establish its credit was useless. Another facet of the problem was the notes' large denominations; they could not easily circulate in New York, hence, recipients turned them in for specie at a state tax office as soon as possible.[31] The problem would not have arisen if the government's credit was more respected and the notes of convenient denominations, and if Duer had not felt himself to be in such dire straits. As things turned out, Duer did not stop the issues, but instead was able to find enough people to accept Morris notes to get him through October, at the end of which Hamilton gave him $1,200 in specie with the promise of an equal amount soon. Morris had asked Hamilton on several occasions to do what he could for Duer; he met the requests so energetically that he disappointed Colonel Timothy Pickering of the Quartermaster's department who had believed himself to have an overriding claim on all $5,200 in Hamilton's public purse. Pickering was not likely to be satisfied soon, as Duer expected more specie from Hamilton in the future.[32] With this generous transfusion of cash, Duer was able to finish the contract without further complaint. Other contractors also suffered because of Morris's inability to pay, but his response was not always as generous as it had been with Duer. Sands, Livingston and Company, holding the West Point and Moving Army contracts, also presented Morris with an ultimatum similar to Duer's of early September. But Morris called their bluff and excused them from the contract. He advised Ezekiel Cornell, Inspector-General of the Army, to make the best terms

he could with Jeremiah Wadsworth for the balance of the contracts. Wadsworth's price was fully one-third higher than Sands,
Livingston's, but he could offer three month's credit, so the
bargain was made.[33] Thus, at the same time Morris was doing
all he could for Duer, he almost pulled their contracts away from
Sands, Livingston. In effect, he sacrificed them to help Duer.
The New Yorker's congressional service was paying off.

It is a statement of the obvious to say that profit was never
too far away from Duer's calculations as he did business; considerations of service and patriotism took a second place—one
is tempted to say, a distant second place—in his hierarchy of
values. This being said, it is nevertheless difficult to establish
what, if any, profit he made on the army contracts. Considerations
such as the fluctuating prices of provisions, the difficulty of purchasing from wary farmers with credit instruments, transport,
and spoilage understandably complicated the picture. So also did
the partnerships and sub-contracts which wound through the
contractors' operations like the paths through a rabbit warren.
Finally, as far as Duer is concerned, many of the firm's records
seem to have been taken away by Daniel Parker when he fled the
country in 1784 to escape prosecution for speculating with the
Company's money, speculations which, as so often happens in
such cases, went bad. He never returned to the United States
and the affairs of Daniel Parker and Company were never settled.
Nevertheless, the possibilities of profit were certainly present.
First, in the basic contract, a profit of one to one and one-half
pennies was figured on a bid of ten to eleven pennies (PA) per
ration; although other contractors believed Duer's bids were often
too low to permit a profit, he did not submit them lightly, but
seems to have calculated them as carefully as circumstances permitted. Second, there were opportunities for profit other than
the difference between the total costs of provisions and administration and the government remittances. One of these was the
use of "due bills," in effect, IOUs issued to the men for a missing
part of the ration; vouchers were then given to the contractor as
if the complete ration had been issued. These were often lost or
used for less valuable items or merchandise at the contractors'
store. One way or another, they could return more profit to the
contractor than the items they represented and they were viewed
as a grievance or abuse by commanding officers who often for-

bade their use. The contractors' store was another source of profit. For a 1783 contract, Daniel Parker and Company backed Melancton Smith in a store at Newburgh, New York, near the principal encampment of the main army. Smith was given an advance capital of $20,000 in January 1783; the partnership was to be dissolved on 1 January 1784, the advance paid back and one-quarter of the profits given to Smith, three-quarters to the company. John Holker estimated profits of $25,000 for this enterprise, but since he did this in the course of supporting claims on Duer and Parker for advances never paid back and profits never remitted, it may well be exaggerated. Duer certainly took almost $1,700 in merchandise from the store, presumably for his personal use, so he derived at least that much "profit" from it. Holker spent the better part of his time after 1784, or so it would seem from his papers, attempting to calculate what was due to him from Parker and Duer. These calculations usually resulted in profits of several hundred thousand dollars from the Army contracts and auxiliary enterprises, but all were made without the necessary vouchers, receipts, etc., which were in the hands of either the government or Daniel Parker and by someone who was obviously very much interested in the results of his labors. Hence, they should not be accepted as *prima facie* evidence of large or even considerable profits. In the end, perhaps the best answer to the question of profits that can be given is the eagerness of Parker and Duer to take up another contract in 1783, even after the difficulty of administering the 1782 contract. They certainly thought they were making money.[34]

The 1783 contract for all troops in New York and New Jersey had first been offered to Jeremiah Wadsworth; when he asked too high a price, Morris offered it to Duer. The New Yorker had been reluctant initially to bid because of the long credit requested by Morris, but after Wadsworth's price, the financier was more amenable and offered to hear any proposals Duer cared to make. He offered to take it up at eleven pennies (PA) per ration, with a $100,000 advance in bills of exchange on France, part of the proceeds of the most recent loan there. After Wadsworth, who had been promised the chance to meet any competing proposal, had turned it down, Morris settled the remaining terms with Duer at his office in Philadelphia. He immediately wrote to Parker, telling him the contract was theirs—"I did not bid for it, nor have I the time to tell you the Extraordinary Manner by which it has become mine." (Other than the circumstances sketched above, there seems to have been nothing to justify Duer's use of "extraordinary," but he did tend to overdramatize things sometimes.) Parker had been afraid he could not raise the money to join the contract, but when Duer was able to offer him a third of it for $10,000, he hurried to Philadelphia to join the talks between Duer and Morris. After further negotiations, a contract was signed on 7 December 1782. Morris gave Daniel Parker and Company a bill of exchange for $99,000, the advance less one percent in consideration of receiving it all at once, instead of equal payments in January and February. The firm began the year with an initial capital of $149,000, the advance plus Parker's $10,000 plus $40,000 from John Holker, who also signed a surety bond for $200,000. Presumably Duer's managerial talents were a sufficient contribution from him.[35]

This contract was not marked by any of the crises which had marred the firm's earlier efforts; Morris notes were circulating well and the contractors themselves had learned to provision troops more efficiently. The three partners also secured a contract to feed troops in New England, a project which Parker supervised. Later in the year, when news came from Europe of the signing of peace terms, Morris decided to move troops from the southern states to New York and New Jersey where they could be fed more cheaply; Daniel Parker and Company handled the transfer satisfactorily. However, in May, General Washington received, through General Heath whose command they concerned, several letters complaining of the quality and quantity of provisions; the Commander-in-Chief sent them to Duer and Parker, commenting that the complaints were of such a "serious & alarming Complexion" that he trusted they would be immediately corrected. Apparently they were, for Holker was able to tell Duer by 6 June that "Everything was going on cleverly." Throughout the year, by dint of frequent visits to Philadelphia, the partners managed to stay in advance on the most important of the contracts, the New York-New Jersey one, and thus had little occasion to test the quality of their own credit, which may well have been stretched by their other enterprises.[36]

Duer's relationship with John Holker deserves a closer examination. Ostensibly, Holker had come to the United States in

1778 to serve as France's naval agent. But he also came armed with a letter of introduction to Robert Morris from Silas Deane, a letter in which Deane urged Morris to give the fullest confidence to whatever Holker had to say on "our Situation here [Paris], whether of a Public or private nature." Deane went on to suggest, probably unnecessarily, that Morris aid the Frenchman in any venture which promised profit, not just to the country, but also to individuals. Holker had more in mind than just naval supplies. Even before he arrived in America, Holker had been in touch with Americans who, if the accusations against Deane are to be credited, were readier to conduct public office with an eye to their personal profit than the public's benefit. After formally welcoming him, Congress referred him to a committee on which Duer was serving. Presently, after Duer left the congress, Holker and he were involved in the mast contracts. Their first formal partnership seems to have been the fall 1781 effort to secure a provision contract with the French army; although that failed, they soon entered into a general partnership which included Duer's share in the mast contracts, a distillery in Poughkeepsie, potential army contracts, and speculations in soldiers' pay certificates and New York land "location certificates." In 1782, when they contracted to feed American troops, they enlarged the partnership to include Daniel Parker, but he was not included in the other enterprises. His role in superintending the New England end of the business, especially the securing there of beef cattle and, eventually, a provisioning contract there also, made him important to Duer and Holker. The latter's importance seemed to be primarily the money he could invest in the different ventures. Although there were sporadic efforts to secure mast cargoes and keep the French effort alive, the slackening of the war made success there less likely than ever and Holker's French contacts less valuable. But his apparently almost unlimited supply of investment funds made Holker invaluable. Shortly after the partnership arrangement began, he complained of making £2,000 (PA) in advances without receiving any return. He also contributed one-half of the purchase price of the distillery and, as noted, part of the start-up funds for the 1782 contract, as well as four-fifths of the $50,000 with which Daniel Parker and Company began the New York-New Jersey contract for 1783. By December 1783, Duer owed Holker almost £8,400 in three accounts covering the army contracts, the distillery, and various commercial ventures.[37]

The army contracts and the attempt to sell masts in Europe have already been touched upon, but the distillery has been mentioned only in passing. Originally begun early in 1782, the works was to provide liquor for the army contracts (a daily ration usually included a gill of rum or whiskey, about four ounces). The distillery succeeded only in consuming money, not in producing liquor. From the beginning, it was not adequately supervised by its owners, Duer being too busy to give it much time and Holker rarely leaving Philadelphia. Duer tried to compensate for his inattention by hiring a series of supervisors who were charged with same duties "as Mr. Duer would execute if he were personally present." During the summer of 1782, John Michael, originally hired as a clerk to keep the books, worked as a manager in place of the distiller, Peter Tappan, who had been hired in February. Tappan had been too devoted to the product of his labors to be effective, yet he lingered on, being of little assistance to Michael who also complained of no money, no materials, and no support from his employers. Duer's only answer was to blame the troubles on Michael's ineptitude and promise Tappan more money to get the still going. He had promises aplenty, but no personal attention to spare and did not visit the still once during 1782. Holker put his finger on the trouble when he observed: "See what it is to Engage in Several objects; one of them Neglected Carries off the profit of all others: we must make it a rule never to have two hares in one chase—this adage at our age comes rather late to observation." (One might add that it is advice Duer never heeded; in 1791, his wife would reprove him in almost identical language.) The next summer saw Duer still trying, this time with John Clarke who had promised to get it going "with little Capital . . . with small expense/to great profit & quick returns." But, after two months, Clarke confessed that the works were a "dead, inanimate mass," and, by the end of the summer, he was making the same complaints Michael had, no money, no instructions. He did not even know if he was to continue in Duer's employ. In December 1783, Duer, while trying to sell it to Udney Hay, estimated he had put £10,000 into the distillery and not received a penny of profit or even return. Hay did not purchase the distillery and, in the late 1780s, the partners still owned the apparently unprofitable enterprise.[38]

Obviously, the Holker partnership had been basic to most of Duer's enterprises since he had left the congress; there was not one of his endeavors, with the exception of the mast contracts, which the Frenchman had not helped to finance. All in all, Holker may have been the most valuable fringe benefit Duer received from his service in Congress and it was little wonder that he had assured him that he felt "the force and value of your friendship," for without that friendship (and loans), he would have had to look far and wide for capital, quite possibly in vain. The relationship was not without its problems, for once Holker advanced funds, he constantly sent Duer queries, suggestions, pointed reminders of how much he had at risk; all in all, he was anything but a silent partner. However, as events would tell, he had good reason to question and suggest and worry.[39]

For the time being, however, things seemed to be going reasonably well. Duer was busily executing the New York-New Jersey contract and looking forward to expanding or altering his operations when peace came. As early as February, there were rumors of a peace treaty with Great Britain and with the rumors, others stirred themselves to consider either the revival of old business connections or branching out into novel ones, in some cases, those made possible by the United States' freedom from Britain's navigation laws. William Constable was not about to be too particular; he wrote to remind Duer of his willingness to participate in "any practicable Scheme . . . when matters become settled." By March, the rumors were so persistent and frequent that Duer bet Colonel Walter Stewart £100 that a treaty would be signed before 1 June. He did not have to wait long to collect; before the end of the month, news of the signing of preliminary articles of peace had arrived from Paris along with the text of a provisional treaty. Daniel Parker happened to be in Philadelphia when the news arrived and, wasting no time in patriotic exultation, sent a pass into New York City which he had obtained from General Benjamin Lincoln, Secretary at War for Congress, urging Duer to use it in an attempt to secure a provision contract for the British forces there. It is certainly good to prepare to beat swords into plowshares when any conflict is winding down, but Parker seemed to be in an indecent hurry. Although Duer was unable to use the pass, Parker managed to get into the city on his own and secured a contract to supply flour to British troops there and in Nova Scotia.[40]

The end of the war brought other concerns to the fore. Duer resumed serving New York State by being a member of a committee which both arranged the details of the British evacuation of Manhattan Island (inasmuch as they concerned the civilian authorities) and governed the area until a new city government could be formed. He also spent a good bit of time at Washington's headquarters at Newburgh and, possibly, at the Army's cantonment at nearby New Windsor, where he might have been on the fringes of the Newburgh Conspiracy, an attempt by some nationalists in Congress and the states to use the debt of the nation to the Army, especially its officer corps, to secure a strengthening of Congress's powers. It was deftly forestalled by Washington who called a meeting of his own, in advance of one called by a few disgruntled officers which was to have kicked off the effort. With the general's disapproval obvious, everyone backed down and the affair collapsed in a hullabaloo of contradictory statements.[41] And it may be wondered if Morris (supposedly one of the Philadelphia group) really cared whether or not the Army was paid. In May, Duer offered to advance the enlisted men three months' pay, part in coin, part in merchandise, in anticipation of a final settlement of their overdue pay. The proposal pleased Washington enough to move him to recommend it to Morris, but the plan failed, for unknown reasons, to gain his approval.[42]

Here, Duer's wartime career as a businessman ends. How profitable had it been? To answer that, one should inquire as to what kind of base he had before the war. He had probably brought over some money of his own when he came to New York in 1768 and he had certainly borrowed £1,400 from his sister to augment this.[43] When the war began, his land and buildings at Fort Miller had to be left in the care of an agent who kept them more or less intact, with some aid from Philip Schuyler, but who could not perform miracles and transact profitable business, especially when the land became a battlefield during the Burgoyne campaign of 1777. Further, the enemy's occupation of New York City from the fall of 1776 to the end of the war ensured that Duer's lumber could not reach its most likely or profitable markets. Hence his efforts on the French and Spanish contracts, provided alternative sources of ship timbers could be found, and the French and American army contracts were not only attempts to exploit his new friends from Congress, but were also the result of necessity. All that could be done at Fort Miller was to hang on until the end of the war. In the meantime, profits might be made in the lower Hudson Valley, both because of Duer's friends as well as the fortunate accident that most of the Continental forces were stationed there during the last two years of the war.

As noted, there is no direct evidence that Duer made substantial sums of money after leaving Congress, but there is an abundance of indirect evidence which certainly shows the possibility of large profits. One estimate of a gross profit of $100,000, excluding the costs of transportation, issuing, and credit, for the New York-New Jersey contract supports this. Attempting a calculation of the omitted costs is just about impossible because, first, the confused bookkeeping of the contractors left their surviving accounts a confused mass (they were never fully settled), second, Daniel Parker's flight to Europe in 1784 with most of the firm's records and, according to Duer and Holker, just about all of its funds. Parker never returned to the United States and no final settlement or liquidation of Daniel Parker and Company was ever executed. However, these costs are not likely to have been so high as to absorb all the gross profits. Also, the contractors were looking to take away some of their profit in pay certificates purchased through their stores. According to an undated memo in Holker's papers, they had accumulated more than £7,000 (NY) of such paper at one point. Apparently, Parker was not able to take these with him and they may have furnished some of Duer's postwar holdings of Continental and state paper. Thus, substantial profits were certainly possible for the contractors, both in the short run, and considering the eventual value of the pay certificates, in the long run as well.[44]

But, as someone once observed, in the long run, we are all dead. Such morbid philosophizing may have occurred to Duer as he contemplated his personal financial situation near the end of 1783. His father-in-law, General Alexander, had always lived in the style of the noble lord he had claimed to be. Thus, when he died in January 1783, leaving one-half of his estate to Kitty Duer, the balance to his widow, the estate turned out to consist mostly of debts. Whatever the bequest to Mrs. Duer might be, after the estate was liquidated, it was not likely to be large, and it was certainly some years in the future.[45] This was important as, towards the end of 1783, he had the reputation in some quarters of a person in serious financial straits. The VanSchaik Brothers of Albany swore out a writ to prevent Duer from leaving the country before he settled a dispute over money he owed them; their fears were shared by Edward Crumpston, a New York merchant, who put his accounts with Duer in the hand of a lawyer, apologizing for his action by citing the latter's plans to leave the continent. Other creditors and former employees were also writing dunning letters.[46] These letters might have been no more than annoyance by his creditors at Duer's inveterate and apparently incurable sloppiness in account keeping and slowness in bill paying. However, there is some evidence that Duer did think of leaving New York. In November 1783, he bemoaned his excessive trust in others to Holker and noted that he could easily make $10,000 by neglecting his estate "in this quarter," and paying attention to the plantations in the Islands and some friends in London.[47] But he may also have simply been exasperated with the difficulties which were beginning to develop with Parker and pessimistically reflecting on the changes which the war's end was bringing. No one lightly abandons the area in which he has been working, in which he is known and also knows reliable colleagues, unless he has clearly failed. However vague his exact situation might seem, it was certainly not one of hopeless failure.

He was bringing away a number of advantages from his wartime service, the most valuable of which was probably the friends and associates he had made during it. His work in the New York Provincial Congress and the Convention had brought him to the attention of highly-placed New York patriots and some figures on the Continental scene such as General Washington. From there, he went to Philadelphia and Congress. Without his service there, it is doubtful he would have met Robert Morris, John Holker, Silas Deane, even Lafayette, who overcame his initial dislike of Duer to help him in the first attempt for a French contract, and others who helped in his business affairs. While his use of these associates and friends did not always measure up to twentieth-century standards of public service, he did not violate the eighteenth-century code by which he was operating. The signing up of Miralles in the Spanish mast contract was perhaps the most questionable move, but there is no evidence to indicate that it was Duer's idea, although he certainly went along with it. His request to General Alexander for a recommendation to the French army was questionable, as Duer himself realized, but the use of well-placed friends and relatives was no less common then than it is now. Whether the request to Luzerne to intercede with Washington for troops to guard the mast cutters was improper is questionable. There was nothing hidden in it and the securing of masts for the French navy could conceivably be of importance to the war effort. Neither the general nor the minister condemned it, and perhaps their judgment should be accepted. Duer's commercial ethics were probably, at this time, no better or worse than most of his contemporaries.

References

1. Wm. Duer to Robert R. Livingston, Mar. 15, 1779, Robert R. Livingston to John Jay, Apr. 20, 1779, Livingston Papers, NYHS; George Washington to Wm. Duer, Mar. 15, 1779, Wm. Duer to George Washington, Mar. 16, 1779, Washington Papers, LC; Duer still owned the Charlotte (Washington) County tract a year later, John Taylor to Robert R. Livingston, Apr. 9, 1780, Livingston Papers, NYHS.
2. *The Pennsylvania Packet*, Apr. 2, 1779; William Constable to Wm. Duer, June 13, 1778, Duer Papers, BV I, NYHS; see Carl VanDoren, *Secret History of the American Revolution* (New York, 1941), 172-76, and East, *Business Enterprise*, 110, 182 for more on Constable's activities; see also Gouverneur Morris to George Clinton, Mar. 2, 1779, George Clinton to Gouverneur Morris, Mar. 22, 1779, *Clinton Papers*, IV, 606-607; see William Davis, "William Constable, New York Merchant and Land Speculator, 1772-1803," unpub. Ph.D. diss, Harvard, 1957 for its subject's career into 1790.
3. Wm. Duer to John Campbell, Feb. 3, 1779, Duer Papers, BV I, NYHS; *The New York Journal* (Poughkeepsie), May 3, 1779; Robert R. Livingston to John Jay, Mar. 4, 1779, Livingston Papers, NYHS; see also *Journals*, I, 929, 936, 954; John Campbell to Wm. Duer, May 20, 1777, Louis DeLavergne to Wm. Duer, May 22, 1777, Duer Papers, BV I, NYHS for some of the reminders sent to Duer. The accounts were not finally settled for several years because of incomplete vouchers, etc.
4. Nelson, *Alexander*, 146; according to the anonymous author of *The Knickerbocker Magazine* sketch (XL, No. 2 [Aug. 1852], 98), Washington stood in for Alexander who was on duty in northern New York, but this is doubtful; John Lansing, Jr. to Philip Schuyler, [1779?], Schuyler Papers, NYPL; Wm. Duer, "aide-de-camp," to Henry Ludinton, Jun. 5, 1779, *Clinton Papers*, V, 34; see also Udney Hay to George Clinton, Jan. 6, 1781, ibid., VI, 553.
5. The contracts and agreements are in Duer Papers, Letter Book and Timber Contracts, 1774-1779, NYHS; Rey deChaumont was Holker's brother-in-law and the owner of the estate at Passy, near Paris, where the American diplomatic mission to France stayed; he held part of the French government's tobacco importing monopoly; he went bankrupt in 1783.
6. See Richard B. Morris, *The Peacemakers* (1965), 9 for an example of a similar attitude by Robert Morris.

7. "Je n'ai absolument aucune opinion à avoir sur cette Matière, et vous sauvez beaucoup mieux que moi, Monsieur, si L' utilité générale peut se Concilier avec ses demands," Chevalier de LaLuzerne to George Washington, Feb. 4, 1780; Wm. Duer to Chevalier de LaLuzerne, Jan. 24, 1780; George Washington to Chevalier de LaLuzerne, Feb. 14, 1780, LC; Washington Papers, LC; _____to Nathanael Greene, Feb. 15, 1780, *Washington Writings*, XVIII, 10-11; Wm. Duer to Silas Deane, Feb. 5, 1780, Duer Papers, NYHS.

8. Silas Deane to Wm. Duer, Aug. 8, 1780, Charles Isham, ed., *The Deane Papers* (New York, 1889), IV, 185-86; _____to Wm. Duer, Aug. 23, 1780, 190-92; _____to John Jay, Aug. 23, 1780, 196; _____to Wm. Duer, Sep. 28, 1780, 234-35; hereafter cited as *Deane Papers*; Peter Whiteside & Co. to Wm. Duer, Sep. 18, 1781; John Holker to Wm. Duer, Jul. 19, 1781, Duer Papers, NYHS; see also Jul. 21, 1781, Diary in the Office of Finance, Robert Morris Papers, LC for an indication that Morris was also interested in the contract, hereafter cited as Morris Papers. This material may also be found, through May 4, 1783, in E. James Ferguson, John Catanzariti, eds., *The Papers of Robert Morris, 1781-1784*, 7 vols. (Pittsburgh, 1973-88).

9. Silas Deane to Barnabas Deane, Jan. 31, 1782, *Deane Papers*, V, 37-38; Thomas Paine to Jonathan Williams, Nov. 26, 1781, IV, 544; Robert R. Livingston to James Duane. Nov. 2, 1781, James Duane to Robert R. Livingston, Nov. 30, 1782, Livingston Papers, NYHS; Silas Deane to Robert Morris, Oct. 10, 1783, *Deane Papers*, V, 201; to James Wilson, Jul. 24, 1783, 163-64; _____to "Le Roy" Chaumont, Feb. 28, 1783, V, 133; Deane ended the war living in London and died in 1784 shortly after taking ship for the United States; see Chap. III, n. 35 for treatments of Deane's activities at this time.

10. John R. Livingston to Wm. Duer, Aug. 2, 1780, Duer Papers, BV I, NYHS.

11. Wm. Duer to Robert Morris, Aug. 27, 1780, cited in East, *Enterprise*, 111-12; Robert Morris to Wm. Duer, Sep. 17, 1780, Duer Papers, BV I, NYHS; Alexander C. Flick, *Loyalism in New York* (New York, 1901), 262; Wm. Duer to Robert Morris, Oct. 12, 1780, Morris Papers, LC; Wm. Duer to John Paine, Mar. 29, 1781, Duer Papers, NYHS.

12. Wm. Duer to William Alexander, Jun. 15, 1781, William Alexander (Lord Stirling) Papers, NYHS; Wm. Duer to Robert Morris, Jul. 11, 1781, Morris Papers, LC; East, *Enterprise*, 93; Bill of lading for rum for French forces, Daniel Parker to Wm. Duer, Jun. 26, 1781, Duer Papers, Box VII; contract between Daniel Parker, Morgan Lewis and Wm. Duer, Jun. 21, 1781, Duer Papers, Box VI; Wm. Duer to Jeremiah Wadsworth, Jun. 20, 1781, Duer Papers, NYHS.

13. Wm. Duer to Jeremiah Wadsworth, Jun. 20, 1781, Jul. 23, 1782, Duer Papers, NYHS.

14. Robert Morris to Wm. Duer, May 29, 1781, Duer Papers, BV I, NYHS; Wm. Duer to Robert Morris, Jul. 11, 1781, Morris Papers, LC; I have followed Wayne Carp's interpretation of these events; it is conveniently given in E. Wayne Carp, "The Origins of the Nationalist Movement of 1780-1783: Congressional administration and the Continental Army," *Pennsylvania Magazine of History & Biography*, 107 (1983): 362-92.

15. Wm. Duer to Charles DeWitt, Oct. 18, 1781, Emmett Coll., Ms. # 13876, NYPL; Wm. Duer to ?, Oct. 17, 1781, Duer Papers; Robert Morris to Wm. Duer, Oct. 16, 1781, Duer Papers, BV I, NYHS; Diary, Oct. 15, 1781, Morris Papers, LC.

16. John Stark to William Alexander, Oct. 28, 1781, William Alexander (Lord Stirling) Papers, Vol. V, NYHS.

17. See Victor L. Johnson, *The Administration of the American Commissariat During the Revolutionary War* (Philadelphia, 1941); E. James Ferguson, *The Power of the Purse* (Chapel Hill, NC, 1961), Part II, hereafter cited as Ferguson, *Purse*, and E. Wayne Carp, *To Starve the Army at Pleasure: Continental Army Administration and American Political Culture, 1775-1783* (Chapel Hill, NC, 1984), Chap. 8 for treatments of the supply problem.

18. Robert Morris to Wm. Duer, Nov. 6, Nov. 13, Dec. 3, Dec. 29, 1781, Letter Book B, Morris Papers, LC.

19. Wm. Duer to Robert R. Livingston, Jan. 25, 1782, Livingston Papers, NYHS; Diary, Feb. 4, 5, 6, 1782, Morris Papers, LC; Contract with Wm. Duer & Co., Feb. 6, 1782, Ms. # 31494, RG 93, Rev. War Ms., War Dept. Coll., NA; Robert Morris to Wm. Duer, Feb. 7, 1782, Duer Papers, NYHS.

20. Elisha Crane to Wm. Duer, Feb. 23, Mar. 11, 1782, Wm. Duer to Elisha Crane, Feb. 18, 1782, Duer Papers, BV I; lease of "Dutch Church" Parsonage, Feb. 14, 1782, Duer Papers, Box VII, NYHS.

21. Wm. Duer to John Holker, Mar. 19, 1782, [Wm. Duer] to Daniel Parker, Apr. 23, 1782, Wm. Duer to ?, [May 1782], Duer Papers, NYHS; Diary, Mar. 29, Apr. 1, 1782, Morris Papers, LC; Enoch Leonard to Wm. Duer, Mar. 25, 1782, Duer Papers, BV I, NYHS.

22. Robert Morris to Wm. Duer, Apr. 3, 1782, Letter Book C; Apr. 2, 4, 6 1782, Diary, Morris Papers, LC.

23. Hugh Hughes to Timothy Pickering, Apr. 10, 1782, Ms. # 23187, RG 93, Rev. War Ms., War Dept. Coll., NA; Enoch Leonard to Wm. Duer, May 1, 2, 13, 16, 23, 29, 1782, Duer Papers, BV I, NYHS; Diary, May 16, 17, 27, Jun. 12, 1782, Robert Morris to Wm. Duer, Jun. 12, 1782, Letter Book C; Wm. Duer to Robert Morris, May 12, 1782, Morris Papers, LC.

24. Robert C. Livingston to Wm. Duer, Jun. 17, 1782, Enoch Leonard to Wm. Duer, May 23, Jun. 20, 24, 1782, Wm. Duer to Marinus Willett, Aug. 2, 1782, Henry Livingston to Wm. Duer, Aug. 9, 1782, see also Timothy Leonard to Wm. Duer, Aug. 16, 1782; see also E. Leonard to Duer letter, May 29, 1782, in BV I; all are in the Duer Papers, NYHS.

25. James Geary to Wm. Duer, Aug. 15, 1782, Duer Papers, NYHS; Diary, Jul. 23, Aug. 26, 28, 29, 1782, Morris Papers, LC.

26. Wm. Duer to Robert Morris, Aug. 2, 1782, Morris Papers, LC; Clarence L. VerSteeg, *Robert Morris, Revolutionary Financier* (Philadelphia, 1959), Chaps. 7, 8, especially 145-49; hereafter cited as VerSteeg, *Robert Morris*.

27. Robert Morris to Wm. Duer, Aug. 29, 1782, Duer Papers, BV I, NYHS; Robert Morris to Wm. Duer, Aug. 30, 1782, Morris Papers, Letter Book C, LC; see VerSteeg, *Robert Morris*, 117-20 for a description of "Morris Notes."

28. Wm. Duer to Robert Morris, Sep. 6, 1782, copy, Washington Papers, LC.

29. Alexander Hamilton to Robert Morris, Aug. 13, 1782, Wm. Duer to Alexander Hamilton, Aug. 16, 1782, Syrett, *Hamilton Papers*, III, 143-46; Morris admitted the possibility of Duer's losses, but promised to alleviate them by liberal advances as soon as possible, ibid., III, 156.

30. Wm. Duer to ?, Oct. 17, 1781, Duer Papers, NYHS.

31. Robert Morris to Wm. Duer, Oct. 2, 1782, Duer Papers, BV I, NYHS; Robert Morris to Alexander Hamilton, Oct. 5, 1782, Syrett, *Hamilton Papers*, III, 177-78.

32. Alexander Hamilton to Robert Morris, Oct. 26, 1782, ibid., III, 190; according to Hugh Hughes, Pickering's assistant, Hamilton was under much pressure from Morris to give all specie to Duer, Hugh Hughes to Timothy Pickering, Oct. 23, 1782, Ms. # 24727, RG 93, Rev. War Ms., War Dept. Coll., NA.

33. VerSteeg, *Robert Morris*, 149-51; although Duer held one-half of Walter Livingston's one-sixth share in Sands, Livingston & Co., he could hardly be considered an important partner because of this small share, one-half of which he had given to John Holker, leaving him with but one twenty-fourth. The officers of the units supplied by Sands, Livingston knew almost immediately of the change and that it had been caused by Morris's acute shortage of funds; see Benj. Gilbert to Daniel Gilbert, Oct. 20, 1782, John Shy, ed., *Winding Down: The Revolutionary War Letters of Lieutenant Benjamin Gilbert* (Ann Arbor, MI, 1989), 71.

34. "Estimate of the Value of a Ration for the Northern Department," "Estimate of Proffits [*sic*] for the Moving Army Contract," n.d., Robert R. Livingston Papers, Uncat., Duer-Flint Corr., NYHS; Lawrence & Smith to Army, Jan. 3, 1782, Lawrence & Smith Papers, I; William Heath to John Lawrence & Co., Jan. 30, 1782, loc. cit., II, NYHS; Contract, Daniel Parker & Co., and Melancton Smith, Jan. 18,

1783, John Holker Papers, LC, hereafter cited as Holker Papers; see vols. XX through XXII, and nos. 4589 and 4611 for details of the store's operations; the same volumes contain many calculations of profits, etc., and depositions by Holker regarding his partnership with Duer and Parker.

35. Wm. Duer to Daniel Parker, Nov. 14, 1782, Duer Papers, NYHS; Diary, Nov. 11 to Dec. 7, 1782, Morris Papers, LC; Daniel Parker to Wm. Duer, Nov. 26, 1782, Duer Papers, NYHS; a copy of the contract is Ms. # 31482, RG 93, Rev. War Ms., War Dept. Coll., NA; there is also a copy, dated Nov. 29, 1782 in Duer Papers, BV I, NYHS; John Holker, "Observations," n.d., Holker Papers, XXX, 5909-10, LC.

36. VerSteeg, *Robert Morris*, 161-62; since Parker supervised both of these contracts, little evidence of them appears in the Duer Papers; some bills, receipts and notes in Box VII belong to them; George Washington to Wm. Duer and Daniel Parker, May 29, 1783, w. encl., Washington Papers, LC; [John] Holker to Wm. Duer, Jun. 6, 1783, Duer Papers, NYHS.

37. Silas Deane to Robert Morris, Dec. 24, 1777, Morris Papers, LC; JCC, XI, 713; John Holker to Wm. Duer, Nov. 16, 1781, Wm. Duer to John Holker, Dec. 11, 1781, Duer Papers; "Credits given in three Distinct Accounts Current Rendered by John Holker to W[illia]m Duer, Esq., January 1782 to October 1783," Duer Papers, Box VII, NYHS.

38. Contract between Peter Tappan and Wm. Duer, Feb. 9, 1782, John Michael to Wm. Duer, Apr.-Oct. 1782, *passim*, Wm. Duer to Peter Tappan, Jul. 6, 1782, John Holker to Wm. Duer, Jun. 19, 1782, Duer Papers; John Clarke to Wm. Duer, Jun. 11, Aug. 22, 30, 1783, BV I, Duer Papers; Udney Hay to Wm. Duer, Dec. 1, 1783, Duer Papers, NYHS; see also "Poughkeepsie Distillery," Duer Papers, Box. V, for receipts and accounts which make Duer's claim of a £10,000 loss plausible.

39. Wm. Duer to John Holker, Mar. 19, 1782, Duer Papers, NYHS.

40. W[illiam]. C[onstable]. to Wm. Duer, Feb. 5, 1783, Duer Papers; see below, for a previous meeting with Constable; "bet with Col. Walter Stewart," Mar. 18, 1783, Duer Papers, Box VIII; Daniel Parker to Wm. Duer, Mar. 26, 1783, Duer Papers, NYHS; Daniel Parker & Co. to John Holker, Apr. 16, 1783, Holker Papers, LC; John Ross to Daniel Parker & Co., Jun. 5, 1783, John Holker Papers, Clements Library, Ann Arbor, MI.

41. "Report of a Conversation with Col. W[illia]m D[ue]r, October 12, 1788," Rufus King Papers, NYHS; King considered the information to be reliable; Richard H. Kohn, *Eagle and Sword: The Beginnings of the Military Establishment in America* (New York, 1975), Chap. 2 has a clear and reliable treatment of a very tangled series of events.

42. George Washington to [Robert Morris], Apr. 9, 1783, *Washington Writings*, XXVI, 309; Diary, May 14, 1783, Morris Papers, LC; Wm. Duer to John Holker, May 2, 1783, Holker Papers, LC.

43. See above, 3.

44. VerSteeg, *Robert Morris*, 247; see also "Calculation . . . Proffits [*sic*] . . .," John Holker Papers, Clements Library, Ann Arbor, MI and Holker Papers, # 3661, 3662, 5554, 5556, LC, for some of Holker's calculations (and laments) as to Daniel Parker & Co.'s profits.

45. "Petition to Change Lord Stirling's Will, March 11, 1785," copy, Duer Papers, NYHS; Thomas Jones, the loyalist historian of New York during the Revolution, wrote that Alexander took advantage of a New Jersey legal-tender law to discharge his debts with depreciated Continental currency at a rate of eighty to one. He also claimed that Duer, "as great a rebel as ever had an existence," took the same dishonorable course. Neither claim seems likely. See Thomas Jones, *History of New York During the Revolutionary War*, Edward E. deLancy, ed. (New York, 1879), II, 234. Duer's son, William Alexander, in his *Life of William Alexander, Earl of Stirling* (New York, 1847), 261-64, wrote that his grandfather sold his estates to pay his debts. But, before he could do so, New Jersey repealed its legal tender law and Alexander was caught with the depreciated Continental currency. All he left his widow was

some New Jersey warrants for back pay. Nelson, *Alexander*, 142-43, confirms the latter version. See also John Holker to Wm. Duer, Mar. 23, 1784, Duer Papers, NYHS, for Duer's receipt of £2,000 in sugar from the estate of "Duer, Rae & Duer," apparently in the West Indies; possibly, this is the liquidated estate which Duer had owned jointly.

46. Jacob Sebor to Silas Deane, Nov. 10, 1784, cited in East, *Business Enterprise*, 123; see East also for the VanSchaik writ; Edward Crumpston to Wm. Duer, Dec. 22, 1783, Elisha Crane to Wm. Duer, May 30, Jun. 28, 1783, Duer Papers; James Lagrange to Wm. Duer, Nov. 20, 1783, Duer Papers, BV I, NYHS.

47. Wm. Duer to John Holker, Nov. 25, 1783, Holker Papers, LC.

Chapter V

Business and Government

January 1784–March 1790

It is not at all certain what William Duer's mood might have been as he transferred his family and business to New York City early in 1784. The end of the war had brought about the end of the familiar environment in which he had been working since he left the congress, but it also brought the first opportunity for the new republic's merchants to try their hands dealing outside the mercantilist restrictions and protections of the British Empire. While they were now free to go wherever profit beckoned and the laws of other states permitted, they lacked the safe market for various of their staple and provision crops which the British Empire had provided. Thus the commercial environment in which American merchants now operated had both its perils and its opportunities and furnished ample material for optimistic or pessimistic expectations. On the scale of personal considerations, the future was also cloudy. While Duer may have gained considerably from his wartime contracting and he had certainly become acquainted with a wide circle of wartime associates, not all the contracts and associated enterprises had been profitable. Daniel Parker's activities especially had become more worrisome as 1783 ended. New opportunities would certainly present themselves, but whether he would be able to take advantage of them was not at all certain.

New York City itself could not have cheered Duer, as the city had suffered severely from the British occupation, two extensive fires having occurred in addition to the neglect any city experiences during a lengthy military occupation. The Duers first lived in a boarding house for several months, moving to a rented house on Broadway opposite St. Paul's Chapel of Trinity Church in May 1784. A year later they moved to "Ranelagh," a country estate located near the village of Greenwich, about two miles above St. Paul's, then the limit of the settled part of the city. There the Duers entertained frequently at dinner parties where business could be discreetly mixed with pleasure. William Alexander Duer describes his father as being intimate with Alexander Hamilton and Robert Troup, prominent attorneys in the city. (It should also be noted that Duer's and Hamilton's wives were cousins.) Other frequent dinner guests included John Jay and Baron Steuben as well as friends from the days of the Convention and the Congress, Egbert Benson, James Duane, John Laurance, and Robert R. Livingston. After the Congress moved to New York in 1785, its president came occasionally, first Nathaniel Gorham of Massachusetts, then Arthur St. Clair of Pennsylvania; Robert Morris, as well as James Madison visited when they were in New York.[1] While most of the guests probably came to enjoy the repartee or the possible business advantages, apparently the meal alone was worth the trip. At least the Reverend Manasseh Cutler, a Massachusetts clergyman and land speculator believed so; during a 1787 visit, he noted that Lady Kitty "performed the honors of the table most gracefully, was constantly attended by two servants in livery. . . . [Duer] lives in the style of a nobleman. I presume he had not less than fifteen sorts of wine at dinner, and after the cloth was removed, besides most excellent bottled cider, porter, and several other kinds of strong beer."[2] Although the moralistic Yankee was dismayed at such Manhattan extravagance, he did not scruple to do business with and through Duer, as will presently be seen.

Duer could also provide shelter of a more homely sort when it was needed. In April 1788, a mob protested the use of exhumed bodies by the medical students of Columbia College, the "Doctors Riot." The mob gathered outside the hospital, close by "Ranelagh." Governor George Clinton had called out the militia, but Baron Steuben was strongly advising him not to use it. Suddenly, the baron was struck by a brickbat thrown from the crowd; he had hardly hit the ground before he was blurting out "fire, Governor, fire." His benevolence had not outlasted his dignity. Duer's son remembers his father and Clinton, who did not get along politically, laughing over the incident as they tended to the baron's superficial wound in "Ranelagh." One may assume Steuben saw nothing funny in it.[3]

His entertaining and binding of wounds, figuratively as well as literally, put Duer in the first ranks of New York society quickly. His wit and charm, attested to by many, plus Lady Kitty's skill as a hostess, also helped. He soon became a trustee of Trinity Church and a member of the Chamber of Commerce, an important body in any city where the merchants had as much influence as they did in New York. On 4 July 1786, the Society of the Cincinnati, a fraternal society of officers of the Continental Army and their descendants, organized a local chapter and made Duer, among others, an honorary member. He was also a member of the "Whig Society," a political discussion club which considered the significant political questions Americans of his generation faced, so he did not concentrate entirely on business, but for a while at least, remained interested in public affairs.[4] Thus, just as at Fort Miller before the war for independence, Duer was able to enter easily into the higher reaches of New York's society. The presence of Congress in the city after 1785 also allowed him to renew and increase his contacts outside of New York as well as to resume public employment; this, plus the expanding commerce of the city, gave anyone as willing as Duer was to mix public office and private profit ample opportunity to do so.

However, before Duer could do much of anything, Daniel Parker would have to be dealt with. Duer and Holker had been uneasy about what Parker might have been doing in New England throughout 1783. Parker had informed Duer in December 1782 that he intended to speculate on the rise and fall of the bill of exchange rate in Boston, presumably with the bill given by Robert Morris for the 1783 contract. In May 1783, Duer told Holker that bill speculation was not a suitable area for the company and that they should distance themselves from Parker's operations as much as possible. Also, he could not understand why the firm was so short of cash at the time. As the war ended, it was very difficult to get Parker to cooperate in settling the affairs of the company. The flour contract with the British in New York City was executed, but then Parker tried to shift the bills from the suppliers to Duer and Holker, while he took the British payments. By the end of November, Duer confessed to Holker that he no longer trusted Parker and would not sign in on any venture entirely under his control; there was more to be made in Britain or the West Indies where he could trust people.

However, for all the brave talk, he and Holker had a bit too much riding with Parker to cut loose from him so quickly.[5] For one thing, Parker had charge of outfitting a novel venture for American merchants, an attempt to trade directly with China. When the effort was first considered, the *Empress of China* was to carry furs from the Pacific Northwest and ginseng, a medicinal herb prized in the Orient. It was to be financed by groups from Boston, New York, and Philadelphia and Duer was to be supercargo. When the vessel finally sailed early in 1784, it was loaded only with ginseng and financed by Morris and some Philadelphia friends, along with Daniel Parker and Company. Samuel Shaw served as supercargo. True to what turned out to be his form, Parker kept the funds advanced for the ship's outfitting and even convinced the inexperienced Shaw that he was entitled to take some of the coin given him for incidental expenses, but that he must not tell any of the other partners of this. Consequently, the partners were faced with most of the cost of outfitting and became involved in a messy legal squabble with Shaw when Parker's theft was disclosed on the ship's return in May 1785. Despite all these problems, the vessel returned a profit of almost $30,000, most of which went to satisfy its impatient creditors.[6] However, as early as March 1784, Holker and Duer were trying to sell or mortgage their share; the following month, Duer assigned his share to Holker in payment of some of the wartime loans. After that, he might have viewed the *Empress*'s fate with a measure of philosophical detachment.

Not so with Parker's fate. In 1784, Duer separated his army contracting in New York from that done in New England by Daniel Parker and Company as a crude form of limited liability. As noted, he had come to distrust Parker as early as November 1783. By April of 1784, he and Holker were dealing with Parker through the Philadelphia merchant, Thomas Fitzsimons, who was trying to rescue the Yankee from the morass of his affairs. Accounts had to be settled immediately for Parker and his friends "would undoubtedly be plotting against us." With this poisonous atmosphere and no good faith on either side, it is no surprise that a reconciliation of the two sides was not achieved before Parker fled the country in August. Duer announced the news to Holker with a self-satisfied, I told you so letter that also pointed out how much better things would have been if only Duer's

earnest entreaties to force Parker to a final accounting had been
followed. What Duer did not point out was that Holker had
been working just as hard as he to bring Parker to a settlement.
This was not the end of their involvement with the slippery
Yankee; both men would spend a good bit of time later in the
1780s dealing with one or another intermediary as they tried to
arrive at a settlement for the more than $300,000 Holker claimed
Parker carried away. Parker lived variously in London, Paris,
Amsterdam, always full of grand plans that were just about to
go through and bring him great wealth, but often short of ready
cash, never returning to the United States.[7]

Nor was Duer free of Parker after the dissolution of Daniel
Parker and Company was begun in the spring of 1784. When
his clerk presented the vouchers for the June issues to the troops,
Robert Morris refused to pay them since a $20,000 advance to
Daniel Parker and Company appeared to be outstanding. Until
it could be accounted for, no further payments would be made
although Duer was to continue as the contractor. The same
sequence was repeated in August. While Morris claimed he was
"particularly distressed that you should (as I fear will happen)
be a Sufferer by the Detention of these Funds," the superintendent would not pay on current vouchers until the Parker balance
was paid. In the fall Duer suggested a linking of several related
matters then pending: claims for damages due him directly and
also as a partner of Sands, Livingston and Company owing to
various actions of the government in 1782, damages which the
superintendent had recommended Congress pay, balances due
on current vouchers, and the Parker advance. Duer's rationale
was that the damages would pay the Parker advance if it was
owing at a final balance; thus the current vouchers could safely
be paid now. Since this implied that Morris's successor (he had
announced his intention of retiring) could not be trusted to do
him justice, which he never tired of asserting was all he wanted,
Morris refused. But, within a month, Morris authorized the payment of the current vouchers with no settlement on the other
matters.[8] Since he did leave public service in mid-November,
perhaps he decided to do a friend a favor as he was leaving, a
favor which would leave no one the loser as he acknowledged
that the current vouchers were owing to Duer.

None of this did John Holker any good. His financial affairs were put into serious disarray by Parker's flight, a state from which they did not soon, if ever, recover. His letters to Duer alternated between threatening and cajoling, all with the purpose of obtaining some kind of an accounting from Duer of the monies and credit lent to Duer and Parker. Holker had been uneasy even before the Parker debacle had started to develop, but had allowed himself to be talked into continuing with his partners, if only because it seemed so difficult to cut loose from them. Now it was proving impossible to bring Duer to a final settlement in spite of all the pressure he could put on him. In addition to the *Empress*, they were still partners in several cargo vessels engaged in trade with Europe, quantities of masts and spars accumulated for the abortive attempts at French and Spanish contracts, the Poughkeepsie distillery, and a quantity of location certificates, vouchers for land bounties given soldiers during the war.[9]

Not one of these ventures was brought to an advantageous, or even a tidy end and to the close of Duer's career and beyond, Holker was trying to get a settlement from him and Parker. Duer's ability to stall Holker seemed unlimited as, for example, in January 1785 when Holker asked, for the third time, for the location certificates, but they were not delivered; in December, he was still asking and, apparently, they were never delivered. Despite his openly expressed suspicions of Duer's honesty and business ability, he nevertheless relied on him for a final settlement, probably because he lacked the necessary documents and accounts himself. On a number of occasions, he lost patience with Duer and started legal action, as in December 1788. Duer responded to the suit and reminded Holker that he had recently received a promise from Parker to pay £5,000 (st.) towards the firm's liabilities; when that was paid, Holker would receive his money. (It was never paid; Parker was as good as Duer at promising, but never delivering.) Perhaps Holker could be taken care of at the general settlement of Daniel Parker and Company—"In this Case you will see the Propriety of the Transa[c]t[ion] . . . not being known to the Company Creditors." Duer also pointed out that Holker was the only one of his creditors to receive any funds; he had not paid a shilling to his own sister on a mortgage made before the war. If Holker would only have patience, he would receive his due. At the moment, Duer could show a profit of over $6,000 gained in stock speculations. Unfortunately, for unspecified reasons, Holker could not be paid this sum immediately. Accepting this transparent deception, Holker withdrew the suit. Several other attempts to settle the mess were made following a trip to Europe by Andrew Craigie in 1787-88. He went to confer with Parker on a large speculation in American stocks by European associates of Parker and also to talk over a possible settlement of the affairs of Daniel Parker and Company, thus freeing the expatriate for further speculation and possibly a return to the United States. In spite of a great deal of effort and trans-Atlantic correspondence, all was in vain, for Duer insisted that he be released from any demand beyond a specific sum in payment of the liabilities of the Company. Holker or Parker, or perhaps both, would have to indemnify the creditors, not him.[10] And so it went, with Duer consciencelessly disregarding the real losses of a man who had been essential to him in his early enterprises. If he had his way, Holker would lose not only what he had invested, but also become liable for any balances due which a settlement of Parker and Company may have discovered. Whether or not Duer shared any responsibility for the collapse of Daniel Parker and Company, and here the evidence is cloudy, he should certainly have aided the Frenchman. Instead he acted as if Holker had no claims on him at all and that, as the latter once complained, he should "pay for losses—when I shared not the Risks, or Chances of Profits."[11] His treatment of Holker was not something of which he should have been proud. Nor was this style of dealing with associates peculiar to his relationship with Holker. When Duer resumed his mercantile career in 1781, Elisha Crane was one of the first persons he employed. In 1786, Crane was finally paid a balance which had been owing since at least 1783 and perhaps earlier. And the balance was not paid freely, but only as a result of an arbitration into which Duer had been forced. Although Duer paid only when he had to pay, like the unjust steward in the New Testament parable, he expected others to pay him promptly. Just as he was shocked when Holker sued, Charles McCann expressed his dismay that Duer should sue his client, a Mr. Roosevelt, over a small sum owed for a short period of time and demand interest as well. But Duer could not see the justice of interest when he was on the paying end. John Miller thanked him in March 1785 for agreeing to pay £81,15/ owed since 1775 but he could not understand his refusal to pay less than £20 interest.[12]

Thus Duer was slow to pay, but quick to demand payment. Although he did not treat everyone as callously as Holker nor was he always as careless as he had been with Crane, incidents such as these are found frequently enough in his business dealings to make one wonder why anyone associated with him. Part of the answer is possibly in the associates, a newcomer like Holker, a man badly needing a job like Crane; part of it is in his manner which could be very persuasive when he wanted it to be, as witness Holker's patience. Also, Duer genuinely believed his schemes were certain to be profitable and this helped him put them over to people who may not have fully understood what he was attempting.

As the eighteenth century would have it, he was exceedingly sanguine. So Duer ended his wartime affairs with a long drawn-out whimper. By fending off Holker and others, he was able to free what capital he had or could borrow for new ventures, some of which were small at first but which quickly grew into efforts spectacular in size, if not in type. Duer was never a pioneer, moving into fields other Americans hesitated to enter. Rather, he was always the speculator, looking for quick returns in familiar pastures.

But he was not so foolish as to pass up or let go enterprises which paid a low but reasonably steady income. There were a few men, scattered at posts throughout New York State, left in service at war's end. General Washington authorized him to continue feeding them at the same rate as the 1783 contract. He also fed some Canadian refugees who had retreated with the American forces in 1776 and were now at West Point. In February 1784, Congress ordered those not needing any further assistance cut off, but there were enough of them who were indigent to require Duer's provisions even through 1789. By the end of 1784, only eighty men were left, guarding stores at West Point and Fort Pitt; except for several hundred men enlisted for three years who were sent to the frontier to guard against Indian attacks, these small units were the United States Army. Duer continued to feed these men through the rest of the decade, as well as units moving west through New York and Pennsylvania. Because of the small size of the Army and the stationing of the bulk of it on the frontier, these contracts could not have been very important to him. Only in 1790 with the renewal of major campaigns against the Indians of the Northwest did contracting again become important to Duer.[13]

Perhaps profit was not the key to Duer's continuing with the provision contracts, but rather a reluctance to cut loose from any enterprise once begun, or a refusal to admit when one was beaten. It is difficult otherwise to explain his attempt to get the distillery in Poughkeepsie to turn a profit. There was a change, but it was not in the accounts. Now Duer's employees were trying to distill gin, an exotic beverage for the rum and whiskey drinking Americans and one which the men never learned to produce satisfactorily, although it was not because they disliked the product— "I believe you had best be done with your Drunken Rectifier— & to send him adrift," Holker advised at one point. His counsel could aptly have been extended to the whole works, but Duer was still plugging away in 1789; by then he had switched back to whiskey, but had not yet turned a profit.[14]

Another wartime venture which continued on, but was at least partially liquidated, was the effort to sell masts and spars to foreign governments. Quantities had been accumulated during the war, but it had proved impossible to ship them to their intended customers and, with hostilities ended, the customers no longer needed them. The timber was sold to various private individuals in 1784 with little, if any, profit apparently being made.[15] Duer also renovated the saw and grist mills at Fort Miller and hired a superintendent for them, but here again, profit seems to have escaped him. As late as 1789, the sale of logs and boards had not repaid the renovation cost, but he hung on stubbornly, turning down at least one offer to buy. In addition to the land around Fort Miller, Duer also purchased, in company with others, 75,000 acres west of Lake Champlain, near Plattsburgh, in May 1785. At least some of the tract was secured with soldiers' bounty or location certificates, bought at a discount through Melancton Smith's store at Newburgh.[16]

The move to New York City would have been ineffectual if Duer had not tried to participate in the far-flung commerce of one of the new republic's fastest growing ports. During the 1780s, he sent the brig *Julia* on several voyages to Europe and opened an account with the Dutch mercantile firm of Wilhelm and Jan

Willink to finance the European sale of masts and spars, but this effort proved unprofitable. He also tried to open a trade in wine with a merchant on Tenerife, the largest of Spain's Canary Islands, but the effort failed when the shipper would not agree to a two year's credit on the wine sent to Duer. Closer to home, an agent, or more likely a junior partner, William Steele went to open up a store in Wilmington, North Carolina. Its initial purpose seems to have been to gather cargoes of naval stores for export by bartering tea and other grocery items as well as general merchandise. Later, when interest in Southern state debt certificates developed, Steele purchased them for Duer as well.[17]

With the end of his partnership with Parker, Duer cast about for new partners as well as new areas of trade. He renewed his acquaintance with Stephen Sayre, a Long Islander who, in the course of a long and varied career, operated a bank in London during the war for American independence. He also introduced Duer to the South American revolutionary Francisco deMiranda whom Duer, in turn, introduced to his brother-in-law, George Rose, a prominent British political figure. Duer and Sayre's closest relationship was an effort in 1786 to open trade with Madras, the British post in India.[18] (It may be noted that Duer served briefly as an aide-de-camp to Lord Clive in India in the 1760s.) The partners employed an unscrupulous and eccentric agent, Charles Henry Lee, to go to Madras. Lee seems unidentifiable; if he was one of the ubiquitous Lees of Virginia, they had good reason to keep it quiet. The "eccentric" label is a personal judgment on anyone who could write with a straight face lines such as: "the Secret Motives that Impulse my Conduct . . . the World Shou'd Deem me Mad in Wandering from my Home like the Accurst Jew." The "unscrupulous" label seems justified by Lee's conduct in India. He left New York in March 1786; by May 1787, he had visited Madras where he bilked a local merchant, I. Popham, of £800. Even before Duer learned of this in 1788, he had disassociated himself from Lee, who was last reported to have taken ship for the Cape of Good Hope. Duer's prompt disavowal may have been owing to his belated discovery that his agent left New York under a financial cloud in 1784.[19] Sayre and Duer also tried to talk a Philadelphia merchant, Paul Vardon, Jr., into a partnership. The cautious Vardon turned it down because he believed the post-war recession they were in at the time would not be friendly to a new firm, especially one which would try to conduct "such an extensive piece of business, without funds to carry it on, but merely supported by Circulation—which at times is dangerous and uncertain."[20] Both the New Yorkers apparently suffered from Duer's old problem, insufficient capital, or perhaps they were willing to risk others' funds in risky enterprises, but not their own. Later, in 1790, Miranda proposed that Sayre and Duer team up to supply the insurgents in a South American revolution being planned by the former; like most of Miranda's plans, nothing came of this. If anything had, it would have been interesting to see how readily Duer, with much more than he could handle in 1790, would have taken on yet another enterprise, no matter how praiseworthy it may have been from a political point of view.[21] Thus, in spite of their best efforts, no Duer-Sayre joint venture ever got underway. Nor, metaphorically, did another of Duer's proposals ever get off the ground, although it concerned the oldest preoccupation of American speculators, land. However, this was not in the West, the New Canaan of the eighteenth century, but right on Manhattan Island. He proposed to buy a belt of land across the Island from the Hudson River through Greenwich Village to Corlear's Hook on the East River and develop it according to a scheme which he had commissioned from Pierre L'Enfant. Insufficient capital again held him back as he could only promise to pay the present owners when development took place. Their refusal to accept this promise was partially based on the notion that the city would never grow that far north, a judgment made time and again, but in 1790, it was enough to end Duer's plans.[22]

Thus Duer used the move to New York City to try himself in larger ventures, ones which would have been difficult if not impossible in Fort Miller. Although several were abortive, this was the case with any venturesome merchant—as well as some conservative ones—of the time. Business conditions were unsettled and profits probably came as much from luck as from skill. He did not seem to have been hurt too much by the failure of Daniel Parker and Company, largely because Parker's flight to Europe permitted him to postpone any serious attempt to reconcile the firm's books, thus putting off a settlement with the hapless Holker. His mercantile business in New York plus a salary for a government position taken in 1785 seem to have provided him with a financial base from which he could venture into his principal preoccupations, stock and land speculation (especially the former), and still survive occasional reverses. But Duer could never do things in moderation and soon went beyond the usual scope of such speculation. Many merchants speculated in government securities, others owned tracts of unsettled land and, while some combined the two, few if any dealt in either as extensively as Duer and no one combined them as he and several associates did in the Scioto Company, a venture involving millions of acres and, if successful, incalculable profits. Since the Scioto grew out of Duer's government service, it would be advisable to examine this and his political activity before dealing with his speculations.

Duer's willingness to subordinate public service to his private concerns is demonstrated in his postwar service in the New York Assembly. While he received two votes in a January 1784 canvass to select New York City's assemblymen, it is doubtful he seriously wanted election at that time.[23] Two years later, the circumstances were very different as the state's politics were agitated by a debate over the congress's request for permission to levy a 5 percent *ad valorem* duty on all foreign goods entering the country. A 1781 attempt to give Congress an independent source of revenue (and thus real strength) had foundered on Rhode Island's refusal. With the end of the war and the recovery of its major port, New York had repealed its consent to the congressional duty and levied one of its own, an import duty on all foreign goods moving through the port of New York. This duty provided more than a third of all state revenues and would have required a doubling of the land tax if it were usurped by the congressional levy. Congress repeated its request in 1784 and, this time, all the states except New York agreed. The mercantile community in the city favored the duty on the grounds that a uniform levy would help to revive trade, seen as being in the doldrums, and the example of the states' cooperation would improve the international image of the new republic; these opinions went along with the general notion by the nationally minded that any step which strengthened Congress was worthwhile. Other than its effect on the state's taxes, New Yorkers who opposed the congressional levy did so on grounds which reduced themselves to states-righters' fears of a too-powerful congress. Duer as a merchant and also as a patriot whose service had been almost entirely on the Continental level strongly favored the levy and accepted appointment in March 1785 to a merchants' committee to draft a remonstrance to the Assembly for its solitary refusal to agree to the tax. Suiting action to words, he stood for election in May to the 1786 Assembly; he and Robert Troup won the canvass. Alexander Hamilton, who had urged him to run, congratulated him on his success: "Abilities like yours ought always to be employed for the public good, and I have no doubt this will be your object."[24]

If Duer did stand for the Assembly in order to serve "the public good," his definition of it was a very restricted one. In sharp contrast to his activity while in the Convention and the congress, he confined himself almost entirely to the congressional tariff bill and to a proposal to print £200,000 of paper currency to alleviate a shortage of circulating currency. He served on no committees and sponsored only unimportant resolutions in addition to his work on these two bills. The Assembly opened its ninth session in January 1786 with a bland message from Governor Clinton, a message whose very blandness was a sign of the difficult time those favoring the congressional levy faced. The governor commented that there were no critical problems facing the state and that he had called the Assembly into session only because he was convinced that it should meet at least once a year. This description of the Assembly's work as being of slight significance showed his disagreement with those who saw the congressional levy as *the* critical issue facing the state and the Union. Clinton did mention Congress's request and urged the Assembly to adopt "every measure calculated to support our national credit, and warranted by the confederation." The qualification was important as Clinton— and a majority of the Assembly—did not think the levy was warranted. Duer demonstrated his restricted definition of the "public good" by not coming to the Assembly until almost a month after its convening. The day after his first attendance (and swearing in), the Assembly began to work on the paper money bill. It was sponsored by an alliance of easy money people and states righters looking to keep Congress as powerless as it then was. The bills of credit (as the currency was properly called) would be given to New Yorkers in return for congressional and New York debt certificates, thus having the state assume a portion of the national debt. Duer and Troup, representing the New York mercantile community, opposed it because, first, by taking up part of the debt, it would remove some of the justification for the levy Congress was requesting, thus weakening the argument that it was needed to permit Congress to deal with the debt, a major point made by those who favored a stronger government. Second, the merchants had come to distrust paper money issues because of the unfortunate experience with such currency during the war.[25]

The opposition's efforts resulted in a paper money bill only slightly more acceptable to them than the one originally introduced. Duer was responsible for this small triumph, making more motions to amend than any of his colleagues and being the first to resist efforts to expand the scope of the bill. The first vote gave Duer an idea of how hopeless his task was; on a motion to issue bills of credit, i. e., whether or not to consider any kind of paper money bill, the vote was forty-nine yeas to ten nays. Later, he moved to make congressional debt certificates unacceptable, thus affecting only the state debt; this went down by a similar margin, forty-seven to ten. An attempt to include other states' certificates and the notes of John Pierce, a Continental paymaster, which had been given to New York troops, was also defeated in several lop-sided votes. Another proposal by Duer that the state discriminate in receiving certificates, refusing to accept them from anyone not an original holder, also failed heavily. After the defeat of other amendments and delaying maneuvers, the bill passed its third reading on 6 March with a vote of forty-three to nine. The only real victory the New York merchants won was a clause in the act making the bills legal tender only in payment of court judgments.[26] Two resolutions passed by the Chamber of Commerce suggest that the merchants got what they reasonably expected, no more. One, sponsored by Duer, argued that a paper money issue would inevitably depreciate and hurt the mercantile community. The other requested that if the bill did pass, the paper money should not be legal tender for ordinary transactions. As a result of the law, New York accumulated enough Continental debt certificates to satisfy her congressional requisitions by indents of interest (actually IOUs) paid on her holdings by Congress.[27]

With the paper money bill passed and sent on to the Senate, the Assembly was able to consider the congressional levy. Action began on 13 April when John Lansing, Jr., moved that the impost be collected according to state regulations; the motion passed thirty-three to twenty-two with those favoring a congressional levy voting against it. If the money was collected according to state rules, it could not then be guaranteed that it would go on to Congress. Also, the other states—New York was the only hold-out at this point—had not put similar provisions in their enabling acts and Congress saw it as a material difference, thus violating the unanimity needed to amend the Articles of Confederation. On the 15th, Duer moved that New York bind itself to accept congressional regulations, when they were adopted. This also lost by eleven votes. With this defeat, the supporters of the impost gave up. Having been defeated on the paper money bill, those who wished Congress to be more powerful, to be able to begin retiring its debt (in practice, two sides of the same coin) saw there was no hope in the New York legislature and looked for their success outside of it. Although no one realized it then, the seed of their eventual victory was planted in this same session of the Assembly, although Duer, because of his restricted definition of the "public good," stopped attending on the 15th and thus did not participate. Before they adjourned, the friends of Congress saw to the appointment of three delegates (Hamilton among them) to represent New York at the famous Annapolis meeting.[28] Although it was convened only to consider ways of improving the commerce of the United States, out of it came the suggestion to Congress which resulted in the call for the Philadelphia Convention of 1787 and, eventually, a new constitution. The gift of prophecy being denied Duer and his more diligent colleagues, all they had to console themselves with at the time was the small victories the session had given them, the very small victories.

Exactly how large a role Duer had played in trying to defeat the paper money bill and pass the federal impost is difficult to estimate. According to his fellow assemblyman, Robert Troup, who was one of Hamilton's closest friends, Duer's "commanding eloquence" and vigor led the effort in trying to carry out what Troup described as Hamilton's plans. He also gave himself and Duer the credit for securing the appointment of delegates to the Annapolis convention, although this is doubtful.[29] Considering his energy in moving amendments and various delaying maneuvers, Duer may well have been the leader of the Hamiltonians in the limited area of the money bill and the federal impost; this was in sharp contrast to Troup who showed no initiative whatever. But Duer's concentration on the money bill and the impost clearly demonstrates his reluctance to become widely involved in politics again. While the Assembly was still sitting, he declined a nomination to the Senate without explanation.[30] Thus, while he would be involved tangentially in the ratification of the Constitution in New York, his service in the Assembly would be the last elective office he would hold, with his limited activities there contrasting with his energy and constancy in the Convention and the Congress.

New York's refusal to agree to the congressional levy proved fatal to it. Congress rejected New York's enabling bill because of the conditions attached and asked Governor Clinton to call a special session of the legislature to consider a suitable bill. Clinton refused, answering that he did not consider the matter of sufficient importance to warrant such a call.[31] The failure of this attempt to give Congress a permanent source of revenue accelerated the movement for a strengthening of the Articles of Confederation. Many thoughtful Americans believed the Articles to be responsible for the various ills from which the country was seen to be suffering, ranging all the way from poor trade to the sorry figure the United States made overseas. From the 1787 Philadelphia meeting came a revolutionary document, a constitution creating a central government with powers of taxation, trade regulation, coercion—in short, all the powers and responsibilities of an effective central government with the means necessary to exercise them. The old Confederation had not been short of power and responsibility; rather, it had lacked the means to exercise its power and carry out its responsibility. The new constitution was revolutionary in that it ignored the provision in the Articles which called for unanimity in amending them. It was to go into effect when conventions of nine of the states approved. Duer quickly and strongly supported the new frame of government. His wife's cousin told of being subjected to a two-hour harangue on Christmas Eve, 1787 by "Duer . . . out of humour . . . horridly with Gov[ernor]. C[linton] who is detected to have been very busy against the new emaculate [sic] Constitution." However Governor Clinton felt about the Constitution (he was opposed), when the legislature opened its 1788 session in January, he asked them to implement the Congress's call for a state ratifying convention, a task which was accomplished by 1 February. Their resolution called for an election in April with all adult white males voting for delegates to a convention to meet in Poughkeepsie in May. The liberal suffrage represented the opposition's judgment as to the unpopularity of the proposed frame of government, not the purported reason, the necessity of consulting as wide a segment of the people as possible in reaching such a momentous decision. Their judgment was correct and the election was a disaster for the Federalists, those who favored the Constitution. They received 6,500 votes and elected 19 delegates; their opposition, tagged by the Federalists with the negative-sounding label, Antifederalist, swept the slate with 14,000 votes and 46 delegates.[32]

As a New York City merchant, a speculator in public securities (which would certainly appreciate with the new government), and a large landowner, it would have been surprising if Duer had not been a Federalist. Probably also of significance was his foreign birth, freeing him from an undue attachment to a native state, and his service in Congress where he became acquainted with the problems of all the states, transcending the parochialism of most Americans. So it should not be startling that he would be enlisted in the work of political evangelization designed to convert New York to Federalism, but it should also not be surprising that his participation would be relatively slight and of a sort which could be fitted into the few open spaces in his busy days. In the fall of 1787, Hamilton recruited James Madison of Virginia and John Jay to assist in writing a series of essays for New York City newspapers, explaining the Constitution and reassuring those who feared the supposed tendency of any central government, except the weakest, toward tyranny. Duer, probably at the request of Hamilton, wrote four essays which James Madison later described as "auxiliary to the numbers of the Federalist," a status nicely expressed by the pen name he took, "Philo-Publius," complementing the "Publius" used by the three main authors. Why Duer, who had shown no special talent for political journalism or analytical writing previously, who had not participated in the Convention, and was much distracted by his business affairs, should have been asked at all is unclear.[33]

"Philo-Publius" first appeared in *The Independent Journal* of New York late in October 1787 and Hamilton may have had immediate misgivings about Duer's suitability. In it Duer commented that the redistribution of powers under the new constitution would not affect individual rights, but would certainly lead to the diminution of some state powers. Since it was a major tenet of the Antifederalists that the new constitution created a despotic central government which would surely reduce the states to political ciphers, this was giving fuel to the opposition's fire. Duer's remaining contributions were not much better, but they did not give the enemy aid and comfort. In the second, he clumsily compared Governor Clinton to Pericles of Athens who used the "specter" of aristocracy to ingratiate himself with the people, ruin his state, and then drive it into a foreign war in which it was defeated. This illogical sequence is as Duer put it down. His third essay was an attempt to add to Hamilton's *Federalist* Number Eleven, "The Utility of the Union in Respect to Commerce and a Navy," and consisted of the unsupported assertion that, while a navy could adequately guard against foreign attacks, it could never threaten individual rights as an army might. It would also guard, in some unspecified manner, against the bad effects of the diverse interests of the states. His fourth contribution pointed out that foreign powers recognized this country only under the title "United States," not as thirteen separate states. He admitted that American independence might survive, even under the weak union of the Articles, but then asked the Antifederalists if they could guarantee we would not become another Poland and be divided by the European powers. Implicitly, they could not. This ignored the Antifederalists' contention that the Articles were adequate to preserve the union and that there was no reason to assume the states would separate if the new constitution was not approved. Also, the use of Poland, which had experienced its first partition in 1775, was certainly a geographically faulty analogy. This turned out to be the last effort of "Philo-Publius."[34] He may have intended more, but he was heavily involved in several business ventures as well as serving as secretary to the Board of Treasury of the Continental Congress. About this time, he did take several pages of notes from Emmerich deVattel's *The Law of Nations* and, in parallel columns, applied them to the controversy over the Constitution. Since none of this material appeared in any of the published essays, he may have intended to write more.[35] This ended Duer's active role in the New York ratification contest. He did help to keep Federalists in the city informed of events during the ratifying convention in Poughkeepsie, relieving Hamilton who led the Federalist forces there, and he also relayed news to James Madison in Virginia at Hamilton's request.[36] He may have made another literary contribution to the controversy, but his authorship survived only in family tradition. While the Poughkeepsie convention was sitting, New Hampshire became the ninth state to ratify, thus putting the Constitution into effect among the states which had approved it. Virginia followed soon after, leaving New York as the only significant state still outside (North Carolina and traditionally perverse Rhode Island were the others). In order to put pressure on the delegates at Poughkeepsie, the Federalists in New York City sponsored a parade, complete with floats, songs, speeches, and bands, to celebrate New Hampshire's ratification and laud the prospective benefits of the new union. According to his son, Duer contributed a song celebrating the advantages to commerce the Constitution was to bring. It may have been better than the essays. Whether the parade or the prospect of being left alone in the world converted the Antifederalists cannot finally be determined, but on 26 July enough of Governor Clinton's group went over to the Federalist side to carry ratification by a three vote margin, thirty to twenty-seven.[37]

Duer again played a small role in Federalist politics during the elections for the first Congress under the new government, December-January 1788-1789, when he wrote to Madison, then standing for election to the House of Representatives in Virginia, wishing him well and letting him know that John Adams would welcome election as vice-president. Duer had discovered that Adams supported the Constitution fully and, in a presumptuous postscript, opined that "A greater knowledge of the world had cured him of his old party prejudices." He urged Madison to ensure some Southern electoral votes for Adams. He returned to his letter writing the following month during the New York gubernatorial election, chairing a committee of correspondence to further the candidacy of Robert Yates, a recently converted Antifederalist. He also took responsibility for a city ward and succeeded in getting the vote out but, as usual, the upstate counties went strongly for Clinton and he won, although by a narrow margin.[38]

In what turned out to be its last move, the Continental Congress came to New York City in January 1785. Coincident with this, Robert Morris made good on his frequently expressed intention to resign as Superintendent of Finance, a step which brought about a reconsideration by Congress of the administration of its finances. Their final decision was to do away with Morris's post and return to a variation of their wartime practice of administering by committee. The Board of Treasury, as the new body was known, consisted of Samuel Osgood, Walter Livingston, and Arthur Lee. Realizing the complexity of their task, the Board decided to employ an assistant to handle the administrative details. In February Morris urged Duer to take the position, advising him to keep the books always in good order so as to be able at a moment's notice to give a clear statement of accounts to the Board, thus entitling him to "their Gratitude at a future day." Duer accepted the Board's offer and took up his duties in May when most of the Congress's public offices moved to Manhattan. The following March, Congress upgraded the position to "Secretary" and increased the salary to $1,850 a year.[39]

Whether the promotion and salary increase were merited may be questioned. James Madison was very concerned when he noticed that Lee was busy in an unnamed intrigue with Arthur St. Clair and was leaving "the business of the treasury b[oar]d to Billy Duer." Madison was properly concerned. Duer used William Constable's firm, Constable and Rucker, to transfer funds and commodities for Congress. He used the same firm for some of his personal business and on several occasions, the accounts became so mixed that he and Constable had to make judicious guesses when balancing the two sets of accounts. Indeed, there is good reason to believe that Duer arranged the manner in which the Board did some of its business in such a way as to give Constable's company interest-free loans. The profits made possible or easier by these loans were shared with Duer who may have originally conceived of this use of the Company's scarce funds. There were occasions when the business of the Board had to wait for Duer's personal affairs, and at least one government creditor, after the formation of the new government, asked that his accounts be submitted directly to the Secretary of the Treasury rather than

Duer because of his past experiences with the latter. Obviously, if Duer intended to earn anyone's gratitude, it was not in the way advised by Morris.[40]

Nor would it be necessarily the Board's (or the public's) gratitude. Certainly, he did not hesitate to use his influence with the Board to aid his friends, or anyone willing to pay for the privilege. As Andrew Craigie noted: "D[uer] has great influence & will use it agreeably to their wishes." He also did not scruple at receiving money from persons doing business with the Board. Craigie knew whereof he spoke when he made the above comment for, shortly thereafter, in April 1788, he promised Duer $8,000 if the Board assigned a claim by the United States against a Dutch mercantile firm to him and also removed an attachment the Board had placed on him. Both actions were taken in May and Duer received his fee. Duer also used information received in the course of his official duties to his personal advantage. In March 1788, Thomas Jefferson, American minister to France, proposed several steps to the Board to reduce foreign speculation in United States debt certificates. Duer immediately used the information to force his way into a speculation Craigie was starting in Europe.[41]

One of the more ambitious schemes by which Duer attempted to profit from his office was a copper coinage proposal presented by James Jarvis, a minor figure in the burgeoning New York City group of speculators. On the surface, it appears that Duer pushed his way into the proposal after it was submitted to the Board, but there is a very strong possibility that he helped to draft the proposal and that his presence was a vital, albeit hidden factor. Be that as it may, the proposal did promise to help alleviate a real problem for the young republic which suffered from a serious shortage of small denomination coins. This affected many people every day and may even have helped to raise prices for daily needs unnecessarily. Congress was properly interested when Jarvis formally approached the Board in October 1786 with a plan to mint three hundred tons of copper into coins and loan them to the government at 6 percent interest. He also offered to coin, at no charge, some copper which Congress already owned. The Board received the proposal cordially and told Jarvis to settle the contract details with Duer. According to Jarvis, at their first meeting, Duer insisted on an IOU for $10,000 "which he demanded as a *sine qua non*." Since Duer refused to give Jarvis a written statement releasing him from liability should the project fail to produce a profit, the latter threatened to withdraw the offer. Duer promised, on his honor, that he would not demand the sum should Jarvis fail, but that he was associated with someone "who could not be mentioned" and who required definite proof of what Duer was to receive. Relying on this promise, Jarvis gave Duer a promissory note and the contract writing began. The finished document called for minting more than 70,000 pounds of copper into eleven coins per pound. Jarvis would receive twenty-year bonds bearing 6 percent interest, but he did not have to post a security bond and there was no penalty for non-fulfillment. Later, when Jarvis did not complete the contract, Duer, despite his promise, did demand the money and since the IOU made no mention of the contract, Jarvis was legally bound to pay. By enlisting Craigie and Melancton Smith in his cause, Jarvis was able to avoid paying anything, but only after some strenuous exertions. As mentioned, it is likely that Duer helped to devise the scheme, indeed that Craigie and Melancton Smith were in on it also, and that the mysterious person who could not be named was a member of the Board of Treasury. Whatever the actual circumstances were, clearly Duer used the occasion to try to profit from his official post to the possible detriment of the public interest.[42]

Another attempt by Duer to profit from his position made the Jarvis contract look like a penny ante poker game. This was an effort to form an international banking house whose initial capital would be the United States debt held by the French government. In the summer of 1788, a French journalist and soon-to-be political figure, J. P. Brissot deWarville, arrived in New York City, ostensibly to gather material for a book on the United States and to spy out possible sites for European settlements. He brought with him a letter of introduction from Daniel Parker to Duer which disclosed his actual purpose: investigating the possibility of a large speculation in United States debt certificates. He represented a French group with very large resources and could be expected, if properly handled, to make all his purchases through Duer and Craigie. Parker urged Duer to give Brissot his "most *confidential* [orig. emph.] communications," to hold nothing back. Presumably, Duer held nothing back and, before Brissot left the city, they were united along with Craigie and others in the most grandiose scheme Duer had ever involved himself in—worthy of a Fugger or a Medici. The new firm was, first, to secure the transfer of the debt the United States owed to France, as well as congressional approval of that transfer. (Jefferson had already advised Congress that such a transfer was not in the best interests of the United States.) Second, they were also to speculate in the domestic debt of the United States. Shares were held by Stephen Claviere, a Paris banker for whom Brissot was acting, Brissot, Duer and Craigie, but the partnership agreement explicitly permitted the division of shares for the benefit of anyone whose assent was needed for the firm's success and Parker was invited to join the firm if he wished.[43]

Brissot returned to Paris at the end of 1788, earlier than he had expected, because of the new firm's needs and the summoning of the Estates General. When he arrived there, he found Parker strangely cold to the idea of the projected house and that there was a rival group of Americans, headed by Robert Morris, also trying to secure the French government's American debt. After some negotiations, the two groups united and began serious dealings with Jacques Necker, the French Minister of Finance. The financiers believed that they were on the verge of success when a loan to the French government by Dutch bankers relieved its fiscal stringency, causing it to lose interest in selling the American debt. With this setback and the outbreak of the French Revolution in May 1789, the defeat of the scheme was recognized.[44]

When one considers the eighteenth century's looser standards governing the private conduct of public officials, Duer's behavior up to this point, while hardly praiseworthy, may not have been especially reprehensible to most of his contemporaries. This is hardly the case for an incident which only came to light after Duer had left public employment. In May 1793, a former board employee, Andrew G. Fraunces, presented two warrants of the Board to the new government's Department of the Treasury for payment. Secretary of the Treasury Alexander Hamilton refused to honor them, because it was impossible to be certain that they had not already been paid. During the controversy which followed, the possibility of Duer having illegally used the warrants was bruited about. It was more than a possibility. He had used one of the warrants, No. 236, as security for a loan made to him by Craigie and Christopher Gore, a Boston merchant, speculator and politician, sometime in 1788. Whether or not the loan was paid back and the warrant redeemed (and Fraunces's possession of it argues against this), the warrant never belonged to Duer and should never, by any stretch of official or unofficial ethics, have been used for his private purposes. Any analysis of the incident reduces itself to plain and simple theft and lends credence to other charges of misconduct made during Duer's later government service.[45] Thus, much of Duer's work for the Board of Treasury seemed to be for his own benefit. He either arranged or pushed his way into the Jarvis contract and he would undoubtedly have used his position to advantage if the venture with Brissot had succeeded. His assistance to Craigie was rewarded by the latter's gratitude and $8,000. All in all, it should not be a surprise that Duer climaxed, in scale if not in time, his service to the Board with the largest example yet of his propensity to use public office for private profit, the Scioto Company.

In Duer's view, the Scioto Company had the unique advantage of combining a stock speculation with a speculation in western lands, the two sure things of late eighteenth-century operators. Land speculation, that is, the holding of large tracts of land in hope of a profitable resale to smaller buyers, has been a constant feature of American economic life from almost the first colonization and such proprietary colonies as Maryland, the Carolinas, and Pennsylvania were large examples of what has been done on a smaller scale by many others ever since, from Jamestown to Levittown. On the other hand, speculation in public and private securities was unknown in America before the war for independence. First, and most important, there were no securities to trade. Second, merchants and landholders were too preoccupied with the work of building an economy, too widely separated from each other, and seldom had any excess capital which they could invest. Stock speculation was a sign of a more mature economy than America possessed before 1775. The war for independence brought about a remarkable change in conditions. The debt certificates issued by the congress and the states now furnished ample stuff for speculation. The war had enriched some, giving them the funds to invest and it had weakened the sectional barriers and acquainted merchants of different areas with one another. It had also put some debt holders—small farmers and veterans, for example—in a financial bind which made them ready to sell off their pay certificates or provision requisitions at a discount to obtain much needed money immediately. Thus, the circumstances necessary for the renewal of land speculation and a beginning to stock speculation were present in the 1780s and Americans took full advantage of them.[46]

The Scioto speculation indirectly came from a petition in June 1783 by a group of veterans asking Congress for permission to purchase a tract of land on the Ohio River with the vouchers they had received in lieu of pay. Although the petition was lost in the press of other business, the idea behind it was not and formed the basis for the Ohio Company of Associates, a New England group organized in 1786. When the Company had some difficulty accumulating its starting capital of $1,000,000 in Continental debt certificates, the Reverend Manasseh Cutler, a Massachusetts clergyman and former army chaplain, was sent to Manhattan to deal directly with Congress. His goal was to negotiate a time payment plan so that the Ohio tract could be secured while—not after—the capital fund was being accumulated. He arrived in the city early in July 1787 and was able to talk with several Congressmen before they passed the Northwest Ordinance for the government of the territory in which the desired land lay. While the terms of the Ordinance were very agreeable to the associates, the terms Congress would accept for a time-payment agreement were not; the price was too high and the time for payment too short. Cutler considered his trip a failure and was preparing to leave in mid-July, when he was approached by Duer who presented him with a plan "from a number of the principal characters in the city, to extend our contract, and take in another Company, but that it should be kept a profound secret. . . . The plan struck me agreeably." The plan which struck Cutler so "agreeably," causing him to unpack his bags, was that the Associates should ask the congress for, not one million acres, but five million acres. Duer argued that Congress might be willing to accept a lower price per acre and a longer term of payment in order to sell such a large tract. A second company, consisting of Duer and friends, would take the additional acres and both Congress and Cutler's associates would be satisfied.[47]

Not surprisingly, Duer was correct about Congress's mood.

Within a week, Cutler and Winthrop Sargent, the company secretary, had congressional approval of the outlines of two contracts
and had submitted the filled-in outlines to the Board of Treasury
for their approval. This had only been done after some astute
and diligent lobbying, especially with Congress. Rising to the
occasion, Cutler observed that "in the true spirit of negotiations
with great bodies; every machine in the city that it was possible
to set to work we now put into motion," that is, Duer and Cutler,
assisted by Samuel Osgood, president of the Board of Treasury,
Arthur Lee, a Board member, Richard Henry Lee of the Virginia
delegation, and Sargent. Added to the usual benefits claimed for
any scheme which would presumably hasten the settling of the
West was the notion that the demand for Continental debt certificates it created would increase their price. (Exactly how the
public would benefit by this was left unspecified.) By the end of
July, Congress had passed the necessary legislation and the completed contracts were on their way to Cutler for signing. In two
separate contracts, one for the Ohio Company, the other for
Cutler, Sargent and associates, Congress agreed to sell five million
acres north and west of the Ohio River for a net price of two-
thirds of a dollar per acre, payable in specie, loan office certificates,
or "certificates of the liquidated debt of the United States." Title
for one and one-half million acres would pass on receipt of the
second of two payments of a half-million dollars each and complete the first contract. The second contract was to be executed
in six equal payments, title being given at each payment for the
acreage purchased. No security was given for the completion of
either contract. By the first contract, the Ohio Company secured
its land at the price it wanted to pay and any failure by Duer
and friends on the second contract would not injure it. A crude
type of limited liability. Few members of Congress were aware
of the maneuvering that had obtained the contracts or that two
separate companies were involved in the purchase. Indeed, many
members expected thirty million dollars (face value) of debt to
be retired by the purchase and were convinced they had struck
a good bargain with Cutler and his Yankee friends.[48]

Shortly after the formal signing of the two contracts, an informal, private ceremony took place. Cutler, Sargent and associates,
and William Duer and associates divided the second purchase
into thirty shares, thirteen for each group with the remaining

four to be sold abroad on joint account. All holders were to share equally in the results of efforts to sell or mortgage the land in the United States or Europe.

This was as much of a formal incorporation as the Scioto Company ever had. This was a very different effort from that of the Ohio Company which seriously intended to try and sell their land to individual farmers. As expressed in its "Articles of Agreement," the Scioto's lands were either to be sold to European holders of American debt certificates willing to exchange them for western lands or mortgaged, with the proceeds being used for debt speculation by the Scioto managers. Either way, its direct goal was speculation in debt certificates for, it was hoped, enormous profits; Congress might have looked to the purchase to reduce the debt and settle the West faster; the Scioto shareholders wanted a fast buck, nothing more.[49]

The number of shareholders was probably not very large. Since it required no starting capital, it needed no contributors on that score and the semi-secret character of the Scioto Company prevented Duer (if he had wished to do so) from opening its doors to many. While no listing of its members can be complete, a partial listing is possible and instructive. The shares taken by Cutler and Sargent were distributed among those who had been active in the Ohio Company's early organization or the first settlement of its lands. These included Generals Benjamin Tupper and Samuel Parsons, Return J. Meigs, Jr., and Daniel Story. Duer's shares went to Andrew Craigie and through Craigie to several Philadelphia and London speculators. For securing some Ohio Company subscriptions, James Jarvis received a partial share and John Holker another partial share in tentative settlement of his claims against Daniel Parker and Company. Baron Steuben was given a share. Duer may also have divided some shares among other New York speculators such as William Constable and Melancton Smith. Samuel Osgood of the Treasury Board probably got a portion. However, as long as the Scioto Company lasted, Duer gave it what direction it had and probably retained the largest single interest.[50]

When Duer's first choice for Scioto's European agency, Royal Flint, fell ill, Cutler pushed forward Joel Barlow, a Hartford editor and lawyer with no direct business experience, but with a well received poem, "The Vision of Columbus" (1787), to his

credit. Failing to see the relevance of poetry to securing speculative capital, Duer resisted hiring him, but, failing to see anyone
better qualified who was willing to go, finally gave in. Duer was
wiser than he knew. On 4 May 1788, he signed a power of
attorney giving Barlow the right to make whatever arrangements
he judged "most suitable" in disposing of the Company's lands
in Europe. Given the problem of communicating across the
Atlantic, there may have been no real alternative to this unlimited
agency, but it would prove to be very troublesome. Barlow arrived
at Le Havre, France, on 24 June in a jaunty mood and eager to
get to work. Whether the mood came from relief that a thirty-
day voyage in which he had been seasick for thirty days was
finally over or a real desire to get on with the job is impossible
to say; it was probably a combination of both. After he met
Parker in Paris, the two went to London where they talked with
prospective purchasers; they returned to Paris by way of Amsterdam and met with the VanStaphorsts, bankers already interested
in American land. However when they got back to Paris in September, they had not made any sales, whereupon they split up.
What moved Parker to break with Barlow is not clear, but Robert
Morris's rival venture in American lands may have led him to
lose any faith he had in the Scioto effort, one in which he had
no vital interest.[51]

Barlow spent the winter of 1788-89 in Paris, circulating in the
city's society, getting to know those worth knowing and apparently enjoying it all very much, but not selling any land. During
the summer, he fell in with an Englishman, William Playfair. The
name did not reveal the man. In August, Barlow and Playfair
along with six Parisians formed the *Compagnie du Scioto*. While
developing the scheme further, a good bit of public enthusiasm
for it was whipped up in Paris. In November, Barlow sold the
Compagnie three million acres of Scioto land for about one and
one-fifth dollars per acre, payable in installments running until
April 1794. The land was to be resold in small lots to individual
farmers, title being given as soon as a portion of the price was
paid in Paris. The purchasers were also guaranteed transport from
an American port to the Ohio, a hut and a year's provisions.
Craigie, commenting on the first fragmentary reports from Paris,
believed Barlow had succeeded "beyond all Expectations" and
thought of giving him the European agency for a land venture

Craigie was putting together. Beyond saying that he was not satisfied with Barlow's information, Duer said nothing.[52]

Barlow had not exceeded his powers (they were too vague to be exceeded), but he had given the Scioto associates in America several serious problems, or rather one serious problem: finding money. Money was needed to pay for the land so the titles Barlow had promised could be given. Money had to be found to transport the emigrants to the Ohio, set them up in cabins, and provision them. From a fairly simple unearned increment land and stock speculation with little possibility of serious loss should things go awry, Barlow had turned the Scioto Company into an agency for colonizing its lands with several thousand French emigrants who expected a considerable amount of help once they landed in the United States. Obviously, the success of the scheme—and with the first unsettling events of the French Revolution, the scheme did not appear as cockeyed as it had at first—depended on the treatment the first group of emigrants received. For a refreshing change, a land shark was going to have to work for his profits. For this dismaying situation, Duer had largely himself to blame. While Barlow was overseas, he was hampered (if that is the correct verb) by a total lack of instructions from Duer. As late as December 1789, he had not received a line since coming to Paris. While Barlow had been less than forthcoming in some of his reports and several times authorized drafts on him based on expectations, not funds in hand, he had at least been reporting to Duer and requesting, vainly, definite instructions.[53] The steps Duer took to redeem the promises made to the French emigrants will be treated below. Part of the reason for Duer's neglect may have been some other land speculations he was engaged in or considering at the time. Late in 1788, he agreed to undertake the sale of some "military lands," that is, land obtained by purchasing land bounty certificates from veterans, around present-day Steubenville, Ohio, well above the Scioto tract. He also thought of starting a company to deal in lands near the confluence of the Ohio and Mississippi rivers, but suddenly, probably because of a lack of funds, dropped the project.[54]

More significant to Duer now was a newer form of investment, that of purchasing the depreciated debt certificates of the United States, whether those of Congress or the states. The Scioto had been simply a complicated form of securing capital to engage in this newer variety of speculation. The certificates presented potentially a very lucrative field for any bold, enterprising speculator. Duer used what capital he possessed, along with whatever he could borrow, to buy up stocks and gamble on a rise large enough to pay the interest costs and return a profit. There were only three banks in the country—Boston, New York, and Philadelphia—prior to the 1790s and, although they loaned at moderate rates of interest, their loans were designed to serve the mercantile community's needs and, besides being limited in size, ran for only three months at a time. Banks often obliged their creditors by rediscounting their notes, but a potential call was never more than three months away. Simple investment in stocks was a fairly safe activity. Buying a congressional debt certificate at a discount of 50 percent or more, especially if it could be done with one's own money, and waiting for a price increase or even, after the ratification of the federal Constitution in 1788, for the new government to fund its debt, was recognized by many as a prudent step. Duer, however, gambled on short term price fluctuations or attempted to create artificial shortages, thus making his own market and, he hoped, profit. Because he was always short of his own money, the necessity of borrowing to pay off maturing loans, or of selling on disadvantageous terms because he had to meet a note, increased the difficulty of his speculations. In his last grand burst of activity, just before he went to the wall, he had to borrow many small sums, usually at usurious rates, to finance his operations. Many of these loans went to pay the interest on previous loans. He was approaching what Eliot Janeway has called "a functional definition of bankruptcy—when you cannot borrow to pay the interest." His constant need for speculating capital explains why he was always associated with others in his speculations although, temperamentally, he was a lone wolf. Walter Livingston and Alexander Macomb, a New York landowner and former British Army contractor, both either supplied him with funds or co-signed notes in return for his presumably informed advice on speculation. Andrew Craigie and Henry Knox also paired up with Duer as did William Constable and John Pintard, a prominent New York merchant. Towards the end, he found it necessary to take in some lesser fry from the New York speculating community, including Isaac Whippo, an erstwhile oysterman.

A further note should be made on the variety of debt certificates Duer and his friends dealt in. A table of prices in Boston, 1789-92, lists twelve different types, including loan office certificates, army certificates, new emission money, and indents of interest (notes issued in lieu of interest on other varieties of Continental debt).[55] This table does not include state certificates whose variety far surpassed those issued by the Congress. The funding of the Continental debt and the assumption by the federal government of the state debts in 1790 vastly simplified speculators' lives, for they then had only three varieties of bonds to deal with: six percent bonds, deferreds, bearing 6 percent interest beginning in 1800, and three percent bonds.

Duer began buying various kinds of Continental debt certificates while he was an army contractor. At least part of the reason for opening the store with Melancton Smith was the hope that the soldiers would cash in their pay certificates at a discount, thus adding to the potential profits of the enterprise. This side of the store was pushed so strongly as to lead to complaints from Washington's staff officers that too much pressure was being applied by the contractors on the enlisted men. Duer's interest in debt certificates did not end with the war and he was sufficiently informed on the topic to advise Holker on a 1784 purchase. His efforts in the New York Assembly in 1786, when he vainly tried to defeat a partial assumption of congressional debt by the state may also indicate substantial holdings. In 1787, he lent the Ohio Company $143,000 in certificates to make their first payment to Congress and the following fall, Craigie sent Parker "50,000 bo[ugh]t of Duer" as part of a shipment of securities. Since holdings of this size were not accumulated quickly in the undeveloped market of the mid-1790s, they probably represented some years' work. In 1785, Jeremiah Wadsworth commented on an effort by Duer and Walter Livingston to start a bank in New York City; they were trying to get Wadsworth to invest in it, but he resisted, believing they only wanted the bank "to play of[f] their Continental paper with." Thus Duer had a well-deserved reputation as a large scale speculator.[56] From 1787, his stock speculations formed an integral part of most of his undertakings. That the Scioto Company failed to secure capital was the fault of those who executed it, not the planners. The attempt to form an international banking house, with Congress's French debt as the capital and in partnership with Brissot and friends, showed, along with the Scioto, Duer's willingness to look abroad for his speculating funds.

But not all of his speculations were such grand projects. Money could be made dealing with small quantities of certificates and Duer wanted to make money. In May 1786, he used an agent, William Hill, to sell fifteen thousand dollars of interest indents in Virginia, although he cautioned Hill to keep his name out of it at all costs. Two years later, some more indents were sent to Europe to be sold, with the proceeds deposited in Duer's account with a Dutch banking firm. Daniel Carthy of New York was used in July 1789 to purchase $2,500 worth of South Carolina certificates, his agent's fee being one-third of the profits.[57] Thus Duer was dealing actively (for these are only representative transactions) in both congressional and state certificates, in large and small quantities, before the federal government was formed. All of this was done while he was holding what was possibly the most important financial office in the Confederation government, but alongside the Scioto venture, the Jarvis contract, the French debt syndicate, and the stolen Treasury warrants, such activities were relatively trivial. Nor was Duer the only one who tried to profit from his official position. Andrew Craigie was refreshingly honest, perhaps even brash, when he described debt certificates as "the best field in the world for Speculation . . . I know of no way of making safe speculations but by being associated with people who from their official situation know all the present & can aid future arrangements either for or against the funds," with Duer understood as one of those fortunate persons. Daniel Parker was just as direct when he wrote Duer to comment on the obvious fact that the latter's position gave him such privileged information: "If any profits can be made by such information, I should willingly share them with you."[58] Enough has already been given about Duer's official conduct to justify the conclusion that, if he could profit by it, he would certainly let his friends in on any good things that happened by.

The most significant "good thing" that was happening in the spring of 1789 was the organization of the new government according to the 1787 Constitution. After its ratification by the required number of states in the summer of 1788, the Continental Congress ordered elections to select the new government's members. Although the new Congress was to convene on the first Wednesday in March 1789, a quorum was not obtained until early April in both houses. The Electoral College's votes for president and vice-president were then counted, with George Washington receiving the College's unanimous choice as president and John Adams, with the next highest number of votes, selected as vice-president. The president-elect arrived in New York City, which was to remain as the seat of government, on 23 April and went to live in a house selected and furnished by Duer and Samuel Osgood; William Alexander's widow and Kitty Duer also helped plan the welcome for Washington. When Mrs. Washington gave her first formal reception on 29 May, the same ladies were prominent.[59] The new government meant no loss in the Duers' social status. What it meant for William Duer's official status remained to be seen.

Before the old congress had been decently interred and the new one out of the nursery, the speculators were second-guessing each other as to two closely related things: the fiscal policy of the new government and who would administer the policy. Representative of these assumptions, although they were not usually as accurate, was William Constable's expectation that the federal government would assume the debts of the state government and fund them at a 5 percent interest rate; his only uncertainty was whether or not this would take place too quickly for him to buy extensively.[60] His assured tone about assumption is surprising at this early date. Everyone knew the federal government would fund the debt owed to France and to foreign bankers as soon as possible; many expected the Congress's debt to American citizens to be paid off, probably at par, but few expected the state debts to be assumed. Some states had paid off most of their war debts, some hardly any, thus an assumption would appear to tax some states to pay off the debts of others, hardly a popular policy. Perhaps Constable was voicing his hopes as much as any considered judgments derived from conversations with some of those who might be expected to guide the new government's fiscal program.

Prior to considering policy, however, it may be advisable to examine who was likely to develop and administer the policy, as their ideas of proper fiscal conduct would be a significant influence on the new congress. In May, Craigie believed that Hamilton would be the secretary of the Treasury and Duer his assistant. Constable was more optimistic, but less accurate, about his friend's chances: "You ask about *Duer* [orig. emph.] & what he is about—making Schemes every hour & abandoning them as instantaneously. I hope He may be Secretary to the New Treasury. . . . He will have to change himself." Although his associates did not waver, Duer apparently sometimes had second thoughts about continuing in government service. "He sometimes appears to think he can do better without," that is, outside the new government, Craigie reported in July. But most of those who had associated with Duer expected him to remain in government if he could, some so confidently that they applied to him for jobs. Edward Fox's request, relayed through Craigie, included a threat to look into "the history of past times, and . . . take the Bull by the Horns" or "to put all my [Fox's] thousand questions together." The point of Fox's questions cannot be determined, but Duer's answer, relayed through Craigie's clerk, was a promise "to render Mr. F. all the services he can." However, the services did not include a job at the Treasury Department.[61]

The guessing as to who would administer the new government's fiscal affairs was ended in September when the Congress created the Department of the Treasury and President Washington appointed Alexander Hamilton its secretary. Hamilton promptly appointed Duer as assistant to the secretary. But the political gossip did not stop, as Craigie passed on the allegation that friends of Duer had altered the bill as it went through the congress to give the secretary the power to appoint his assistant. In its original version, the president had the appointment of both positions. This was done, according to Craigie, to make it more certain that Duer would get the position.[62] Probably less significant than who would make the appointment are the reasons Hamilton may have had to appoint—or not to appoint—Duer as his assistant, for even if the president had the power, Washington would certainly have given Hamilton's wishes great weight in making the selection. In favor of the appointment, it can be said that Duer knew as much about the recent fiscal affairs of the Confederation as anyone else in New York. His reputation as a businessman with a wide circle of acquaintances might help the performance of his official duties; Duer may be said to have represented the business community in the new government and he represented it directly, as only a businessman could, and not indirectly as Hamilton, too devoted a public servant for his own financial good, could do. Also, the personal element should not be ignored. Hamilton and Duer had known each other since at least 1777 and had been friendly since the end of the war when both had moved to New York City and they were married to cousins. They both agreed on the necessity of a stronger central government and on funding the public debt. But the reasons for not appointing Duer were also considerable. He was already known as a speculator in debt certificates and Hamilton could not have been entirely ignorant of the Scioto and Brissot ventures. In establishing the Department of the Treasury, Congress had forbidden its employees from dealing in public securities. Unless Hamilton was ready to require Duer to give up his private holdings and speculations, he could only expect him to follow the path of least resistance and most profit, for if there was a choice to be made between rectitude and profit, Duer's conscience would not trouble him unduly as he went for the latter. Constable's suggestion that he would have to change if he accepted a position in the new government was not likely to be followed. More representative of his attitude was a promise he made to Christopher Gore of Boston. In thanking Gore for an unspecified personal favor, Duer offered to perform "Every Service I can render to yourself or Friends, either in a private or Public line."[63] If he was going to do friends favors, he was certainly going to do himself some as well.

His official duties began immediately with a trip to Philadelphia to arrange for a loan from the Bank of North America. Unofficially, he continued as before, giving what direction he cared to the old projects involving public securities and embarking on new ones. He was not even careful about his casual conversation and less than a week after he started his new position, some speculators were acting on guesses derived from the "outdoor talk of Col. Duer, the Vice-Secretary." In October, he talked briefly with Robert Morris, through William Constable, about joining the Philadelphia financier, now a senator for Pennsylvania, in a new debt speculation, clearly indicating he intended to disregard the Treasury prohibition on dealing in public securities. If he did not recognize the dangers in his conduct, Constable did and commented, in connection with his acquisition of some pay certificates, that Duer "may not only incur censure but be turned out." Actually, he did recognize some limitations, for Constable reported him ready to do anything "he may do with Safety" for Morris. But it was not clear what this caution amounted to, for he had already told Constable that the indents of interest were to be funded with the rest of the debt certificates.[64] Whether these disclosures were significant or not is another question. Hamilton's ideas as to the proper fiscal course for the new government were well known when he entered office and, try as he might, he could not avoid showing his cards to the New York speculators.[65]

Duer began several new speculating partnerships after he joined the Treasury Department. In December, he pooled resources with Constable and Richard Platt to put $170,000 into North and South Carolina certificates, two wells of profit which had not previously been drawn on deeply. He also purchased indents from Walter Livingston at the relatively high price of eight shillings (no matter what currency they had been issued in, the market price of a certificate was always spoken of as if the face value was twenty shillings or a pound) or 40 percent of their face value. He feared the purchase might turn into a losing proposition as Congress had received Hamilton's proposals for funding the public debt with limited enthusiasm. "Both the Language & the Conduct of the Members in the house will (for two months, at least) depress public credit." It would actually be closer to eight months before a funding bill would be signed into law.[66]

The Secretary had delivered his Report on the Public Credit, containing his fiscal proposals to the House of Representatives on 14 January 1790. The speculators' judgments on the probable course of the new government had been reasonably accurate. Hamilton suggested the funding of the foreign and domestic debt, and the assumption by the central government of those state debts incurred in the cause of American freedom during the war for American independence. The certificates were to be received at face value and new bonds issued, both 6 percent bonds and bonds on which 6 percent interest was deferred until 1800, which, in combination would give an investor a little more than 4 percent interest. The indents were to be funded at 3 percent interest. The arguments Hamilton advanced to support his suggestions were as much political as fiscal and need not be gone into here.[67] It is impossible to say how much Duer may have influenced the writing of the report. The two men met on a daily basis, so the assistant secretary's views, if they were requested, could have been given orally. Nothing in the report conflicts with what Hamilton was known to have held before he entered office, and since Duer probably agreed with him, any influence that he had was complementary to Hamilton's ideas.

Although the speculators had been busily trading before the submission of Hamilton's report, once it went to Congress, public attention was directed to their activities more than ever before. William Maclay, representing Pennsylvania in the Senate, noted acidly in his one-sided diary that a colleague had seen two "expresses" heading south with money to buy underpriced Southern state securities before the news of the proposal of assumption should arrive: "Nobody doubts but all this commotion originated from the Treasury. but the fault is laid on Duer but *respondeat Superior*." Maclay was not the only one who suspected Duer's superior of connivance in stirring up the speculating fever. Unfortunately for Hamilton, the apparent corruption, information peddling, and "stock-jobbing" surrounding Duer and his associates made accusations against the secretary more plausible. As we know, Duer was certainly guilty of trading in government bonds when such trading was expressly forbidden by Congress. Accusations of more substantial misconduct were made later, after he left the Treasury but they were either political rumors or garbled versions of the stolen Board of Treasury warrants mentioned above. It is certainly possible that Duer used his official position to do more than get an unfair advantage over the other speculators, but until more substantial evidence is discovered, the Scottish verdict of "not proven," inspired mainly by his past disregard for public ethics, is the most severe judgment that should be rendered. It should be noted, however, that it is not an acquittal.[68]

Although Hamilton's program was eventually adopted, the congressional debate on it lasted from the submission of the report through August 1790. Initially, the program's opponents demanded that there be some kind of discrimination in favor of the original holders of the domestic debt certificates. They argued that it was the original holders who had actually fought, or had their crops taken for the Army, or who had been in some direct way, of service during the war, but now the speculators who had taken advantage of their necessity to buy up the certificates at depreciated prices would receive the entire amount. Representative James Madison led an effort to get 50 percent of the face value for the original holders, with the remainder going to the present holders. It was also Madison who received a letter signed "A Foreigner," which detailed the assurances the Board had given Dutch buyers in 1787 as to the certificates' transferability. Since the letter to Holland had been written by Duer, it is reasonable to suppose he may also have written the letter to Madison, who failed to be convinced by its arguments. But it should also be noted that Madison failed to convert Congress to discrimination and that part of Hamilton's program passed easily. Madison, who continued his opposition, especially on the assumption of state debts, became the special target of Duer's malice.[69]

The delay in congressional action, while it very much annoyed the speculators, actually worked to their advantage in that it gave more time for purchases, time of which Duer made the most use he could. He, Walter Livingston, and Joseph Hardy sent an agent, George Reid, to South Carolina to buy whatever certificates he could, while Duer and Livingston went in with Royal Flint for a flier in North Carolina certificates. Yet another venture brought Duer, Flint, Constable, and Craigie together. Most of the capital for Duer's part in these ventures was borrowed from various sources on Walter Livingston's guarantee as a co-signer. Duer was also associated with Richard Platt and Theodosius Fowler, city merchants lately turned speculators, although these may have acted only as his agents, not partners.[70]

It is difficult, because of the very incomplete state of Duer's correspondence and accounts, to estimate the scale of his dealings. Few of his speculations seem to have been for less than $5,000 while a good number were for much more than that. In March 1790, the highest priced certificates, specie orders, were selling in Boston for only ten shillings or one-half their face value.[71] Most of Duer's purchases were of the less-valued certificates, e.g., indents at six shillings, eight pence, and some were bought in the Southern states where prices were lower than in Boston. With figures like these in mind, it is plausible that he may have been dealing, at this time, in certificates worth $500,000 to $750,000 in face value. Assuming the successful resale of the certificates or holding them until they were funded in the Loan of 1790, a profit of up to one-half the principal could have been made, or from $250,000 to $375,000 federal dollars, a sum well worth breaking a Treasury regulation for.

Within weeks of becoming Hamilton's assistant, Duer was himself doubting whether he would stay with the post for very long, but when the end came, it was with startling suddenness. In mid-March, Constable wondered how much longer Duer would stay; early in April, Hamilton accepted his resignation. On 1 May, Tench Coxe of Philadelphia was appointed in Duer's place. The rush may have been owing to pressure from Hamilton. Constable, in commenting on the possibility in March, thought this was the case and Hamilton, in accepting Duer's resignation, was ambiguous: "I confess, too, that upon *reflection* [orig. emph.] I cannot help thinking you have decided rightly." The reasons for any pressure by Hamilton are readily apparent. The funding program's chances in Congress were hardly improved by the presence of a notorious speculator in the Treasury, something which was probably much more obvious in March than it had been in September. Aside from his speculating, Duer's other business affairs were also intruding. In January, Hamilton had to write Holker and ask that he postpone or put aside a suit he was filing against Duer in another attempt to settle their affairs. His main point in making the request was the embarrassment the suit would cause the Treasury. An assistant without such liabilities would certainly be attractive to Hamilton. Although Duer's friends claimed he left of his own free will, their statements do not have to be taken as indicative of anything other than what Duer may have said to them. Finally, Duer, in explaining his resignation to a friend, gave what was, for him, the best reason: "I have left to do better."[72] Perhaps he should have the last word on this point.

William Duer's stay in the Treasury Department was probably of significance mainly to himself. His presence there in a consequential position gave apparent substance to the charges of impropriety made against Hamilton but, whether he was there or not, the charges would still have been made as they were directed as much against the substance of the program as against any irregularities in its execution. Duer, however, had used his offices under both the old and new governments to move himself up from a New York figure to an internationally known financier, land speculator, and promoter. The Scioto might yet turn a profit, Brissot had not yet despaired of bringing off the transfer of the

French debt, the federal debt was, in Craigie's phrase, "an immense field of Speculation," and there were several more ideas he had not yet had an opportunity to try. Now, free of the demands of public service, however lightly he may have felt them, Duer's future seemed bright indeed.

References

1. William Alexander Duer, *New York As It Was* (New York, 1849), 9, 10, 18, 28-29.
2. William P. Cutler, ed., *The Life, Journals and Correspondence of Reverend Manasseh Cutler* (Cincinnati, 1888), I, 240-41; hereafter cited as Cutler, *Journals*.
3. William Alexander Duer, *Reminiscences of an Old New Yorker* (New York, 1867), 34; hereafter cited as Duer, *Reminiscences*.
4. *The New York Packet*, Feb. 2, 1784; East, *Business Enterprise*, 237; Henry P. Johnston, "New York After the Revolution," *Magazine of American History*, 29 (1893): 312; *Institution of the Society of the Cincinnati* (New York, 1851), 87; Alfred F. Young, *The Democratic Republicans of New York: The Origins, 1763-1797* (Chapel Hill, 1967), 173-74 for the Cincinnati's politics, hereafter cited as Young, *Republicans*; Duer kept up his membership, Theo[doric] Bland to Alexander Hamilton, James Duane, and Wm. Duer, Mar. 20, 1787, James Duane Papers, NYHS; document appointing Duer, among others, as a delegate to the General Meeting of the Society, May 3, 1788, Syrett, *Hamilton Papers*, IV, 647; Wm. Duer to Pres., Whig Society, Misc. Ms., # 15017, NYSL.
5. Daniel Parker to Wm. Duer, Dec. 1, 1782, Wm. Duer to John Holker, May 2, 1783, John Ross to Daniel Parker and Co., Aug. 4, 1783; for trouble regarding the payment for flour delivered to the British forces, Wm. Duer to John Holker, Nov. 25, 1783, Holker Papers, LC.
6. Philip C. F. Smith, *The Empress of China* (Phila., 1984) is a full narrative of the origin, progress, and consequences of this initial voyage.
7. Wm. Duer to Thomas Fitzsimons, Apr. 11, 1784, Ms. Coll., # 15016, NYSL; Wm. Duer to John Holker, Aug. ?, 1784, Holker Papers, LC; "Observations in General respecting Dan: Parker . . . ," loc. cit., XXVIII, 5556, LC; Clifford Egan, "Daniel Parker: An Exploratory Sketch," paper presented at the July 1981 meeting of the Society for Historians of the Early American Republic, Siena College, Loudonville, NY; see also "Estimate of the Engagements of Daniel Parker and Company," Duer Papers, Box IX, f. 1, NYHS; see Emden Grant to Andrew Craigie, Aug. 21, Sep. 1, Sep. 13, Sep. 17, Nov. 16, 1784, Craigie Papers, AAS, for the apparently successful efforts of Parker's clerk to spirit the firm's papers away from Duer and Holker.
8. James Geary to Wm. Duer, Jul. 11, 1784, Duer Papers, NYHS; before Geary, Duer's messenger to Philadelphia, could get the letter off, the supposed advance had risen to $38,000; "Report to Congress on the Memorial of William Duer, Esq., April 8, 1784," Letter Book G, Morris Papers, LC; the report was submitted to Congress on Apr. 13, JCC, XXVI, 219-20, XXVII, 404; Morris's willingness to admit damages was not new; in October 1782, Parker urged Duer to pad the vouchers for that month's issues since "I have every Reason to believe that Mr. Morris Intends to make ample representations for all Damages we have sustained by his non-performance," Daniel Parker to Wm. Duer, Oct. 26, 1792, Duer Papers, NYHS; Robert Morris to Wm. Duer, _____to Daniel Parker and Co., Aug. 11, 1784, Morris Papers, Letter Book G, the letter to Parker called for immediate action on the balance; for the July vouchers, see Diary, Aug. 9, 11, 23, 30, 1784, Morris Papers, LC; Robert Morris to Wm. Duer, Oct. 19, Nov. 22, 1784, Duer Papers, BV II, NYHS.
9. Thomas Fitzsimons to Wm. Duer, Apr. 13, 1784, Jan. 25, 1785, John Holker to Wm. Duer, Jun. 4, 1784, Jan. 22, Dec. 17, 1785, Duer Papers, NYHS.

10. John Holker to Wm. Duer, Jan. 22, Dec. 17, 1785, Duer Papers; Wm. Duer to John Holker, Dec. 10, 1788, Duer Papers, BV II; for the English debt, see George Rose to Wm. Duer, Apr. 3, 1788, loc. cit.; Daniel Parker to Wm. Duer, Jun. 2, 1788, Duer Papers, NYHS.

11. John Holker to Wm. Duer, May 16, 1786, Duer Papers; see also Thomas Fitzsimons to Wm. Duer, Jan. 25, 1786, Duer Papers, NYHS, where Fitzsimons rejects allegations of Duer's about the *Empress*; it could hardly be believed, Fitzsimons commented, that Holker could receive only a portion of the profits, but bear the entire loss.

12. Wm. Duer to Daniel Hale, Jan. 10, 1787, Daniel Hale to Wm. Duer, Jan. 14, 1787, Duer Papers, BV II, Charles McCann to Wm. Duer, Jul. 22, 1784, Duer Papers, McCann does not specify how small a sum or how short a time; John Miller to Wm. Duer, Mar. 14, 1785, NYHS; see also Alexander Hamilton to Wm. Duer, May 14, 1785, Syrett, *Hamilton Papers*, III, 610 for another successful suit against Duer for a debt owed since 1776.

13. George Washington to Wm. Duer, Jan. 22, Jan. 24, 1784, Washington Papers, LC; Washington had formally resigned his commission in December 1783; JCC, XXVI, 76-77; vouchers for rations, Duer Papers, Box V, NYHS; Diary, Sep. 2, 6, 7, 9, 1784, Morris Papers, LC; Robert Morris to Wm. Duer, Sep. 6, 1784, Duer Papers, BV II, NYHS; Timothy Pickering to Wm. Duer, Nov. 25, Nov. 30, 1784, Letters of Colonel Timothy Pickering, Vol. 88, Rev. War Mss., RG 93, NA; JCC, XXVII, 681; J. R. Jacobs, *The Beginning of the U. S. Army, 1783-1812* (Princeton, 1947), 15-16; Henry Greene to Wm. Duer, Jul. 21, 1785, Duer Papers, NYHS; F. V. Greene, *The Revolutionary War and the Military Policy of the United States* (New York, 1911), 297; from April 1784 to March 1789, provisions for the Army cost an average of $45,000 a year. Duer probably did not receive more than one-fifth of this sum, "U. S. Treasury, General Account of Receipts and Expenditures, 1785-1789," Livingston Papers, Box 16, NYHS.

14. John Holker to Wm. Duer, Oct. 10, 1784, Duer Papers; Udney Hay to Wm. Duer, Mar. 11, Jun. 30, 1785, John Brickhout to Wm. Duer, Oct. 7, 1786, Poughkeepsie Distillery folder, Duer Papers, Box V, NYHS.

15. Lumber Contracts, Box V; Bills, receipts, notes, etc., Box VIII, Samuel Hammer to Daniel Parker, Apr. 26, 1784 (copy), William Page to Daniel Parker and Co., Jun. 1, 1784, Duer Papers, NYHS.

16. Hugh Peebles to Wm. Duer, Mar. 18, 1789, Duer Papers, Wm. Dunwoodie to Wm. Duer, Jun. 23, 1787, Duer Papers, BV II, also Bills, Receipts, Notes, etc., Box VIII, Duer Papers, NYHS; *Calendar of Land Papers* (Albany, 1864), 695-96, 725; "Description of a Tract of Land adjoining Plattsburgh...," Misc. Mss., Clinton County, NYHS; "Order from Governor George Clinton to Simeon DeWitt, Surveyor-General of New York, Dec. 3, 1785," Morris Papers, LC.

17. Ships Invoices folder, Box V, Duer Papers; Wilhelm and Jan Willink to Wm. Duer, Feb. 12, 19, Sep. 19, Dec. 8, 1785, Jan. 11, Dec. 16, 1786, Duer Papers, in the last letter, the Willinks complained they had not heard from Duer for a year and his account showed a balance due of £1241; no further correspondence with them appears; Wm. Duer to Don Joseph deLugo, Apr. 24, 1784, Duer Papers; see also bill of Thomas McFee for drawing up articles of agreement between Duer and Don Joseph, Duer Papers, Box VIII; William Steele to Wm. Duer, Oct. 16, 1785, Duer Papers, NYHS.

18. See John R. Alden, *Stephen Sayre, American Revolutionary Adventurer* (Baton Rouge, 1983) for a full recounting of Sayre's career, hereafter cited as Alden, *Sayre*.

19. Charles Henry Lee to Henry Farrar, Mar. 6, 1786, Duer Papers; I. Popham to Wm. Duer, Oct. 9, 1787, Peter Leyns to Wm. Duer, Sep. 15; Nov. 10, 1788, Duer Papers, NYHS; see also Wm. Duer to George Washington, Jun. 5, 1784, Washington Papers, LC.

20. Paul Vardon, Jr., to Wm. Duer, Dec. 9, 1784, Duer Papers, NYHS.

21. Alden, *Sayre*, 159-60.

22. Duer, *Reminiscences*, 44-45.

23. *The New York Packet*, Jan. 1, 1784.
24. E. Wilder Spaulding, *New York in the Critical Period, 1783-1789* (New York, 1932), 155, estimates that the removal of this tax would have meant the doubling of the land tax; see *The New York Packet*, Mar. 17, Apr. 21, Jul. 14, 1785 for representative articles and letters on the congressional tax issue, Mar. 14, May 2, 1785 for Duer's actions; Alexander Hamilton to Wm. Duer, May 14, 1785, Syrett, *Hamilton Papers*, III, 611; Hamilton's role in the contest was so important or noticeable, perhaps both, that those favoring the impost bill were called Hamiltonians; those who opposed it were called Clintonians, Spaulding, *New York*, 177-79.
25. *The Journal of the Assembly of the State of New York* (New York, 1786), 39 [to order the compiling of a list of defaulters on state land purchases], 147-48 [election of delegates to the Continental Congress], 166 [to fix the city of Hudson as the meeting place of the Assembly]; this last failed, the others passed; 5-6 [Clinton's speech], 36 [Duer's swearing in], hereafter cited as *Assembly Journal*; Ferguson, *Purse*, Chap. 11, has an extended discussion of state assumption of the federal debt during the 1780s, New York is on 231-32.
26. *Assembly Journal*, 38, 41, 43-45, 47, 49-50, 70-71; Pierce's notes were being settled by the sale of land reserved for the soldiers; the *Assembly Journal* recorded only the proceedings; the judgment as to Duer's activity assumes that if he made a motion for amendment, he supported it with a speech; Ferguson, *Purse*, 232.
27. *The New York Packet*, Feb. 16, 1786; Ferguson, *Purse*, 232.
28. *Assembly Journal*, 134, 137-38, 150.
29. Quoted in Herbert P. Johnston, "New York After the Revolution," *Magazine of American History*, 29 (1893): 327.
30. *The New York Packet*, Apr. 3, 7, 1786.
31. Spaulding, *New York*, 178-80; Thomas C. Cochran, *New York in the Confederation: An Economic Study* (Phila., 1932), 175-77, hereafter cited as Cochran, *New York*; both these writers agree that the special session would not have made any difference; the 1786 votes were repeated by even more decisive margins in 1787.
32. Young, *Republicans*, Chaps. 4, 5; see Linda Grant DePauw, *The Eleventh Pillar: New York State and the Federal Constitution* (Ithaca, NY, 1966) for a sound, extended treatment of the election and the ratifying convention; hereafter cited as DePauw, *Pillar*. [Walter Rutherfurd] to John Rutherfurd, Dec. 27, 1787, Rutherfurd Collection, vol. V, NYHS. For an analysis of how the Constitution affected Duer's various speculations, both directly and indirectly, see Robert F. Jones, "Economic Opportunism and the Constitution in New York State: The Example of William Duer," *New York History*, 68 (1987): 357-72, esp. 369-72.
33. James Madison to William Alexander Duer, May 5, 1835, William Alexander Duer, *A Course of Lectures . . .* (New York, 1874), 373; hereafter cited as Duer, *Lectures*. On another occasion, Madison described Duer's efforts as "intelligent and sprightly," "The Federalist," unpublished paper in the State Department Archives, cited in John C. Hamilton, ed., *The Federalist* (Phila., 1865), I, lxxxv. John C. Miller, *Alexander Hamilton: Portrait in Paradox* (New York, 1961) believes Duer was asked by Hamilton and did not volunteer himself; hereafter cited as Miller, *Hamilton*. Most of Hamilton's biographers and practically all editors of *The Federalist* have ignored Duer's contributions.
34. Duer's essays were published in *The Independent Journal* (New York), Oct. 30 for the first, Nov. 28 for the third; the fourth was printed in *The Daily Advertiser* (New York), Dec. 1, 1787. The second essay was published in *The New York Packet* on November 16. The first three essays are included in John C. Hamilton, ed., *The Federalist* (Phila., 1865), II, 655-59; I have not found any other edition of *The Federalist* which includes the "Philo-Publius" essays and even Hamilton missed the fourth; according to him, they were to be published in the edition printed by J. & A. McLean in New York City in 1788. They were not.
35. Undated notes, Duer Papers, BV II, # 239, NYHS; the notes consider weightier topics than "Philo-Publius" wrote on; perhaps they were the beginning of the really

important book that most authors intend to write some day; they were taken from Emmerich deVattel, *The Law of Nations* . . . (London, 1760).

36. C. E. Miner, *The Ratification of the Federal Constitution by the State of New York* (New York, 1921) does not mention Duer; a search of New York City newspapers for the period did not disclose Duer's name connected with any political activity; James Kent to Robert Troup, Jun. 29, 1788, Duer, *Lectures*, 369; Wm. Duer to James Madison, Jun. 23, 1788, BV Sec. A (Misc. Letters), Green Folio Vol., Case I, NYHS; Alexander Hamilton to Wm. Duer, Jul. 19, 1788, Syrett, *Hamilton Papers*, V, 177.

37. Duer, *Reminiscences*, 61; see Sarah H. J. Simpson, "The Federal Procession of 1788," NYHS *Quarterly Bulletin*, 2: (1925): 39-56 for a detailed description of the parade; Simpson does not mention Duer's contribution; see DePauw, *Pillar*, Chaps. 18, 19 for a convincing argument that it was the prospect of being left alone that moved ratification in New York.

38. Wm. Duer to James Madison, n.d., BV Sec. A (Misc. Letters), Green Folio Vol., Case I, NYHS; also in Duer, *Lectures*, 369-70; Adams had been approached by Henry Knox, acting for Hamilton, about not taking the vice-presidency, for which someone more docile was preferred. Knox's report convinced Hamilton that Adams would not step down; see Alexander Hamilton to Theodore Sedgewick, Nov. 7, 1788, Syrett, *Hamilton Papers*, V, 230-31. Duer simply paraphrased Hamilton's comment; *The Daily Advertiser*, Feb. 13—Mar. 6, 1789; Broadus Mitchell, *Alexander Hamilton* (New York, 1962), II, 8-9; hereafter cited as Mitchell, *Hamilton*; D. S. Alexander, *A Political History of New York* (New York, 1906), I, 44, mentions the "arguments of Duer" as a Federalist advantage.

39. JCC, XXVIII, 18; Robert Morris to Wm. Duer, Feb. 12, 1785, Duer Papers, BV II, NYHS; Rufus King to Elbridge Gerry, Apr. 18, 1785, Burnett, *Letters*, VIII, 68; Garrett Cottringer to Wm. Duer, May 2, Jul. 15, Aug. 3, 1785, Duer Papers, NYHS; Rufus King to Elbridge Gerry, Mar. 29, 1786, Burnett, *Letters*, VIII, 335; JCC, XXX, 135-36; see Liston L. Baker, "The Board of Treasury, 1784-1789: Responsibility Without Power," Ph.D. diss., Univ. of Wisconsin, 1972 for a detailed treatment of the work of the Board.

40. James Madison to James Monroe, Sep. 24, 1786, Burnett, *Letters*, VIII, 473; Wm. Duer to William Constable, Mar. 21, 1787, William Constable to Wm. Duer, Dec. 12, 1787, Constable-Pierrepont Papers, NYPL; hereafter cited as Constable Papers; William Constable to William Duer, Oct. 25, 1791, Duer Papers, NYHS; Donald G. Tailby, "Foreign Interest Remittances by the United States, 1785-1787: A Story of Malfeasance," *Business History Review*, 41, no. 2 (Summer 1967): 161-76; Wm. Duer to Walter Livingston, Oct. ?, 1788, Mar. 4, 24, 1789, Livingston Coll., NYHS; Henry Glen to Philip Schuyler, Nov. 2, 1789, Schuyler Papers, NYPL.

41. Andrew Craigie to Daniel Parker, Feb. 20, 1788, _____, to William Duer, Apr. 17, 1788, _____, to Daniel Parker, [May ?], 1788, Craigie Papers, AAS; Thomas Jefferson to the Board of Treasury, Mar. 29, 1788, Duer Papers, NYHS; Duer knew the information was confidential; "I must now caution you to avoid communicating [Jefferson's plans] to anyone—as it was not perhaps intended to be known beyond the Treasury," Andrew Craigie to Daniel Parker, Sep. 3, 1788, Craigie Papers, AAS.

42. See Pierre Brissot deWarville, *New Travels in the United States* . . ., 2nd ed. (London, 1794), I, 378 for the difficulties caused by this shortage; hereafter cited as Brissot, *New Travels*; John Holker to Wm. Duer, Mar. 11, 1786, Duer Papers; J[ames] Jarvis to [Wm. Duer], Oct. 26, 1786, Duer Papers, BV II, NYHS; James Jarvis to Melancton Smith and Andrew Craigie, Nov. 5, 1790, Craigie Papers, AAS; this is an explanation by Jarvis as to why he should not pay the $10,000 which Duer was demanding; Duer had insisted that there could be nothing written to link him with the contract: "Mr. D[uer] had ever said, that it was not proper for him to enter into written engagements." JCC, XXXI, 921n, XXXII:II, 160-64, 221, 223-25 for congressional action; a copy of the contract, dated May 12, 1787, is in Duer Papers, BV II, NYHS. A small quantity of copper was coined by Jarvis in New Haven. The dies were made by Abel Buel of that city after a design ordered by Congress. They

were marked with the thirteen states in linked circles with the motto "We Are One" on their face. The reverse had a sun dial, the Sun and the mottoes "Fugio" [i.e., I flee or time flies], and "Mind Your Business," with the date, 1787. The mottoes and design were probably suggested by Benjamin Franklin and the coins are called "Franklin" or "Fugio" cents. They are rare today. JCC, XXXII, 303-304; R. S. Yoeman, *A Guide Book of United States Coins*, 19th ed. (Racine, WI, 1966), 56; R. E. Davis, "The Circulating Medium of the Period of the Confederation," *The Numismatic Scrapbook Magazine*, 6, 1 (Jan. 1938): 6. See also "W. Duer's calculation of profits which might be made on the supply of copper to the U. States," n.d., Craigie Papers, Bills, etc., I, f. 1, AAS; the document mentions Jarvis, although the numbers do not correspond with those on the actual contract.

43. Daniel Parker to Wm. Duer, Jun. 2, 1788, Duer Papers, BV II, NYHS; Daniel Parker to Andrew Craigie, Jun. 2, 1788, Craigie Papers, AAS. See Eloise Ellery, *Brissot deWarville* (New York, 1915) for a general treatment; Brissot died on the guillotine in 1793, a victim of the French Revolution, hereafter cited as Ellery, *Brissot*. In *New Travels*, I, 139, Brissot thanked Duer: "it is to his obliging character and his zeal, that I owe much valuable information on the finances of this country." See Duer's jottings on the back of Nathan McFarland to Thomas Hutchins, Jul. 23, 1788, Duer Papers, BV II, NYHS, for his expected profits from the house; the text of the agreement is in Ellery, *Brissot*, 72-73; the shares were apparently spread quite widely with Baron Steuben receiving one, J. A. Palmer, *General Steuben* (New Haven, 1971), 371; hereafter cited as Palmer, *Steuben*.

44. Andrew Craigie to Daniel Parker, Oct. 29, Nov. 19, 1788, Craigie Papers, AAS; Memorandum by Rufus King of a conversation with Wm. Duer, Dec. 21, 1788, Rufus King Papers, NYHS; according to this, Duer offered to help King get the ministry to Holland if he would help secure the transfer of the American debt; King equivocated and Duer dropped the matter; King also noted that Duer said that Samuel Osgood of the Board of Treasury had been given a share. There is no record that Thomas Jefferson, Minister to France, was consulted. Joseph S. Davis, "William Duer, Entrepreneur," *Essays in the Earlier History of American Corporations* (Cambridge, 1917), I, 172-73; hereafter cited as Davis, "Duer Essay."

45. Andrew G. Fraunces to Alexander Hamilton, May 16, 1793, Syrett, *Hamilton Papers*, XIV, 470-71, see also "Introductory Note," 460-70; Alexander Hamilton to George Washington, Aug. 9, 1793, ibid., XV, 197-201; Oliver Wolcott, Jr., to Alexander Hamilton, Aug. 7, 1793, ibid., 201-203; Andrew G. Fraunces to George Washington, Jul. 30, 1793, State Dept., Misc. Letters Rec'd, RG 59, M 179, Roll 10, NA. See "Copy of a Rect. to W. Duer . . .," 1788, Craigie Papers, Bills, etc., I, f. 3, Craigie Papers, AAS. In the "Introductory Note" cited above, Warrant No. 236 is misdated 1789 instead of 1787. Julian Boyd, "Appendix: The First Conflict in the Cabinet," *The Papers of Thomas Jefferson* (Princeton, 1971), 18, 611-88, treats the matter exhaustively. "The Opinion of Thomas Jefferson," Jun. 3, 1790, ibid., 16, 468, refers to another misdeed of Duer's, but the evidence is rather slight.

46. The "stocks" referred to here would be called bonds today. They were usually certificates of indebtedness issued by a government and bearing a stated interest. After the funding of the congressional and assumed state debts by the federal government in 1790, they were redeemable only after some years had elapsed and thus resemble, in all important characteristics, a modern government or corporate bond. The only speculative instruments circulating during this period which would today be called stocks were shares of the few banks which existed and shares in the Society for Establishing Useful Manufactures, chartered in New Jersey in 1791. Duer was the first governor of the Society and it will be treated in Chapter VI. It has been thought best to keep the c. 1790 labels to avoid awkward bracketing in quotations and to make more intelligible contemporary observations on "stock-jobbing." The various debt certificates of the Congress and the states are described in William G. Anderson, *The Price of Liberty: The Public Debt of the American Revolution* (Charlottesville, VA, 1983).

47. Theodore T. Belote, "The Scioto Speculation and the French Settlement at Galli-

polis," *University of Cincinnati Studies*, s. 2, III (1907); hereafter cited as Belote, *University Studies*; Archer B. Hulburt, "Methods and Operations of the Scioto Group of Speculators," *Mississippi Valley Historical Review*, 2 (1915): 56-73, hereafter cited as Hulburt, "Scioto Group"; JCC, XXXIII, 334-43; Cutler, *Journals*, I, 242, 293, 294-95.

48. Cutler, *Journals*, I, 301; Manasseh Cutler to Honorable, the Board of Treasury, Aug. 11, 1787, Livingston Coll., NYHS; JCC, XXXIII, 399-401, 427-30; *American State Papers: Public Lands* (Washington, 1832), I, 23 for text of contracts and attorney general's opinion on the intent of Congress to deal with only one company; see Burnett, *Letters*, VIII, 619-20, 622, 630, 631, 644, 655-56 for the impressions and hopes of Congressmen at this time.

49. "Articles of Agreement of the Scioto Company," Oct. 29, 1787, Craigie Papers, Box 13, f. 3, AAS.

50. Davis, "Duer Essay," 140-41; Andrew Craigie to Narlbro Frazier, May 22, 1788, to Samuel Rodgers, Apr. 10, 1790, _____, to John Holker, Sep. 1, 1790, Craigie Papers, AAS; Hulburt, "Scioto Group," 20-21.

51. Charles Todd, *The Life and Letters of Joel Barlow* (New York, 1886), 46-54, 63, 68, 70; Barlow was the most successful business man Duer ever associated with; a speculation in European government bonds later made him a rich man, 117; hereafter cited as Todd, *Barlow*; Cutler, *Journals*, I, 381-82, Davis, "Duer Essay," 147; Joel Barlow to Wm. Duer, Jun. 25, 1788, Duer Papers, NYHS.

52. Todd, *Barlow*, 73-85; Belote, *University Studies*, 23-28, 68-70; Hulburt, "Scioto Group," 24-25; see also Edward Haskell to William Constable, Nov. 30, 1789, Constable Papers, NYPL, for Parisian reaction to the Scioto scheme; Andrew Craigie to Narlbro Frazier, Mar. 11, 1790, to Joel Barlow, Apr. 10, 1790, Craigie Papers, AAS.

53. Joel Barlow to Wm. Duer, Nov. 29, Dec. 8, 1789, Jan. 25, 1790, Scioto and Ohio Land Company Papers, "Barlow" fol., I, NYHS, hereafter cited as Scioto Papers; Joel Barlow to Royal Flint, Dec. 8, 1789, Craigie Papers, AAS. Despite his apparent conduct on this occasion, Playfair may have been a person of some achievement and stature, see "Obituary—Mr. William Playfair," *The Gentleman's Magazine and Historical Chronicle* (London), new ser., 93, no. 1 (Jan.-Jun. 1823): 564-66.

54. "Agreement to sell land in Northwestern Territory, Oct. 24, 1788," Nathan McFarland to Wm. Duer, Jul. 23, 1788, Duer Papers, BV II, NYHS; James Jarvis to Melancton Smith and Andrew Craigie, Nov. 5, 1790, Craigie Papers, AAS; Baron Steuben to Benjamin Walker, May 23, 1788, cited in Palmer, *Steuben*, 359.

55. Davis, "Duer Essay," 339.

56. B[enjamin] W[alker] to The Contractors, Jun. 3, 1783, Washington Papers, LC; Wm. Duer to [John Holker], [1784], Duer Papers, Box III, Undated Letters, NYHS; Belote, *University Studies*, 65-67; Andrew Craigie to Daniel Parker, Oct. 27, 1788, Craigie Papers, AAS; Jeremiah Wadsworth to Alexander Hamilton, Nov. 11, 1785, Syrett, *Hamilton Papers*, III, 634.

57. Wm. Duer to William Hill, May 28, 1786, _____, to Joel Barlow, May 17, 1788, Agreement between Daniel Carthy and Wm. Duer, Jul. 11, 1789; see Andrew Craigie to Wm. Duer, Jul. 28, 1788, Duer Papers, NYHS, for earlier speculation in state debts.

58. Andrew Craigie to Daniel Parker, n.d., Craigie Papers, Letter Book, I, 5, AAS; Daniel Parker to Wm. Duer, Jun. 1, 1787, Duer Papers, NYHS.

59. "Washington in 1789: A Contemporary Account of His Reception in New York," *Pennsylvania Magazine of History & Biography*, 13 (1889): 115-16; T. E. V. Smith, *The City of New York in the Year of Washington's Inauguration, 1789* (New York, 1889), 240.

60. See Robert F. Jones, "Stock Speculation and the Revolutionary Debt: Andrew Craigie, 1787-1792," paper presented at the July 1981 meeting of the Society for Historians of the Early American Republic, Siena College, Loudonville, NY, for an active speculator's fears, assumptions, and operations.

61. William Constable to James Seagrave, Jun. 8, 1789, Constable Papers, NYPL; Andrew

Craigie to Brissot deWarville, Jul. 28, 1789, Scioto Papers, "Craigie-Brissot" folder, Box II, NYHS; see also Andrew Craigie to N. and J. VanStaphorst, Jun. 27, 1789, _____to Daniel Parker, Jul. 11, 1789, Edward Fox to Andrew Craigie, Nov. 19, 1788, Jul. 30, 1789, see also Aug. 5, 1789, Oct. 25, 1789, Seth Johnson to Andrew Craigie, Aug. 30, 1789 for Duer's reaction to Fox's message.

62. *U. S. Statutes at Large*, I, 66-67 (Sep. 2, 1789); Alexander Hamilton to Samuel Osgood, Walter Livingston, and Arthur Lee, Sep. 4 [14?], 1789, Livingston Coll., NYHS.

63. Wm. Duer to Christopher Gore, [1789], cited in Davis, "Duer Essay," 337.

64. Alexander Hamilton to Thomas Willing, Sep. 13, 1789, Syrett, *Hamilton Papers*, V, 371; Noah Webster to James Greenleaf, Sep. 20, 1789, cited in Mitchell, *Hamilton*, II, 162; William Constable to Robert Morris, Oct. 19, 28, 1789, Constable Papers, NYPL.

65. William Constable to Robert Morris, Nov. 9, 26, 1789, Constable Papers, NYPL.

66. "Contract between William Duer, William Constable, and Richard Platt, Dec. 23, 1789," Constable Papers, NYPL; Wm. Duer to Walter Livingston, Jan. 27, 1790, Livingston Coll., NYHS.

67. "Report on the Public Credit," Jan. 9, 1790, Syrett, *Hamilton Papers*, VI, 56 ff.

68. Kenneth R. Bowling, Helen E. Veit, eds., *The Diary of William Maclay* (Baltimore, 1988), 185; James T. Callender, *Sketches of the History of America* (Phila., 1798), 107; Callender was one of the most virulent critics of Hamilton's program, but his entire lack of scruples makes all his writing suspect; John Beckley to James Monroe, Jun. 22, 27, 1793, photostats, Monroe Papers, NYPL; Seth Johnson to Andrew Craigie, Dec. 24, 1793, Craigie Papers, AAS; William Campbell to David Ross, Nov. 18, 1790, cited in Mitchell, *Hamilton*, II, 280, 604; also see above, 117-18, for the affair of the stolen Treasury warrant.

69. "A Foreigner [Wm. Duer?]," to James Madison, Feb. 17, 1790, James Madison Papers, NYPL; see also Daniel Parker to Wm. Duer, Jun. 1, 1787, Duer Papers, NYHS; Walter Rutherfurd to John Rutherfurd, Mar. 3, 1790, Rutherfurd Collection, NYHS; see Ferguson, *Purse*, Chaps. 13 and 14, for a clear and cogent treatment of the congressional debate and action on Hamilton's first Report.

70. Wm. Duer to George Reid [Mar. 1790?], Duer Papers, Box III, undated folder, NYHS; Walter Livingston to Wm. Duer and Joseph Hardy, Mar. 1, 1790; "Agreement of Walter Livingston and Wm. Duer with Royal Flint, Mar. 15, 1790"; Wm. Duer to Walter Livingston, Mar. 30, 1790, Livingston Coll., NYHS; Wm. Constable to Andrew Craigie, Mar. 29, 1790, Constable Papers, NYPL; Davis, "Duer Essay," 190-92.

71. Ibid., 339.

72. William Constable to Robert Morris, Nov. 9, 1789, _____to James Seagrave, Mar. 13, 1790, Constable Papers, NYPL; Alexander Hamilton to Wm. Duer, [Apr. 4-7, 1790], Syrett, *Hamilton Papers*, VI, 346-47, to Tench Coxe, May 1, 1790, ibid., 401, _____to John Holker, Jan. 8, 1790, ibid., XXVI, 503 (and Holker Papers, LC); see John Holker to Alexander Hamilton, Jan. 13, 1790 for Holker's agreement to suspend the suit, ibid., XXVI, 507; Wm. Duer to George Reid, [Mar. 1790?], Duer Papers, Box III, undated folder, NYHS.

Chapter VI

The Speculator Triumphant

March 1790–March 1792

It took little time for William Duer to immerse himself in his several private projects. For one thing, he probably had not been giving the Treasury Department fair value for the money, distracted as he was by his speculating, land projects, and the like, so full time to his private affairs did not mean the reallocation of that much effort. For another, the Scioto project seemed to be coming to a head and, while it promised great profit, it now threatened considerable losses should it fail. Barlow's letters from Paris were optimistic, giving glowing reports of a growing volume of sales and the sterling qualities of those who were planning to emigrate; they would certainly succeed in the Ohio Country. Speaking in terms Duer could easily understand, Barlow authorized a draft on himself for one hundred thousand livres (about $20,000) to help pay the cost of sending the first emigrants, even then crossing the Atlantic, from Alexandria to the Ohio. All seemed bright and promising. In March, Barlow suddenly changed his tone and informed Duer that the *Compagnie du Scioto* could not make its first payment and he had abandoned it. Barlow would now make the sales in his own name. With no mention of the draft, Duer assumed it could still be paid. However, the funds collected by the *Compagnie* had been left in Playfair's hands where apparently even Barlow was unable to get to them. In July, Barlow, Playfair, and several Frenchmen formed a second land company which took over the assets and obligations of the first. If this contract had ever been executed, the Scioto Associates would have received very little money and been left with a large tract of hard-to-sell interior lots, well away from the Ohio and its tributaries. As Barlow had by now fallen into Duer's habit of not writing, the news of the second company came to the latter indirectly, but quite tangibly, when the drafts on Barlow were returned protested and unpaid.[1]

Confronted with this rude surprise, Duer now did what he should have done long before and sent Benjamin Walker, then serving as federal naval officer for the Port of New York, to Paris to find out what was going on. Secretary Hamilton, perhaps intent on showing his good will toward his former assistant, gave Walker a leave of absence and he left for Paris in mid-September. Duer equipped him with three letters, one making him joint agent with Barlow, another authorizing him to examine the books of the various *Compagnies*, and a third, to be used only if absolutely necessary, removing Barlow as agent and giving Walker sole authority. Not really knowing what he would find, the American trustees authorized Walker to buy American stocks in Europe, using as capital a draft for 532,267 livres on Barlow. At least they were keeping the original goal of the Scioto in mind, even though by this time a draft on Barlow represented little more than a forlorn hope, but hope they did.[2] Finally bestirred to action, Duer followed Walker with several letters, charging him with selling several bills of exchange and a draft by one of the emigrants, M. deBoulogne, on Playfair, accompanying the last with a legal opinion fixing responsibility for the draft on the Englishman. A recurrent theme in these letters was that Duer had advanced significant sums to move the emigrants to the Ohio, but had not received a penny from Barlow or Playfair; this had put him in serious difficulties and he had had to borrow at usurious interest—"any sacrifice is better than the enormous one now being paid to keep up Circulation for what has been expended." Although it sounds as though Duer was ready to cut his losses and let the Scioto go, this was not to be the case. Some saw things more clearly and William Constable predicted early in November that, with "respect to Duer's land Speculation I believe the Dog is born to be unfortunate."[3]

Constable's prophecy was correct. Walker had arrived in Paris late in October and, after examining the accounts, acquitted Barlow of wrongdoing, although not of foolishness. For a time, even Walker was hopeful of working with Playfair (who must have been as adept at selling himself as he claimed to be at selling land), but he soon found reason to advertise in the Paris journals that he alone was legally able to sell Scioto lands. Playfair then disappeared with what *Compagnie* funds there were, leaving Walker holding an empty bag. Not realizing this immediately, Walker formed yet another company to sell the Scioto lands, entrusted it to a Colonel Rochefontaine, and took ship for America, convinced he had done what he could. Although Barlow was relieved to be free finally of a charge he had apparently never enjoyed, he was also unfairly critical of Duer, generously giving the New Yorker all the discredit for the scheme's failure in Paris, although there was blame enough for everyone. Rochefontaine worked on for a long while, but the venture was ended by both the bad news filtering back from the first emigrants to the Ohio and the increasing violence of the French Revolution; the latter caused Rochefontaine himself to flee France in 1792 and the Scioto became a bad memory in Paris, nothing more. Unaware for a time of these events in Paris, Duer convinced himself that all the trouble there had been owing to Barlow. Remove him, and all would be well. He was so certain of this that he talked Hamilton into giving Walker permission to remain abroad another few months, permission Walker wisely did not take up.[4]

Given the difficulties the Scioto venture began causing Duer in the spring of 1790, his anxiety about getting some profit out of it is easy to understand. It is difficult, if not impossible, to say just where his troubles with the effort started. Aside from the original concept, which may or may not have worked, depending on, among other things, the sequence of events both in Europe and the United States, the project began to go sour with the choice of Barlow as agent. Although, as noted, he proved to be a successful investor in European bonds, he was no land salesman. Compounding Barlow's inadequacy was the lack of direction by Duer. Despite the difficulties of any direction when a questioner had to wait four to six months for an answer, some kind of counsel might have helped Barlow steer away from Playfair and his Parisian friends. After he fell into their hands and the Scioto became a colonizing venture, it was probably doomed. None of those active in its origin and subsequent direction had expected that to happen and while they probably lacked the funds for heavy start-up costs, they certainly lacked the desire to become the promoters of a French colony in the Ohio Country. All this was compounded by the *Compagnie* allowing credit sales, but giving titles immediately. The Scioto partners now had either to pay for the land before receiving any large sums from Europe or secure changes in the agreement with Congress. Barlow realized the difficulty and suggested several alternative concessions that could be sought from Congress. Although Duer made no formal request to change the agreement, one of Barlow's suggestions, that the price of land be lowered to take into account the increase in the value of securities, was included in Hamilton's Report on the Public Credit, submitted to Congress in January 1790. While Duer could have influenced Hamilton in this, there is no evidence of it. Since the Ohio Company promoters had originally urged their plan on the old congress as a way of increasing the market value of government debt certificates, it was very neat logic to turn the rise in value which did occur into a reason for lowering the price of the land. Congress left land prices unchanged.[5]

Barlow increased Duer's difficulties when he began to sell specific lots. Most of those he sold were on the west bank of the Ohio, across from the mouth of the Great Kanawha River of western Virginia. The lots were very desirable, especially because of their location, but it was a location within the bounds of the Ohio Company tract, not the Scioto. Duer now had to bargain with the Ohio promoters, who were having problems of their own. A late February meeting at his home with Manasseh Cutler and Rufus Putnam produced a tentative agreement, held in abeyance for a while in case Congress acted on Hamilton's proposal. When the legislators did not move, the agreement was put into final form in late April. The Scioto group agreed to purchase 148 forfeited shares of the Ohio Company (200,000 acres) for which they paid $10 a share in sixty and ninety-day notes, $8,880 in indents, to be paid in six months, and a final balance, the size of which depended on the price the Ohio Company finally paid for its land. If Duer should help the Ohio people strike a better deal with Congress, then his price would be lower. The arrangement promised benefits for both groups and Duer's political influence was as much a part of the price paid as were the indents of interest.[6]

The first emigrants were scheduled to leave Le Havre in January 1790; this group included both purchasers of small lots as well as members of the *Société des Vingt-Quatres* (the Twenty-four), each of whom had bought 1,000 acres. To the latter, Barlow had promised passage west, provisions for a year, and workmen to aid in clearing the land. The small purchasers claimed that the Paris agents had also promised them passage west. Finally, some of the emigrants had prepaid Barlow and company in Paris the costs of their transportation from the port of debarkation, Alexandria, Virginia, to the Ohio. Thus, when they began to arrive in the spring of 1790, Duer was expected to move all the emigrants on to the Ohio at no further cost to them, but without having received a sou from France. Probably with a good bit of grumbling, but not seeing any other practicable course of action, Duer set out to see the French on their way west and to redeem as much as he could the promises made in Paris. He began by offering Captain Isaac Guion the job of receiving the emigrants in Alexandria and getting them started to the Ohio. Rufus Putnam was started preparing the future settlement's site and a Major John Burnham given the supervision of fifty men raising cabins for the settlers. If offers and promises could do the job, it would be accomplished.[7]

But complications began to occur immediately. Some of the emigrants arrived unexpectedly in Philadelphia; Colonel David S. Franks was deputed to deliver them to Alexandria with most of his compensation apparently being Duer's influence regarding a claim he had against the government. On arriving in Alexandria in late March with the French, he found no one preparing for the main party, expected daily. Ostensibly, that was Colonel Guion's job, but he was nowhere in sight. Craigie had conscripted a friend, Alexandria merchant Thomas Porter, to assist Guion but Porter had not been hired directly by Duer nor was he given any specific powers or instructions. Franks returned to Philadelphia and left Porter holding the bag. He had to wait until early May before the emigrants arrived. When they did, Porter, who had still received no instructions from Duer and no further letters from Craigie who was ill, and who had thought of doing nothing more than a favor for a friend, found himself alone in dealing with the importunities of more than 200 Frenchmen. How long he would have to deal with them was also something of a question. Duer had written Putnam to come east and escort the emigrants to the Ohio and, as he had with Guion, assumed his offer meant Putnam's acceptance. It did not. In addition to the discouraging news that he wanted nothing whatever to do with bringing the French west, Putnam also informed Duer that provisions there were extremely scarce and could be purchased only for ready cash, not the credit Duer offered. The emigrants should be held in the east until after the harvest and provided with two year's provisions. Putnam added a singularly unpleasant post-script to all this by asking for more than $8,000 to pay for work already done for the Scioto Company.[8]

One bright spot was Porter who, in spite of his uncertain position, took care of the prospective settlers in Alexandria, feed-ing and sheltering them, even trying to keep them from being lured away by the local people, some of whom tried to de-monstrate the good sense of staying in the east by pointing out the dangers along the Ohio. How effective this was is not clear, but it impressed Duer sufficiently for him to write, or cause to be written, a pamphlet pointing out the benefits to the area and the country of the kind of settlement and settlers the Scioto proposed. The Alexandrians' advice, however negative, was cer-tainly preferable to the actions of some townsmen in Winchester, where the emigrants stopped on their way west—"the affray between the Emigrants and Some of the Country people is ami-cably settled – Two of the latter were very much cut & mangled with Swords – and three or four of the former shot – but no lives lost." Perhaps an early example of nativist agitation? The "affray" must have occurred in late June or early July when Guion, who had finally appeared late in May, managed to send the French on in several parties. By 7 July, 220 of them had left Alexandria for the new settlement, aptly named Gallipolis, where they arrived in October. There the preparations to receive them were reason-ably near completion and they settled down in rude, but adequate comfort.[9]

By this time, Porter may well have wished he had gone west with the settlers; he was left in Alexandria, fending off creditors with little more than Duer's promises to pay. The New Yorker dealt with the expenses by questioning all expenditures as to authority, amount, economy exercised, with no apparent purpose other than delaying payment as long as possible. Also left in the lurch was William Armstrong of Winchester who had hired the wagons, teams, and drivers, giving them one-half of the hire out of his own funds. Now he found himself facing angry teamsters demanding the remainder of their wages, all without a penny having come from Duer. If Porter and Armstrong were eventually paid, and it is by no means certain they were, they were hardly compensated for their aggravation. Finally, if Duer seems to have followed with Porter and Armstrong (and other Scioto creditors) the same practice he followed with Holker, it should be noted that he was dealing with bills he never expected to see for a company which had apparently received substantial sums in Paris, but which had not remitted anything to him or the other Scioto trustees. While this does not in any way excuse his shabby treatment of men who were practically drafted into his service, it does help to explain it.[10]

Things seem to have gone somewhat more smoothly at Gallipolis. Visiting the settlement in November, the governor of the Northwest Territory, Arthur St. Clair, found them at least physically comfortable, but their situation differed so greatly from what the *Compagnie* agents had led them to expect (apparently a cross between the Garden of Eden and the south of France) that they were sullen and discontented, what St. Clair described as a "mutinous disposition." The governor believed that, even if the settlement did establish itself, it could never "in any degree answer the expectations that had been raised." And the dissatisfaction seems to have been mutual; one of Duer's agents at the settlement, Benjamin Thompson, advised the dismissal of all the servants brought over by the "Twenty-four," for "they will never pay their salt." Only soldiers and a "very summary mode of procedure . . . will ever reduce these people to order & keep them within the bounds of decency." If Thompson was correct, and others said the same thing, it was small wonder that St. Clair judged them to be of a "mutinous disposition." That seems to have been normal.[11] To add to the difficulties of starting any new settlement, the Indians chose this time to resume their resistance to the westward advance of settlers away from the Ohio River. A series of raids threw the whites back to the river and inspired a move against the Indians by Colonel Josiah Harmar and a militia force, a move which ended in disaster for Harmar and his men in October 1790. Following this convincing demonstration of the inability of the new government to protect the new settlers, the Indians grew even bolder and began to harass those along the river, killing one man near Gallipolis. One of the "Twenty-four" who had intended to settle away from the town gave the Indian problems as his major reason for going back to France.

The panic caused by these attacks was serious enough for Rufus
Putnam to fear for the safety of all those in the Ohio country
and he urged Duer to use his influence in Congress to have
another armed force sent to the area. Duer could have been
anything but single-minded in his supervision of the Scioto at
this time, distracted as he was by his stock speculations, the
continuing maneuvers of Barlow in Paris and an army provision
contract which he took over early in 1791 when President Washington did decide to send another force against the Indians. Also,
these different ventures did not necessarily complement one another
as, for example, when Duer ordered Guion to stop issuing food
to the French settlers in February 1791 rather than fall short on
issues to the army. Fortunately, for the settlers, there proved to
be enough to go around, but the incident showed clearly where
Duer's priorities lay.[12]

Enough of the French stayed through the winter of 1790-91
to make it seem as if Gallipolis had a chance. The return of warm
weather in the spring coincided with the arrival of Walker's first,
hopeful reports from Paris. Duer stirred himself and sent out a
M. Claudius to begin a store and instructed Guion to have more
surveys made, preparatory to giving titles—"Exert yourself, my
Friend, to promote the Welfare and c[redi]t of the Colony: – to
Encourage the Industrious." But the hopeful signs were illusory.
Also with the spring, several who had been waiting for good
weather left the settlement and returned to the east before taking
ship for France. Naturally, their reports were not optimistic and
they even complained of the tyranny of Guion, one commenting
wryly that the settlers had stopped talking of killing him, and
that was an improvement. These reports helped to turn back
several parties who had wintered along the trail, with some of
these asking to be settled elsewhere, and others just going back
to France. Few of the "Twenty-four" were left, some going further down the Ohio, others returning east. Most of those who
were left at Gallipolis were the poorer settlers; their resources
were exhausted and they had no alternative but to remain. Several
travelers reported they were working hard, even making wine
from some native grapes, and that all they needed to make them
"heureux comme Dieux" ("as happy as lords") was a firm title
to their lands and safety from the Indians. Few settlers along the
Ohio in the 1790s wanted very much more than that. Duer

remained in touch with them during the summer, replacing Thompson with a new superintendent, Medad Mitchell, and instructing him to make more surveys.[13] This last was window dressing, nothing more, as there was no prospect of a firm title until the Ohio Company was paid and Duer, given the news from Paris, had neither the inclination nor the money to do that.

As the nucleus of a French colony, Gallipolis died a slow, lingering death over the next few years. When Duer failed in March 1792, the company issues of grain which had continued during the winter of 1791-92 were stopped; this and the near-certainty that good titles would either never be obtained or obtained only with great difficulty and after much time, caused more settlers to leave. By November 1795, of the five to six hundred emigrants who had moved through Alexandria, only eighty-five were still at Gallipolis. In May 1792, Royal Flint refused Rufus Putnam's request that a sum owed by Duer as the superintendent of the Scioto Company be paid, stating that he and the other trustees were not liable as they regarded the company as dissolved. Although this was as much of a funeral as it ever had, not all of its survivors were willing to let the Scioto slip away. In May 1792, when the Ohio Company wanted to reclaim the site of Gallipolis as part of its original purchase, Duer, from debtors' prison, protested to Secretaries Hamilton and Knox that he could not, in honor, leave the poor French settlers to the "tender mercies" of Cutler and Putnam. Such a move would endanger the settlers' land titles, titles which they did not have and which Duer could not give them, but this was not pointed out. His final point, and this was the rub, was that such a move might involve him in a lawsuit "such as may defeat my present efforts to extricate myself."[14]

The Scioto's failure to achieve any of its sponsors' hopes should not obscure the possibilities for profit which it contained. When it was begun in 1787, public securities sold for about three shillings in the pound; within three years, they were nine shillings and going up. The 1787 price had given the promoters an 85 percent discount from the one-third of a dollar per acre price Congress had set. The increase not only wiped out much of this advantage, it also made the securities more attractive as financial speculations rather than simply a cheap way to buy western land. The rise, of course, was owing to the series of events which ended

in the ratification of the Constitution and the establishment of a
new central government for the young republic, neither of which
events were foreseen by the Scioto promoters, who probably
expected or hoped for a slow, but steady increase in the securities'
value. As already noted, the Scioto was basically a securities speculation, not a land speculation, but it was not founded on the
quick realization of the hopes for a strong central government
with taxing power which could redeem the debt certificates, in
short, the Constitution.

The choice of Barlow as agent also hurt the venture's chances.
A more experienced person might have stayed clear of Playfair
and company. Once he had fallen in with them, and the *Compagnie du Scioto* was formed, little could have been done to save
the project. Although Barlow had been pressed on Duer, he did
assent to hiring the young man, probably because he did not
want to be distracted long enough from his other affairs to search
out a suitable replacement himself. He also left him alone in Paris
without any kind of direction, even the slight direction given
through the slow communications of the time. With so much at
stake, why Duer was so inattentive to this remains a mystery.
He was always a sloppy correspondent, but that hardly constitutes
a full explanation for his inaction in this case.

The conversion by Playfair of the Scioto from an unearned
increment land speculation into a colonizing project posed an
entirely new set of problems for the American promoters. Playfair's role will have to remain a mystery. Here he seems to have
been nothing more than a confidence man, in the game for as
much as he could carry away. But he did have a substantial career,
at other times, as a writer on economics and was something of
a minor inventor. It is possible that he really believed in the
Compagnie idea and, when it failed, was hurt as much as Duer
or Barlow. That having been said, it remains to note that he
seemed to be the one in custody of the apparently considerable
sums collected from the "Twenty-four" and the smaller purchasers in Paris, funds which were never sent to the United States.
What happened to Playfair and the money is not known. Duer's
neglect of his agents, whether at Alexandria or on the way west
or at Gallipolis, does not seem to have hurt the settlement's
chances for survival. The agents' work was much more effective
than Duer deserved and the emigrants do not seem to have

suffered badly from inadequate food, shelter, and the like. The
settlement's chances were injured much more seriously by the
selection or recruitment in Paris of emigrants lacking the skills
essential for survival along the Ohio and by the depiction of that
wilderness as a gentle, clement land, just waiting for the culti-
vating touch of man to blossom into an agrarian paradise. The
reality was, of course, quite different. Finally, the eruption of the
French Revolution may have been one of the arguments used to
convince Barlow of the feasibility of a colonizing project, but the
French, even under the spur of the Revolution's anarchic violence, were not interested in leaving their homeland. As R. R.
Palmer has pointed out, proportionally many more American
loyalists left the United States, most of them permanently, at the
conclusion of the war for American independence, than Frenchmen left their country temporarily, during their Revolution.[15]
Emigration, even to such garden spots as the Ohio Valley during
the 1790s, has never been popular with the French. A Gallipolis
which met the Parisian promoters' pictures probably would still
not have drawn enough Frenchmen to the Ohio to be profitable.

How much the Scioto failure may have cost Duer cannot be
stated definitely. Searching the incomplete records left behind
gives the impression that a few small balances were paid, but that
the bulk of them were ignored and, after Duer's financial failure,
were lost. The largest single sum owed was $80,000 to the Ohio
Company for the cabins, clearing of land, and various other
expenses incidental to establishing Gallipolis, including the cost
of the land; none of this was paid.[16] While Duer did miss the
chance to get control of a large amount of speculating capital,
the attempt did not apparently cost very much. Further, the
Scioto failure did not affect Duer's reputation significantly because
he already had the reputation of a high flier who, inevitably,
would have some failures. Also, this was a failure which happened
out on the Ohio and which did not involve the loss of significant
sums of money by well-known persons. It probably did not attract
very much attention. What he did lose on the Scioto was a good
bit of time and effort in lobbying the project through Congress
and getting it under way, as well as trying to redeem the promises
made to the Gallipolis settlers. It certainly served as a further
distraction from his other affairs. But one also has the impression
that, if Duer did not have the distraction of the Scioto, it would

have been some other scheme. He always had to have, in Holker's apt phrase, more than one hare in a chase.

Supporting the truth of this observation, Duer was involving himself in yet another colonization project even while the Scioto was dying. The Maine land project grew out of the coincidence of several developments. First, some of the "Twenty-four," although disillusioned with the prospects of the Scioto, were still eager to find American homes. Apparently, they did not blame Duer, but rather the Parisian promoters for the extravagant promises and misleading pictures of life on the Ohio and hence were willing to try it again with Duer. For his part, he had recently renewed his friendship with Henry Knox, Washington's chief of artillery during the war who acted as Secretary of War for both the old and new governments. Knox's wife had inherited a large tract of land in the District of Maine, than a part of Massachusetts. Although Knox was content to hold the land for the foreseeable future, anything which promoted the settlement of the District could be seen as increasing its value and he was not averse to risking some money to bring that about. Thus Duer had the customers, Knox the interest, some capital, and some people in Maine who could help the settlers. There may, also, have been some less creditable influences working.

In May 1791, William Tudor, a member of the Massachusetts Assembly, got in touch with Richard Soderstrom, former Swedish consul in Boston. Soderstrom had moved to Philadelphia when his diplomatic immunity did not cover suits for debt against him. Tudor mentioned rumors of the impending separation of Maine from the rest of Massachusetts and noted that the parent state might consider selling large tracts of land before losing them. He closed by identifying himself as a member of the Assembly, "a Circumstance which may not impede your views." Soderstrom relayed the news to William Constable who may have brought Duer into the venture, having heard of his interest. After some discussion, Henry Knox and associates agreed with William Duer and associates, among whom Constable was included, to attempt to purchase one to four million acres in Maine at not more than twelve cents an acre, payable in at least five installments. Duer insisted on two clauses, one permitting aliens to hold mortgages on the land, the other granting a bounty of one hundred acres for every foreign artisan who would settle on the tract. The emphasis on foreign-held mortgages and artisans indicates that, while he may have given up on the Scioto, he had not given up on the idea and that his recent interest in a manufacturing society along the lines suggested in Alexander Hamilton's forthcoming Report on Manufactures (December 1791) may have been part of his plans for the Maine venture also.[17]

Both parties chose agents to act in their names, not only for convenience, but also because it was policy in Massachusetts to avoid large sales, so as to prevent a monopoly of the land. But monopoly was just what Knox and Duer wanted and hence different names might have to be used to disguise the actual purchasers. Also the agents, Henry Jackson and Royal Flint, were reminded that since the cultivable land in the area concerned comprised about four million acres, a purchase of about one-half "would operate as a Monopoly of the whole, and enable us to fix the Price." They also understood that there was some kind of an Indian claim to lands on the Penobscot River. After the broad terms of the agreement were reached, the agents should use this claim either to drive down the price or secure the state's assistance to erase the claim. Other desirable provisions show that some of the lessons of the Scioto had been learned: title would be given in units of as little as 50,000 acres as payment was made, settlement requirements were not to be applied for at least five years, and the requirements were to be as lenient as possible.[18] Of course, they had not learned the most obvious lesson of the Scioto: do not do it at all.

Jackson went at once to Boston where he got down to work. Less than two weeks after the groups had agreed on the terms of their cooperation, Jackson had established that the Assembly held to a minimum price of fourteen cents per acre in Massachusetts certificates, then at about twelve shillings to twelve shillings, six pence, and that not more than one million acres would be sold to any one company; "but as I did not conceive these to be their ultimatum, I shall advise with my friends & come forward with my proposals tomorrow." Jackson's intuition (or perhaps it was Tudor's guidance) was correct and on July 1st, he "& others" signed an agreement with the Commonwealth of Massachusetts to purchase two million acres, generally between the Penobscot and "Schoodyck" Rivers, for ten cents an acre. But, while Duer and Knox had gotten the quantity they wanted, for the price they were willing to pay, the Assembly had not agreed with several of their other stipulations and they were going to have to scramble to meet settlement requirements and to pay 6 percent interest on the balances owing to the Commonwealth. Still, Knox was sufficiently encouraged by the prospect of the settlement that he urged Duer to start negotiations for another million acres in August. A good occasion to open up on this would be when Flint delivered $5,000 to the committee. Knox did not specify what the money was for, but since the formal contract provided for no payments to be made until surveying had been done by the Commonwealth, the committee was possibly being rewarded for their reasonableness during the negotiations.[19]

Late in August, Duer told Knox he was thinking of selling part of their new purchase to Mme. DelaVal and Mons. DelaRoche of the "Twenty-four" under conditions that resembled those given by Playfair and the *Compagnie* in Paris. The principal argument he advanced for its likely success was the present state of France which he expected would drive many French, especially the lesser nobility, out. The climatic difficulties in Maine would have to be outweighed by giving the first settlers many advantages. Duer realized the cost of this, but he would see to the money. He also revealed to Knox that he was giving up the Scioto in favor of this project—"What I have done is the Result of Mature Reflection." Just how mature this reflection could have been is questionable in the light of what the French wanted, and which Duer was apparently willing to give. On 27 August, they offered one and one-half dollars per acre for five townships and Mt. Desert Island, one half down, the remainder in four equal annual payments starting on 1 May 1793. Provisions, livestock, houses would be provided, but to be paid for in a year at 6 percent interest, with a chartered vessel to carry persons and provisions between New York and the settlement at the sellers' expense for a year. In reply, Knox accepted most of the stipulations, simply desiring that they be stated more precisely, for example, how many rations would be required, what size and type of house, and insisting that title to the land be held as security against all advances. He would not accept the vessel. Apparently most of the conditions were met, for in October the French were calling on Duer's credit for supplies, clothing, etc., in the name of the

"Company of the Union," the name for the proposed venture. However, before it could fairly be got off the ground, Duer's failure ended his association with it and the entire Maine purchase.[20] Eventually, Duer's share in the original purchase was sold to William Bingham of Philadelphia; as far as is known, the "Company of the Union" collapsed in the wake of the extensive panic Duer's failure set off.

The Scioto and the Maine projects were not the only land speculations Duer contemplated or actually began. During the first flush of interest in the Scioto, May 1788, he talked with General Steuben about a speculation in the Illinois country, in which Royal Flint and a Joseph Parker were also associated. Later, James Jarvis of the coinage contract complained that Duer had talked with him about going to Europe to sell land at Cape au Gris:

> snug, neat-concern, un-fettered, the land as to its legality and quality, superior to any of the Western-world—The Missouri, the Illinois & the Mississippi had wandered this immeasurable territory in pursuit of some favorable spot to disembarque their wealth and treasures of the happy regions of the west, and finally united in this Cape au gris.

Ignoring the hyperbole, the Cape (not on modern maps) must have been in the St. Louis area and may have been near Cahokia where Medad Mitchell scouted out some land for Duer sometime before October 1791. (Cahokia is on the east bank of the Mississippi, opposite St. Louis.) Duer was associated with a store in Cahokia which may have been the first step in establishing a new settlement in the area. Jarvis's main complaint about the Cape au Gris project was that he had not been given the opportunity to sell the land in Europe. If he had, he could not only have made a large profit, but also given many happy settlers new homes. He felt so strongly about it that he thought of suing Duer for damages, if he could only remember the name proposed for the city! If Duer could sell others as well as he had sold Jarvis, it is little wonder he was able to secure capital for his various speculations. He also agreed in July 1791 to purchase a tract on the Schuylkill River in eastern Pennsylvania with Mons. deBarth, identified as one of the French settlers at Gallipolis, possibly one of the "Twenty-four." This, like the other land ventures, had either died by the time of Duer's failure or was killed by it.[21]

With the failure of the Harmar expedition in October 1790, Indian attacks on the Ohio settlements increased considerably. While this was one of the several developments which helped put an end to Gallipolis, it also gave Duer an opportunity to exploit his western connections and concerns by returning to his old occupation of army contractor. Just about the entire army of 800 men was stationed along the Ohio River where their principal duty seems to have been to chase squatters from public land and Duer was already supplying some of these posts by arrangement with the local commanders. In October 1790, the supply of provisions for the troops through civilian contractors was officially revived with the granting of a contract to Theodosius Fowler of New York by Secretary Hamilton; the contract was to supply the "Western Army" for one year. Within four months, however, the contract was formally transferred to Duer, whose agent Fowler had been all along. Why an agent was used to give a contract to a man who was experienced in the field and who already had the nucleus of a supply organization in the area where the provisions were to be issued is not clear at all. Granted that the accounts between the old congress and Daniel Parker and Company had never been settled and that some of Duer's accounts as Secretary to the Board of Treasury were also still open, these would argue for no contract at all with him. Why would a contract be granted to a known associate of his and then transferred to Duer himself within a few months, first, avoiding the difficulty a contract with Duer might invite, then inviting trouble by sanctioning the transfer? One inadequate explanation is that giving the contract to Fowler may have been a kind of test of the water; when no one complained, the transfer to Duer was made.[22] Whatever the private arrangements might have been, Duer was quite confident of getting the contract and even before Fowler signed, was corresponding with a Captain Hills at "Fort St. Vincent" (possibly Vincennes, where the formal name for the federal fort was Fort Knox), advising him that, as the contract price was very low, wild meat and Indian meal would be used as much as possible to lower the cost. Duer remained in New York and did all the business of the contract through agents, some already hired to handle the Gallipolis business, some added for the Army provisioning. For a change, he seems to have corresponded systematically with the agents and administered the contract about as well as it could be done at a distance. But the use of so many agents, many of them personally unknown to Duer, was bound to create some difficulties. Quite a bit of time was lost, for example, when one agent, John McFarland, killed himself and all the local arrangements he had made had to be remade in the name of his replacement. Given the inevitable snags, things seemed to go along fairly well until the Army was expanded in March 1791 by a brigade of infantry, about 900 men, and the enlistment of up to 2,000 men, either militia or volunteers, for six months. This force would attempt what General Harmar had failed to do, discipline the Indians and push them back from the Ohio. Governor St. Clair was commissioned a major general and given overall command of the expedition. At this time, Duer was given a contract in his own name.[23]

The expansion, naturally put strains on the system of agents and supervision at a distance and the flaws or weaknesses began to show themselves. Also, Duer was now even more distracted by Gallipolis and his increasing stock speculations. In June, troops who had been ordered to the Gallipolis area could not go because the agent had neither placed food there nor did he have the money to purchase it in the locale. Even working with an agent as close as Philadelphia created difficulties. Duer either misplaced or ignored a letter from Governor St. Clair notifying him of the purchase of pack horses at Pittsburgh; in the meantime, John Wilkins in Philadelphia purchased the animals there. After being informed by an angry Duer of the duplication, Wilkins inquired plaintively if he should not arrange for a deposit of six months' provisions at Fort Pitt as they had more than enough horses to do it. Delays brought about by incidents such as these slowed down an expedition already badly behind schedule and St. Clair did not leave Fort Washington (Cincinnati) until 7 September. Moving in a leisurely fashion, his animals were deprived of grass by an early frost and he was delayed even more. On the morning of 7 November, St. Clair's men were attacked by a force of Indians one-half as large. In spite of the disparity in number, the Indian surprise was so complete that about 1,000 of the soldiers were killed or wounded; the rest abandoned their equipment and fled to Fort Washington without order or discipline.[24]

Frightened and angered by this second humiliation at the hands of the Indians, Congress, for the first time, used its investigatory power to discover the reasons for St. Clair's defeat. The report disclosed a number of shortcomings and could have been used to distribute guilt for the expedition's failure widely among those associated with it. However, by the time the report was released, Duer had defaulted and was in debtors' prison, so fire was concentrated on the contractor's shortcomings.[25] While these were quite real, not all of them hurt the military effectiveness and physical safety of the expedition; some were questionable on other grounds. Officers, for example, were given extra rations; they customarily took them in the form of cash when they were not needed. Also, if a portion of an enlisted man's ration was not available, cash could be substituted there also. However, Duer's clerks were not supplied with cash and had to give "due bills" instead. When a force was routed as completely as St. Clair's was, the loss in due bills was considerable. Even when the due bills were not lost, the contractor often either offered to purchase them at a discount or exchanged them for merchandise—just as Duer instructed the Vincennes agent mentioned above: "such Articles of Merchandise as you think will be advantageous." All in all, the due bills worked to Duer's advantage, not that of the officers and men.

More significant to the success and safety of the expedition was the contractor's delay in supplying provisions and horses at several rendezvous points, a delay caused by agents attempting to buy on credit, even though Duer had been advanced $70,000 by the government. On several occasions, the officers at the rendezvous points advanced the agents cash, just to get the men moving out. There was the utmost difficulty in getting a sufficient number of pack horses (despite the Philadelphia surplus) at the points where they were needed. St. Clair's purchase of several hundred at Pittsburgh has already been noted, but Duer refused to pay for them and eventually the Treasury Department picked up the bill. The teamsters employed by the contractor were either incompetent or so badly supervised and equipped that horses were lost or maimed, with a further delay to secure replacements. Duer attempted to defend himself from the committee's charges in *The National Gazette* (Philadelphia) in May 1792. But his effort was awkward and unconvincing, probably in part because it was composed in debtors' prison, but also because the deficiencies were real; the misleading aspect of the report was its concentration only on the shortcomings of the contractor. And by the contract, Duer lost not only reputation; he may have lost money also.[26]

Never happy unless super-active, or perhaps so avaricious, or perhaps so self-confident in his ability to handle almost an infinity of projects, or perhaps all of these, just when Duer should have been concentrating on his stock speculations, he engaged himself in yet another enterprise. His replacement at the Treasury had been the Philadelphia merchant and one of the country's most prolific writers on economic subjects, Tench Coxe. In the course of preparing an answer to a January 1790 inquiry by Congress as to how the United States might render herself independent of other nations for materiel needed for defense, Coxe devised and Hamilton circulated a plan for a society to encourage the establishment of manufacturing enterprises in the United States. In the spring of 1791, what would become the Society for Establishing Useful Manufactures (SEUM) was set underway. Hamilton contacted, among others, Duer in an effort to secure assistance. During the summer and fall of 1791, subscriptions for SEUM stock were sold. Duer's efforts were amply repaid for, of the first sixty-five stockholders, twenty-eight were New Yorkers and, when the stockholders elected the first thirteen-member board of directors, seven were from the city. While some of these were recruited by others, or perhaps just by Hamilton's obvious approval of the project, it is significant that, of the seven New Yorkers, six had been or were then associated with Duer in his other speculations. His work for the SEUM did not stop with soliciting for stock subscriptions, for in September and October he interviewed prospective employees and directed a search for a suitable site in New Jersey. In November, he helped to lobby the SEUM's charter through the state legislature in Trenton. New Jersey began its generous treatment of corporations with this charter. About the only thing the SEUM could not do was to become a general trading or banking company, and even this restriction was worded indefinitely. Several features accommodated Duer's speculative nature. Not only could the Society accept government stocks as part of its capital fund, it could also invest in them for its own benefit. Its own shares could also become the object of speculation and it could conduct lotteries. It is no wonder Duer was attracted to it.[27]

For a time, Duer was amply rewarded for his efforts on behalf of SEUM. When the stockholders held their first formal meeting in December, he was elected governor of the Society, in effect chairman of the board and president. He then directed the final selection of the site, named after New Jersey's cooperative governor, William Paterson, located at the falls of the Passaic River, twenty-four miles from New York City. In these early days, Duer's direction of SEUM's affairs was so self-contained, discreet, and complete, that when he went to the wall in March 1792, Archibald Mercer, the deputy-governor, had not the least idea what he had been doing.[28]

There was a reason for this. As early as September, John Rutherfurd, meeting Duer on his way to a SEUM meeting in New Jersey, put down his impressions that "they are making a Buble [*sic*] of this business. Duer said he had already £200.000 subscribed." Rutherfurd deplored this. Some welcomed it. Alexander Macomb noted in December that "Duer, as is usual with him, is very sanguine in hopes of it being a good speculation." Early in the new year, Macomb made clear just what a good speculation entailed. Duer had gathered a group of New York speculators, all but one of them also SEUM shareholders, to put together a fund to buy 3,000 shares "in order to have the management of the Directors, and by that means to promote its interest *& our own* [orig. emph.] . . . Duer, whose fertile genius is always suggesting new speculations, proposed this."[29] As noted, the plan succeeded and Duer secured control of SEUM. Even the most adept casuist would have difficulty refuting the charge that Duer's continued control of the Society would not have meant his continued use of it for his own enrichment and that of his colleagues. Whether this would have meant a prudent direction of its affairs or a shameless looting of what assets it had would have depended on where Duer saw his best interest. As Macomb had said, Duer viewed everything as a speculation and would have run great risks in the hope of great profits. There was enough risk already in SEUM and Duer would certainly have increased it if he had control for long. Prudence was not a strong element in his character; indeed, it was hardly to be found at all.

When Duer did fall, he held $10,000 of the Society's funds; despite assurances that the money was secure, it was never paid back. Fifty thousand dollars had been paid to John Dewhurst, a

SEUM director, New York merchant, and associate of Duer's, to be sent to Britain in the form of a draft on Dewhurst's London partner to pay for machinery. Affected by the general panic which Duer's failure set off, Dewhurst failed himself on 9 April 1792; this set off a desperate and unsuccessful attempt by the SEUM directors to save the money. Two other directors were bank-rupted by the panic and many of the stockholders were prevented from filling their subscriptions. Thus, directly Duer lost at least $10,000 for the Society, and an incalculable sum indirectly. Also, the later course of the SEUM was made rougher by the reputation which Duer had given it of being a playground for speculators. If it never completely fulfilled the hopes of its originators, and it never did, much of the blame can be placed on Duer.[30]

Not only did Duer involve himself in new major projects, he continued several of the miscellaneous enterprises he had begun after he left Congress. Active operations at the Poughkeepsie distillery had stopped with the war contracts, but Duer held on to the property, even though its unguarded state invited the theft of the valuable copper stills and worms, until the end. He also continued importing and exporting, sending cargoes to India via the ship *America*, owned jointly with Walter Livingston. The profits of this vessel's last voyage were lost to Livingston, when Duer gave over his share as security for $100,000 in notes. Although William Constable did not think highly of the captain and crew, Duer never mentioned the *America*'s voyages as losing ones, so some profit was probably realized.[31] He also planned a new undertaking which, despite its small beginning, might have been significant. In November 1790, he hired a M. Trennet, one of the Scioto emigrants, to supervise the construction and operation of a mill, principally for the drawing of iron and copper wire. Trennet was sent back to Paris to hire a skilled work force for the mill. A location was not mentioned, but there was talk at the time of reviving "Schuyler's Mine," an old copper mine in Essex County, New Jersey, and the mill could have been intended to use ore from this mine. However, Duer failed before the mine could be reopened and the mill remained only a plan.[32] Except for these, Duer seems to have concentrated on his large-scale ventures, but for someone involved in floating a land company and a manufacturing society, executing an army provisioning contract at a distance of 500 miles, and speculating in a volatile, complicated securities market, any dissipation of effort was foolish.

Duer did take one hare out of his headlong chase for fortune politics. He ran for no office nor did he play an active role in state or national politics in the early 1790s. On the eve of Duer's failure, Richard Platt, a New York speculating associate, apologized for their inaction in the gubernatorial election of 1792: "Duer & myself who have worked on all former Occasions" had to stay out that year because of business pressures. Any political work Duer might have done was very much behind-the-scenes, as during the state legislature's election of a new federal senator in January 1791. One of New York's senators, Philip Schuyler, had drawn a short, two-year term when the first Senate was divided into thirds so that the constitutionally prescribed order of election and term of office could be effected. With a Federalist controlled legislature, Schuyler's re-appointment was assumed, but some Federalists, led by Robert R. Livingston of that important and numerous clan, defected and, in union with Governor Clinton, selected Aaron Burr. From the sidelines, Duer, seeing the drift of things, had suggested that voting be delayed in the hopes of attracting a few more votes for Schuyler, but he was overruled by Hamilton's group in the legislature. Now he could see no way of rescuing the "Federal Cause from utter Depression," except by placing a branch of the Bank of the United States (still one month away from approval by President Washington) in New York City and having Schuyler make his residence there. Presumably, the branch bank would demonstrate the beneficial work of the federal government and Schuyler could rally the troops as no one else available could. The situation required "the Exertion of all our Fortitude—God knows, that my own private Concerns require all that I can summon. . . . Point out what is to be done, to rally a broken Party—and trust to my Exertions to carry your Vision into Execution." Either Hamilton's vision failed him at this point or he heeded the advice of others on the scene, such as Joseph Tillery who counseled the secretary that there was no one in New York to lead the Federalists; "Duer can never prop up the *good old cause* [orig. emph.] here. He is unfit as a Leader, & unpopular as a man besides."[33]

When Duer left the Treasury Department, the questions of funding and assumption were still before Congress and their fate appeared uncertain to many people. Duer's old associate, Andrew Craigie, however, was positive the fiscal program would pass in all its essential points. Not only had Hamilton told the Yankee speculator it would pass, but Craigie had moved in with Caleb Strong, Fisher Ames, Theodore Sedgewick, and other members of Congress so as to be better informed of the progress of the debates. Thus Craigie was redeeming fully his earlier pledge to "cultivate & improve" such sources of information. However, Craigie's sources were all ardent supporters of the secretary's program and their wishes did not immediately translate into enough votes to pass the program into law. In June, the question was still before the Congress. The feature that had prevented passage up to then was that of the assumption of state debts, something opposed with special vehemence by Virginia and supported equally strongly by Massachusetts and South Carolina. William Constable fretted over the delay and complained that "Congress employ themselves on the question of residence and removal instead of the public Concerns and parties run so high that nothing can be done." (Residence and removal concerned where the permanent capital was to be and how soon it would be moved there, if it was not to be New York City.) Constable hoped that such unimportant questions would not either delay or prevent the passage of the fiscal program. He was no prophet, so he could not know that Madison and Hamilton would reach a bargain during June by which Southern votes for assumption would be exchanged for a capital located on the Potomac River. A ten-year stay in Philadelphia secured some needed Pennsylvania votes. While Craigie was not a prophet either, he learned of the bargain almost before it was made. Hamilton first approached Secretary of State Thomas Jefferson about mid-June, asking him to act as an intermediary with Madison; several meetings were needed to put the agreement into final form. This was not accomplished much before the end of June, yet on 8 July, Craigie was able to inform Daniel Parker "By the *best information* [orig. emph.] . . . it is evident that an accommodation has been made (call it a bargain if you please)" and then described the terms of the "accommodation" quite accurately. He immodestly, but correctly, boasted that the transaction was not public knowledge, although it was "by some people suspected." The fiscal bills passed through Congress by early August, so enterprising speculators such as Craigie had about a month's prior knowledge of the assumption of the state debt.[34]

Duer was certainly one of the enterprising brethren. Well before the passage of assumption, he had someone in South Carolina purchasing state certificates. His resources, just after he left the Treasury, may have been slim, for he directed the Carolina agent to hold on to $5,000 in drafts if he could not make any purchases within specified limits. Any failure to follow instructions "might Expose me to Embarassments of a very Injurious Nature." The amount seems small to warrant such severe language, although Duer may have been going through a cash flow crisis at the time. Despite the injunction and caution, he was able to accumulate a large amount of state certificates; he and Walter Livingston held almost £16,000 face value of South Carolina indents of interest, an especially low priced certificate, which they had secured for an expenditure of less that £1,900, or about 11 1/2 percent of face value. Since few speculators held on to their certificates for long, trading them when it was either profitable or necessary, it is doubtful the partners got the face value. Even if they had, indents were exchanged for bonds bearing 3 percent interest which, a year later, were selling for nine shillings three or four pence, or about 46 percent of face value. A sale at that time would have given a gross profit of £5,460, exclusive of acquisition and carrying costs, or about 350 percent on the £1,900. Again, this is simply an illustration of the possible profits; interest costs could be quite high and some agents' commissions ran to 50 percent of profits. In July 1791, Royal Flint, probably a more conservative operator than Duer, was quite pleased to make 9 percent net profit in a speculation involving Carolina certificates. Duer continued to purchase Southern state securities, especially in the Carolinas where the quantities were greatest and, initially, the prices lowest, throughout the summer of 1790. Sometimes local agents had to be employed because the natives had started to expect higher prices from Northerners than from their fellow Carolinians. This was one indication, among others, that the mother lode of Carolina state securities was petering out. By October, the gold rush was over and Duer's agent could make no buys at the indicated prices, "for the assumption business was so generally known here . . . I have not heard of a single contract being formed . . . [under] advantageous circumstances."[35]

Although the gradual spread of news about assumption and the funding of the debt certificates, both congressional and state, cut off potentially lucrative sources of depreciated certificates for the speculators, it also simplified their operations considerably. Holders turned in their old certificates and received three varieties of federal bonds, a process known as the Loan of 1790; depending on whether one's certificates were congressional or state and whether they represented principal or were indents of interest, various combinations of federal bonds were issued, 6 percent bonds, 3 percent bonds, or deferreds, bearing 6 percent interest starting in 1800. With only three kinds of bonds circulating, the beginnings of an organized securities market appeared. Devices such as borrowing stock, buying on credit, sales at auction, and stock jobbing became common. The last operation, jobbing (although the term was frequently used loosely and pejoratively to describe speculation) was really a bet on where the market price would be at some future date. Two operators would agree on a date, price, and the type and quantity of stocks and, on the stipulated date, pay or receive the difference between the market price and the projected price without any shares actually changing hands, without the "jobbers" necessarily even owning any certificates of the type. Such phantom stock was sometimes called "wager stock."[36] Stock price quotations had appeared in newspapers before 1790, but they now became more frequent and systematic. These developments both allowed and aided an acceleration of stock speculating which brought prices to new heights.

While the market was evolving, so also were Duer's various partnerships and enterprises. William Constable had come to distrust him and was considering breaking entirely with him— "I fear he is not true at bottom." With some coaxing by Duer, Constable overcame some of his fears, but he cut down the scale of their joint dealings and, at the time of Duer's failure, was virtually unconnected with him. Baron Steuben, who had taken a share in an Illinois project with Duer, secured a pension from Congress in June 1790. In considering how to keep him from squandering it, his adopted son, William North, knew one thing; keep him away from Duer, who owed the old soldier money: "Let such gentlemen and such friends go to Hell." As old sources of money dried up or lessened, Duer turned to others and, in the fall of 1790, associated himself with the Roosevelt brothers,

John and Nicholas. They supplied the capital and the effort involved in securing the certificates; Duer supplied the direction and information needed to make their transactions profitable, or so it was hoped. He also provided some funds. Implicit in the agreement was the assumption that Duer would be able to determine or guess what Treasury Department policy was likely to be. For a time, he did not do badly. During a temporary fall in stock prices in October, Hamilton decided to use Sinking Fund purchases to bring prices back up, thus bolstering the credit of the new government. Duer was able to tell the Roosevelts of this in advance and prevent a sale at twelve shillings, two pence. Soon after, the Treasury began buying at twelve shillings, six pence and prices began recovering. But things did not always go this smoothly. In April 1791, the Roosevelts were faced with several large notes coming due simultaneously, and little on hand with which to meet them. Angry with Duer's initial refusal to help them, Nicholas pointedly asked him: did he ever lend to the company without receiving collateral, did he ever co-sign a note for the company without requiring a similar favor for his own concerns? "These are ideas I never would have reminded you of if every thing were done in the manner it ought." The Roosevelts were able to lessen the crisis by paying $15,000, but even that left $16,000 still owing. Unless Duer aided them, they were going to have to resort to usurers; "it is not the Premium alone which hurts a Man but his Paper goes through a Channel which disgraces it." Duer's own paper would suffer much in the future from just such a channel, but on this occasion, he was able to help his partners and the company survived the crisis.[37]

One partner who stayed, although not without difficulty, was Walter Livingston, who often had to be coaxed out of a pessimistic pout by the ebullient Duer. In March 1791, Livingston could not meet several notes coming due and, as often happened, panicked: "You can command my Services if you will religiously comply with your agreement, if not . . . the country will become my place of residence." But greed for expected profits overcame his fears (as it always did) and, when Duer fell, Livingston was affected almost as badly. During 1791 and through the first quarter of 1792, he endorsed more than $250,000 for Duer. How much of this paper was still outstanding is clouded in the fog of charge and counter-charge made at that time, but Livingston was certainly one of the largest, if not the largest, of Duer's co-signers in his last few years. Although he was given mortgages on upstate land and bonds as security for co-signing, he never felt secure, partly because he was never quite certain as to what else Duer was involving himself (and Livingston) in. He certainly had no better idea than most as to how thin the ice was on which Duer was skating. The difficulty his partners, the Roosevelts, were having meeting notes illustrates this. Not surprisingly, Duer's risk-taking became the matter for coffee-house gossip, with William Steele reporting that "many men who pass for your friends attack you . . . by seeming to lament what they propagate." His business affairs even upset the peace of his home, with Mrs. Duer being hounded by several note-holders, some of whom she appeased out of her household funds. This sort of thing induced her, on at least one occasion, to be a perceptive and severe critic of her husband's affairs. Duer was away on business, probably in Philadelphia, and she dropped him a line to tell him that, basically, everything was all right at home, but that she could not help wishing

> for the sake of your own Happiness that you could divest yourself of some affairs – entangled in a multiplicity of perplexities to follow some *one* [orig. emph.] steady line: that may leave a little leisure: to enjoy and improve the fleeting hours as they pass – don't laugh at all this – this is a Sunday night's lecture – my mind is in a serious vein. & I am sick of such a herd of Frenchmen who seem all to consider themselves in the stile of agents & look to you as their banker – without rendering you the least service.

The letter's tone suggests she often gave this talk to an amused husband, one who would have been a good bit better off had he heeded her advice, a more profound and loving version of Holker's counsel about not having two hares in one chase.[38]

Although he was no longer employed in the Treasury Department, Duer continued to enjoy some of the benefits of a person reputed to have influential connections. Joseph Hardy, a Treasury clerk in Philadelphia, where Congress and all government offices had moved in November 1790, assured Duer that he had "sufficient time to attend to your demands without interfering with my official duty." These demands had him buying and selling stock in Philadelphia as well as acting as an intermediary between

Duer and other Treasury officials who were interested in balancing his accounts as Secretary to the Board of Treasury and
some of the wartime Army contracts. Hardy also obligated himself to pay substantial sums of money on Duer's behalf, and then
was left to meet the obligations as best he could when Duer was
delayed in remitting. Most of this was done without any salary
or commission being paid Hardy, as the latter wanted his payoff
to come after he left the Treasury. He was planning to leave and
set up as a broker to receive interest payments and buy and sell
for European investors in American debt certificates. Others were
already doing this, but he hoped to get an edge on the competition by being endorsed as "Broker to the Treasury" by Secretary
Hamilton, an endorsement Duer apparently gave him reason to
expect. Failing in this, he hoped for Duer's assistance in securing
a transfer to the Treasury's New York City office. Neither ever
came about, and these two vain hopes may have been all Hardy
ever got by way of salary from Duer.[39]

As might be expected, after his resignation from the Treasury,
Duer's stock dealings increased and, had it not been for the arrival
of the Scioto emigrants and the resumption of the Army contracting, might have increased still more. Given the amount of
Livingston's endorsements and their dealings in Carolina certificates, it is not surprising that Duer was able to give Livingston
more than £69,000 in such certificates as security. In a three-
month period, December 1790 through February 1791, Duer
sold $25,000 in certificates through just one New York broker,
George Sutton. While these amounts alone would be sufficient
to mark him as a major operator, he was certainly engaged in
other stock speculations through other brokers.[40]

The expected financial stability of the new government was
not the only factor (other than market operations) bringing about
an increase in the market price of its securities. In December
1790, Secretary Hamilton proposed the establishment of the
Bank of the United States, a federally chartered but essentially
private corporation; the bank was to act as the government's
fiscal agent as well as be a kind of rudimentary central bank for
the country's burgeoning economy. The charter passed Congress
easily in February 1791, but underwent an intra-Cabinet debate
on its constitutionality before President Washington signed it
into law on 25 February. The BUS was to have a capital of

$10,000,000, $6,000,000 in federal 6 percent bonds (thus creating a use for them other than investment and speculation), the balance in specie. The first public sale of stock took place in Philadelphia, New York, and Boston on 4 July under conditions approaching a riot. All that was sold on that day was a right to buy a share, the full cost of which was $400, one-quarter in specie, three-quarters in bonds. Initially, one paid twenty-five dollars in specie. These rights, called "scrip," were soon being traded back and forth. Naturally, Duer was awake to the possible profit in them and inquired, before the sale, as to the acceptability of Bank of New York notes for the rights. By the end of July, he had at least 355 scrips, bought at prices ranging from $133 to $138.50. The narrow range of prices suggests that they were purchased recently and within a short period of time; under the pressure of feverish speculation, prices mounted quickly and before the end of August were at $185. They peaked at $325.[41]

Recall that all a scrip represented was a payment of twenty-five dollars, so that the highest price, $325, represented an advance of 1,200 percent on the original purchase. Since they were going to be needed to fill up subscriptions, 6 percents rose to par, and 3 percents, made receivable at 50 percent of face value in place of 6 percents, to twelve shillings, six pence. While the objections of Madison, who had held the BUS charter to be unconstitutional, to all this speculative clatter were only to be expected, not so expected were the objections of Secretary Hamilton. Shortly before the peak of scrip speculation in August, under the pseudonym "A Real Friend to Public Credit," the Secretary warned speculators that their fond hopes that what went up would keep going up were both foolish and dangerous—to themselves and to the government's credit. This essay, published in *The Gazette of the United States*, was backed by letters to friends, giving what Hamilton considered fair prices and explaining the effect a "bubble" or speculative craze could have on the government's credit. Duer was one of those warned by Hamilton; he was suspected of leading a New York group and was urged to lessen the pace of his operations. Hamilton's fears were well-founded. On 11 August, the Bank of New York refused to make any further loans to speculators or renew those coming due; a drop in prices occurred which spread quickly to Boston and Philadelphia. This drop must have caused Duer to take umbrage for, when Hamilton replied, he was trying to mollify his former assistant by quoting some of the rumors he had heard. Duer and Constable, for example, were trying to corner scrip, that is, command or monopolize the market for it. Hamilton realized that Duer would never wander from the path of either public good or private integrity. "But I will honestly own I have serious fears for you—for your purse and your reputation. . . . You are sanguine . . . I feared lest it might carry you further than was consistent either with your own safety or the public good."[42]

Hamilton was writing to the correct person for Duer was a large holder and trader of scrip. However, more important for the immediate future were Hamilton's orders to William Seton, Cashier of the Bank of New York, the federal government's fiscal agent in the city, to purchase stock for the Treasury's Sinking Fund. He was instructed to buy from those whose operations raised prices, not lowered them, the bulls, not the bears. Seton followed these orders, given in "great confidence," so literally that, of the $200,000 purchased, $52,695 was obtained from the super-bullish Duer. Assisted by these purchases, Duer survived the August break and may even have profited as the general price levels soon surpassed those which had already made Hamilton nervous.[43]

While fortunes could be made—and lost—in the unpredictable rise and fall of this new market, that few managed to keep their fortunes for long was a truth not yet realized by many of those in it. Even if it had been known, it would probably not have deterred most from trying their hand. Many believed they possessed the requisite wit and nerve to succeed, while some recognized that a willingness to be less than scrupulous would also help. Duer was one of these. In October 1791, the stock holders of the Bank of the United States held an organizational meeting in Philadelphia, where its headquarters was to be. Duer attended and was elected to a committee to prepare the bank's by-laws, but committee service was probably not uppermost on his mind. On Monday, 31 October, the stockholders were to decide whether branches would be opened in other cities. Duer prepared for this, whichever way it might go, by arranging to sell scrips on Tuesday, 1 November, after the news of the decision arrived in New York. His agent was to contract to sell 600 scrips sixty days hence at the highest price possible. Duer reasoned that any raise "cannot be permanent and Scrips can be delivered at least as low as what you sell at; if it has no Effect the Depression will be great." But, in order to ensure a high price, the agent was to place "five or Six persons in different Quarters of the Room to bid them up . . . You . . . must be kept out of view." These instructions give a rare clue to Duer's trading morals; whether such tactics were habitual or not cannot be determined, but other facets of his business conduct already noted bring the Scottish verdict of not proven again to mind. And, with a nice turn of hypocrisy, he asked his New York correspondent to do some discreet checking on John Pintard, a broker with whom Duer had recently associated himself. He was afraid of his own "over-Confidence" in others; it had too often led him into "Error." He had especially to remind himself that there was such a "cursed Temptation in this Abominable Scrip—that a Man's Honesty must be like adamant, to resist the Temptation of making a fortune, without the Possibility of Conviction, by sacrificing his Principal [i.e., Duer]." We have seen how much like "adamant" Duer's own honesty was.[44]

Duer recovered quickly from the fall in August and within the month he was buying scrip again, at a price $17 higher than Hamilton's recommendation. The general level of prices continued to rise steadily. He obtained his speculating capital from a variety of sources. He used his own assets, the Carolina certificates already mentioned, for example, also upstate New York lands and some of the new federal bonds. He was able to borrow on a limited basis from the Bank of New York, but its lending policies prevented it from being used as the source for any long term capital. During the summer and fall of 1791, he received advances for the Army provision contract and he had effectively relieved himself of most of the Scioto expenses. But his own assets and credit could not support his extensive operations. As early as January 1791, Gouverneur Morris wondered why Duer was so ready to lend his name "cheaply" and he commented that the astute (and conservative) Amsterdam bankers "have no high Idea of his Credit or Fortune." In August, Madison recorded his belief that speculators generally were forced to borrow at usurious rates, ranging from 2 1/2 percent a month to 1 percent a week. Apparently Duer had not yet been reduced to this, for in July he borrowed from Richard Platt at 10 percent a year, considering the risk, a reasonable rate. His joint operations with Walter Livingston have already been described and his dependence on him seems to have grown during the summer of 1791. If he was having trouble securing funds, his operations show no sign of it; from July through September, transactions through only two New York brokers totaled almost $95,000. If all the dealings of Pintard, the Roosevelt brothers, Livingston, and others who may have been allied with Duer could be traced, it could be that most of the stock speculating in New York at this time was under his influence.[45]

As 1791 came to an end, speculators everywhere recovered from the August fall—Duer's brashness and possibly Hamilton's aid had allowed him to recover much faster—and new speculations, projects, companies, and banks were planned or begun. The SEUM is only one example. Others were a Pennsylvania canal company, a Boston bridge company, new banks in Providence, Boston, New Hampshire, and Albany. In New York City alone, three new banks were planned; these would be in addition to the Bank of New York and the BUS branch, scheduled to open on 1 April 1792. Before the end of January, the three projects were merged into one to improve chances of acceptance by a hostile state legislature. Associates of Duer's, such as Alexander Macomb, Walter Livingston, and Richard Platt, were connected with these plans, but, incredibly, Duer seems to have kept away from them, or was content to play a very secondary role. In the end, the state legislature refused to charter any new bank for New York City. Not all states were quite so opposed to new style corporate ventures, however, and from October 1791 to April 1792, seventeen new companies were chartered in the United States, as many as in the previous seven years. All of these required capital, secured by selling shares, which in turn added to the total available for speculation.[46]

Intent on riding this new wave—indeed, it may be said that he was one of the principal wave makers—Duer must have had little time to talk or think of anything else. Late in November, Walter Rutherfurd dined with him and found him "immersed with Speculations of all Classes, Money Land and Manufactures, enough to turn an ordinary Brain. We had most talk on the last Subject." But Duer needed more than talk to get in and stay in the game and in December, he was able to enlist a new partner and source of capital in Alexander Macomb, an Irish-born land speculator who had recently made an especially advantageous purchase from New York State. Since the Irishman had previously been unconnected with stock speculation, Duer probably hoped to do business through Macomb with some who had come to distrust him. The two men had been connected only through SEUM, where Macomb was a director. On 27 December 1791, they agreed to speculate in United States bonds and the stocks of the Bank of the United States and the Bank of New York, with all purchases made in Macomb's name. Macomb was also to keep all records, with Duer's contribution restricted to advice on all transactions. The partnership was for one year.[47]

Aside from making a profit, just what the partnership intended is not clear. Macomb described a number of projects, but only one of them, a speculation in federal bonds, belonged solely to the new association. William Constable, then in London, was offered a half-share through his younger brother, James, left tending the store in New York. James turned it down. Thus, it was left to Macomb and Duer to embark "upon an adventure which before the end of the Year may amount to a pretty large Sum," according to Macomb, whose faith in his new partner knew no bounds. He assured the absent Constable that Duer's "genius assures him that it shall all be done without any active capital farther than can be raised upon our joint Credit at the Bank." Macomb described an attempt to control the SEUM as well as a plan of Duer's to turn its right to conduct lotteries to their advantage. Here, however, they found themselves forestalled by the Roosevelt brothers and decided to combine under their name in order to run lotteries for the construction of bridges across the Hackensack and Passaic Rivers in New Jersey. Again, a share was offered to Constable, who was cautioned that everything had to be done "with great secrecy." Macomb also agreed to buy a share in the *America* when she returned from her current voyage.[48]

A contract to purchase 290 shares of Bank of New York stock started the new partnership off and Duer went to Philadelphia over the New Year to purchase some other securities and sound out people there about a New York branch for the BUS. While the directors had decided earlier that there would be branches, they had not yet located them. The conventional wisdom of the

time had a New York branch competing so effectively with the
Bank of New York that its only prospect for long term survival
would be to merge with the BUS branch, in which case its
position would be improved considerably. There was also thought
to be a possibility that the BUS would buy the local bank and
thus accomplish in the short run that which was expected to
happen in the long run. However the BUS was going to arrange
its affairs, Duer soon showed how he was to conduct the new
partnership. He instructed Walter Livingston to sell 100 shares
of New York bank stock, deliverable in May, but through a
reliable, confidential agent. Neither man was to be connected
with the transaction. He then told Macomb to buy New York
stock on the supposition that a branch bank, if established, "will
not continue for many months, as the Secretary . . . is very anxious for the Coalition, and his Influence will in all probability
effect it." Handsome profits were possible for those in the know
and Macomb assumed blithely that he was in the know. What
he was not aware of was that Duer was lying to him, so that his
purchases might help to make a market in Bank of New York
shares. While Macomb was doing this, Duer was selling at a
higher price than he would otherwise have gotten. This broke
eighteenth-century business practice, the Duer-Macomb agreement which the latter interpreted as forbidding separate dealing,
the contemporary code of honor, and the Ten Commandments.
Macomb knew nothing of this and continued in deeper and
deeper with Duer. On 28 January, he, Duer, and Isaac Whippo
borrowed $100,000 from William G. Smith. While Whippo's
role in the transaction is not entirely clear, he does seem to have
been more than an agent; perhaps the money was borrowed for
a specific transaction, one to which Whippo had been admitted
as a partner.[49]

In the meantime, Constable was sending advice from London
which, could it have been transmitted by modern means of com-
munication, might have done some good, but in 1792 could only
be a kind of ironic post-script to Macomb's venture into stock
speculating. He strongly counseled Macomb against continuing
in a partnership already six weeks old when he was writing. Duer
will "speculate upon you—as often leading you into all the advance
& risque. He will reap the profit." On Duer's advice, Constable
had once sold short some Southern state certificates, only to

discover later that the buyer was Duer. He accused him of milking the Maine land company and probably planning the same with the SEUM. All those associated with him were, in some way, under his control and there was something in all his ventures "which would not bear the light," so that if a loss did occur, one simply had to bear it quietly. The only way to take advantage of Duer's undoubted talents, information, and resources, Constable believed, was to be constantly on one's guard. That was too high a price for Macomb, with his good name and wealth, to pay. Constable asserted that he never made a penny on any project he entered with Duer, chiefly because of the latter's fickleness: "Duer could have made a Million if he would have Confined himself to any one object—but his Genius will not permit it."[50] Holker, Catherine Duer, now Constable, the speculator did not lack for perceptive critics.

However, Macomb was happily unaware of Constable's experiences with his new partner and was getting in deeper and deeper with him, all the while becoming more impressed: "You know Duer's fertile head and genius at resource—it astonishes me. He thinks very little of raising in a few days some hundred thousand Dollars—such operations come perfectly easy to him." But the ease was deceptive, especially to Alexander Macomb. By early March, Duer's notes, co-signed by Macomb, were being peddled around New York at very high rates of interest. According to Seth Johnson, a former clerk of Craigie's (now semi-retired from the speculating game and living in Cambridge, Massachusetts), Duer was attempting nothing less than a corner on government bonds, especially 6 percents, to oblige those who needed them to fill long term contracts or to pay in for shares of the BUS (payments of specie and bonds were to be made in four equal payments on 1 January and 1 July until the shares were filled), in short, to squeeze their fellow speculators. Whatever his objective, and the 6 percent corner is the most plausible explanation, Duer's credit needs were becoming more and more critical. Walter Livingston had one of his periodic failures of nerve early in January: "Do not my friend urge me further. I have already exceeded the value of your property added to mine." Duer tried to allay Livingston's fears and prevent him from liquidating the partnership, a move which, he argued, was against "your Interest and Reputation as well as the Public Good." He added, cryptically, that some of Livingston's fears were caused by friends whose true character would soon be seen, a possible reference to another group of speculators—Livingstons among them also— who were working to bring prices down. Duer and Livingston met in mid-February and, for the last time, Duer was able to talk the other man out of his fears, or perhaps he showed him that the situation was so critical that they had to go forward, for they could not stop. If their joint obligations were truly more than the value of their property, liquidation meant ruin. In an application of the old saying, "in for a lamb, in for a sheep," Livingston went in with the whole flock and agreed to underwrite $800,000 for Duer, nothing to last beyond 31 December 1792, collateral in the form of stocks and land to be handed over. But this did little to ease the pressure on Duer and, before the end of the month, he admitted that their affairs needed the closest of attention, but that and faithful adherence to their latest agreement would carry them through. They had to stay together—to illustrate what this meant in practice, Duer asked Livingston for all the cash he had in the bank. He would need it for only a day.[51]

Duer had just about exhausted all possible sources of credit. He borrowed $10,000 from John Dewhurst and applied $10,000 of SEUM money which he held to his speculations, in addition to borrowing $50,000 which Macomb held for the Society; he paid 7 percent for this and gave Macomb stocks as collateral. So far the sources of his money were conventional enough, even if they were not all ethical, but now he had outrun both the conventional and the ethical. He started borrowing through Whippo and Pintard small sums, as little as $500, from "shopkeepers, widows, orphans, butchers, cartmen, Gardeners, market women & even the noted Bawd Mrs. McCarty," at usurious rates of interest.[52]

Duer might have covered all these expenses in a rising market, but early in March, prices started to fall; this was partly the result of the bearish operations of Brockholst Livingston and others, partly simply the quantity of stocks which had been drawn to New York, beyond the ability of that market to support, especially when Duer was so influential. His contracts to buy were coming due in late March, early April. But on 8 March, uncomfortable with the quantity of loans being discounted by speculators and nervous about its prospects once the local branch of the BUS opened on 1 April, the Bank of New York stopped all loans. Duer's house of cards began to collapse around him. His credit situation was so precarious that he could not afford to lose any source of cash, but he had exhausted all the possible and some of the impossible sources, so he cut loose some of the impossible ones and announced on the 9th that he had just discovered that his agents had contracted usurious loans in his absence; he was stopping payments on these loans until he could determine their true character. Within three days, Philadelphia speculators knew of Duer's action and realized it meant a general fall was coming. Although prices apparently stayed steady for a few days yet, their verdict was the correct one.[53]

Almost as though it had been waiting for the least sign of weakness on Duer's part, the Treasury Department chose this time to start a suit against Duer for the settlement of some long overdue accounts. This impression is wrong. The Treasury had been pressing Duer for some years about several different sets of accounts stemming from the war contracts and his service as Secretary to the Board of Treasury. Oliver Wolcott, Jr., Comptroller of the Treasury, was probably concerned that his office secure what it could of Duer's assets in case of a general debacle. They had already shown more than enough patience. Little if any of this was generally known, however. What was known was that Duer had stopped paying some of his notes and the United States was now suing him for more than $100,000. Stock prices resumed their fall and Duer began casting about frantically for help. He wrote Hamilton and other friends in Philadelphia, asking that they intercede at the Treasury for him, but there was nothing anyone, even the secretary could do. Any action on Hamilton's part would be ineffectual as well as unethical, and probably illegal. The comptroller was a semi-judicial official from whose decisions there was no appeal within the Treasury. Hamilton could only give sensible advice—"If you cannot reasonably hope for a favorable extrication, do not plunge deeper. Have the courage to make a full stop." This was not what Duer wanted to hear and he ignored it, instead pleading that the secretary "use for once your influence to defer this [suit] until my arrival [in Philadelphia]. . . . If a suit should be brought on the part of the public,—and in my present distressed circumstances—my ruin is complete."[54]

Although there was little Duer could do except talk bravely, he could do that. He assured the justifiably nervous Livingston that the collateral he held was more than enough to pay the notes for which he was responsible. Although the last agreement, 18 February, could not now be executed, Duer promised to indemnify Livingston should any losses result from it; this would injure Duer, but it was needed if the two men were to act honorably towards each other. But the brave talk was no longer effective and Livingston delayed coming forward to support Duer, even though the latter warned that "by this conduct, you Destroy all future Utility of your Name to you, or myself." Not at all reassured, Livingston continued to hang back. And there was little, aside from Duer's talk, to reassure him. Six percents, which had been as high as twenty-five shillings, were now at par and seemed ready to fall further. A committee of Duer's creditors advertised a meeting for Saturday, 24 March, at which the financier would reveal how he was to meet his obligations, for he had now stopped paying on all his notes.[55]

The meeting was not to be held. Since he had stopped paying on the small, usurious notes, their holders had despaired of ever getting their money back and some decided to take their principal satisfaction in manhandling, or worse, their debtor. For the last few days before his scheduled meeting with his creditors, Duer was virtually a prisoner in his house, instructing potential callers to come by the back alley, rather than Broadway, and to "Reconnoiter well" before they entered. As much for his physical safety as for any debt guaranty, several of his creditors had him committed to city prison on 23 March.[56] No one, least of all Duer, expected this to be as final a step as it was.

References

1. Joel Barlow to Wm. Duer, Nov. 29, Dec. 8, 29, 1789, Jan. 25, Mar. 3, 1790, Scioto Papers, "Barlow" folder, NYHS; Davis, "Duer Essay," 239-40; Rochefontaine to Wm. Duer, Aug. 15, Scioto Papers, "Duer" folder, NYHS; David S. Franks to Wm. Duer, Nov. 2, 1790, Duer Papers, NYHS; Harrison Ansley & Co. to Walter Livingston, Oct. 6, 1791, Livingston Coll., Uncat., Duer-Flint Corr., NYHS; see also the Barlow-Constable correspondence for this period in the Constable Papers, NYPL, for details of Barlow's work in Paris.
2. Tobias Lear to Alexander Hamilton, Aug. 28, 1790, Alexander Hamilton to George Washington, Aug. 28, 1790, Syrett, *Hamilton Papers*, VI, 575-78; Wm. Duer, Andrew Craigie and Royal Flint, Trustees for the Scioto Purchase, to Benjamin Walker, Sep. 11, 1790, Agreement between Andrew Craigie, Wm. Duer, Royal Flint, and Ben-

jamin Walker, Sep. 11, 1790, Scioto Papers, "Duer" folder, NYHS; there are also items in the Winthrop Sargent Papers, MHS, Josiah Harmar Papers, Clements Library, and the "Records of the Original Proceedings of the Ohio Company," ed. by Archer B. Hulburt, *Marietta College Historical Collections* (1917), I & II, pertaining to the Scioto Company; hereafter cited as "Records of . . . Ohio Company."

3. Wm. Duer to Benjamin Walker, Nov. 20, 1790, Scioto Papers, "Duer" folder, NYHS; see also [Wm. Duer] to Benjamin Walker, Nov. 6, Dec. 2, 1790, Duer Papers, NYHS; Walter Livingston to Benjamin Walker, Nov. 6, 1790, Livingston Coll, NYHS; William Constable to James Seagrave, Nov. 10, 1790, Constable Papers, NYPL.

4. Davis, "Duer Essay," 244-47; Wm. Duer to Benjamin Walker, Mar. 26, 1791, Scioto Papers, "Duer" folder, NYHS; see William Playfair to Wm. Dewer [*sic*], Dec. 27, 1790, loc. cit. for an example of Playfair's salesmanship.

5. Belote, University Studies, 76; Alexander Hamilton, "Report on Public Credit," January 1790, Syrett, *Hamilton Papers*, VI, 91; Davis, "Duer Essay," 223, thinks Duer was possibly responsible for this; see J. C. Mountflorence to Wm. Duer, Oct. 7, 1790, Duer Papers, NYHS, for evidence that Duer considered sending the emigrants to Kentucky, rather than buy Ohio Company land.

6. Cutler, *Journals*, I, 508-11; see also Andrew Craigie to Joel Barlow, Apr. 10, 1790, Craigie Papers, AAS; see "Records of . . . Ohio Company," II, 23-25, for the sale of Gallipolis to the Scioto Company.

7. Joel Barlow to M. Boulogne, Jan. 1, 1790, Duer Papers, BV II, NYHS; Thomas Porter to Andrew Craigie, May 14, Jul. 19, 1790, Craigie Papers, AAS; [Wm. Duer to Isaac Guion], Mar. 9, 1790, Duer Papers, BV II, Rufus Putnam to Wm. Duer, May 28, 1790, Duer Papers, NYHS; see also Agreement of Wm. Duer with John Wilkins, Jun. 14, 1790, Scioto Papers, "Duer" folder, NYHS for a supply of flour in Ohio; Agreement of Wm. Duer with William McMahon, Aug. 14, 1790, Duer Papers, NYHS, for a supply of beef in Ohio.

8. David S. Franks to Andrew Craigie, Mar. 26, 1790, Thomas Porter to Andrew Craigie, Mar. 18, May 5, 7, 19, 1790, Craigie Papers, AAS; Rufus Putnam to Wm. Duer, May 28, 1790, Duer Papers, NYHS.

9. [Wm. Duer?], *Address to the Inhabitants Of Alexandria and Other sea-ports in the United States of America. From a proprietor of lands on the Scioto* (New York,1790); attributed to Duer by R. W. G. Vail, *The Voice of the Old Frontier* (Phila., 1949), 349; see also 194 letters from the emigrants to various persons, mostly Duer describing the alternative plans offered to them in Alexandria and complaining about their accommodations, food, wine, etc. there, Scioto Papers, "Trenet and Bretsche deboulogne" folder, NYHS; Thomas Porter to Wm. Duer, Sep. 30, 1790, Duer Papers, NYHS; Belote, *University Studies*, III, 51-54; see also Isaac Guion to Wm. Duer, Jun. 2, 1790, Duer Papers, BV II, Wm. Duer to Peter Marmie, Jun. 9, 1790, Thomas Porter to Wm. Duer, Jul. 12, 1790, Duer Papers, NYHS; Thomas Porter to Andrew Craigie, Jul. 7, 1790, Craigie Papers, AAS.

10. Thomas Porter to Wm. Duer, Oct. 11, 1790, Duer Papers, Wm. Duer to Thomas Porter, Nov. 10, 1790, Duer Papers, BV II, NYHS; Thomas Porter to Andrew Craigie, Jun. 30, Jul. 5, 7, 12, 16, Oct. 22, Nov. 3, 4, 10, Dec. 10, 13, 1790, Craigie Papers, AAS; see especially Duer to Porter, Nov. 10, 1790 for one of Duer's quibbles and Porter to Craigie, Dec. 13, 1790 for Porter's reaction; see the Scioto Papers, NYHS, for accounts rendered and, occasionally, amounts paid by Duer; the Craigie-Porter letters referred to above also have information on the costs of the Gallipolis colony. It is my opinion that, prior to his failure, Duer avoided paying most of these costs. Davis, "Duer Essay," 237, asserts the contrary, but cites no evidence to support it. See also Wm. Duer to Benjamin Walker, May 14, 1790, MS # 15015, NYSL,"A New Colony of Frenchmen is upon me . . .," asking for a loan from Walker; even George Washington was brought in, see George Washington to DuChesne, et al., Jun. 30, 1790, Fitzpatrick, *Washington Writings*, XXXI, 64-65.

11. Arthur St. Clair to Henry Knox, Nov. 26, 1790, William H. Smith, ed., *The Life and Correspondence of Arthur St. Clair* (Cinc., 1882), II, 195; hereafter cited as Smith,

St. Clair; see also Arthur St. Clair to George Washington, Nov. 21, 1790, ibid., I, 180; Arthur St. Clair to the French Inhabitants of Gallipolis, Nov. 21, 1790, ibid., 190-91; Benjamin Thompson to Wm. Duer, Jan. 6, 1790 [1791?], Duer Papers, BV II; David S. Franks to Wm. Duer, Sep. 11, 1790, Duer Papers, NYHS.

12. Isaac Ludlow to Wm. Duer, Jan. 10, 1791, Duer Papers, NYHS; Rufus Putnam to Wm. Duer, Jan. 9, 1791, Scioto Papers, "Putnam" folder, NYHS; contrast these with Duer's rosy report on Indian affairs to Benjamin Walker, Mar. 29, 1791, Scioto Papers, "Duer" folder, NYHS; Isaac Guion to Wm. Duer, Feb. 16, 1791, Duer Papers, NYHS.

13. Wm. Duer to Isaac Guion, May 1, 1791, Duer Papers, NYHS; M. DuPlaine to Wm. Duer, May 17, 1791, Scioto Papers, "D-E-F" folder, see also M. Sallot to Wm. Duer, Jun. 20, 1791, "S-T-U-V" folder, NYHS; Laban Bronson to Wm. Duer, Mar. 17, 1791, Duer Papers, BV II, NYHS; Cutler, *Journals*, I, 519; M. Mitchell to Wm. Duer, Jul. 31, 1791, Duer Papers, NYHS.

14. John Mathews to Wm. Duer, Apr. 5, 1792, Duer Papers, BV II; see also B. J. DeLeTure to Wm. Duer, Mar. 19, 1792, Duer Papers, NYHS, for reports of rumors at Gallipolis that Duer kept back letters from and to France which had been sent through him; this also discouraged the emigrants; Davis, "Duer Essay," 328; "John Heckewelder's Journey to the Wabash in 1792," *Pennsylvania Magazine of History & Biography*, 12 (1888): 35-36, 181-82, for a description of Gallipolis; Belote, *University Studies*, 57-59; Rowena Buell, ed., *The Memoirs of Rufus Putnam* (Boston, 1903), 123, 125, 409; Report of Attorney General on Gallipolis, Mar. 24, 1794, 3 Cong., 1 Sess., *American State Papers: Public Lands* (Washington, 1832), I, 23-24, for the final settlement with the Gallipolis settlers; Royal Flint to Rufus Putnam, May 26, 1792, Wm. Duer to Alexander Hamilton, to Henry Knox, May 30, 1792, Craigie Papers, AAS.

15. R. R. Palmer, *The Age of the Democratic Revolution: The Challenge* (Princeton, 1959), 188; see also the Report of a Conversation with Alexander Hamilton by Comte deMoustier, Sep. 13, 1789, Syrett, *Hamilton Papers*, V, 368, for a prediction by the French minister to the United States that very few Frenchmen would go to America.

16. See the sources cited in n. 10 and Hulburt, "Scioto Group," 26.

17. William Tudor to Richard Soderstrom, May 11, 1791, Richard Soderstrom to William Constable, May 16, 1791, Constable Papers, NYPL; Wm. Duer to [Royal Flint?], Jun. 5, 1791, Emmett Coll., Ms. # 11011, NYPL; see Charles R. King, ed., *The Life and Correspondence of Rufus King* (New York, 1894), I, 75-80, for Soderstrom's financial difficulties; see Alexander Macomb to William Constable, Dec. 2, 1792, Constable Papers, NYPL, for a later report on Tudor's bribe.

18. Wm. Duer and Henry Knox to [Royal Flint, Henry Jackson], Jun. 2, 1791, "Principles of Agreement . . ., Jun. 2, 1791," Henry Knox Papers, XXVIII, MHS [microfilm]; hereafter referred to as Knox Papers.

19. Henry Jackson to Henry Knox, Jun. 12, 1791, "Commonwealth of Massachusetts to Henry Jackson & others . . .," Jul. 1, 1791, Knox Papers, XXVIII; Henry Knox to Wm. Duer, Aug. 4, 1791, loc. cit. XXIX, MHS.

20. Wm. Duer to Henry Knox, Aug. 27, 1791, "The Present State of Confusion . . ." Aug. 27, 1791, Memorandum, Henry Knox, Sep. 3, 1791, Bacler DeLaVal, DeLaRoche to [George] Jackson, Oct. 22, 1791, Knox Papers, XXIX, MHS; see "Copy of Agreement" between Jackson and Flint and Mme. DeLaVal and Mons. DeLaRoche, n.d., Scioto Papers, Box II, misc. folder, NYHS, for what may be a later draft of the agreement.

21. Friedrich Steuben to Benjamin Walker, May 23, 1788, cited in Palmer, *Steuben*, 359; James Jarvis to Melancton Smith and Andrew Craigie, Nov. 5, 1790, Craigie Papers, AAS; John Edgar to Wm. Duer, Oct. 29, 1791, Duer Papers, BV II, "Remarks on the Illinois Settlement," n. d., Duer Papers, BV II, James Mackey to Wm. Duer, Dec. 29, 1792, Duer Papers, NYHS; Duer-deBarth Agreement, Jul. ?, 1791, Scioto Papers, "deBarth" folder, NYHS; see also J. C. Mountflorence to Wm. Duer, Oct. 7, 1790, Duer Papers, NYHS for the possibility that Duer was interested in a Kentucky settlement as well. "Petition for Land by Flint and Parker, Oct. 18,

1787," C. W. Alvord, ed., *Kaskaskia Records, 1778-1790* (Springfield, IL, 1909), 449-51 for identification of Parker as "Joseph" and for a location north and east of the Wood River opposite St. Louis for the land.

22. Randolph C. Downes, *Council Fires on the Upper Ohio* (Pittsburgh, 1940, repr. 1968), Chaps. 12, 13; Francis P. Prucha, *The Sword of the Republic* (New York, 1969), Chap. 2, for background; bills of exchange for meat supplied the Western Army, Jul.-Aug. 1790, Scioto Papers, "Duer" folder, NYHS; contract in Syrett, Hamilton Papers, VII, 127; assignment by Fowler to Duer, Jan. 3, 1791, Duer Papers, Box IV, Legal Papers, NYHS; after a congressional report critical of the contractor was issued, Fowler objected to Hamilton and described himself as "an innocent person in the whole of this Transaction, which no doubt you are perfectly senciable [*sic*] of," T. Fowler to Alexander Hamilton, Feb. 2, 1793, Syrett, *Hamilton Papers*, XXVI, 693-94; see also William Campbell to David Ross, Nov. 18, 1792, ibid., XIII, 222-23, n. 6, for the allegation that Hamilton knew from the beginning that Duer was to be the contractor.

23. [Wm. Duer] to Capt. Hills, Oct. 18, 1790, Duer Papers; J. C. Mountflorence to Wm. Duer, Oct. 21, 1790, Duer Papers, BV II; John T. Halstead to Wm. Duer, Jan. 8, 1791, Duer Papers, NYHS; *Annals of Congress*, 2 Cong., 2 Sess., 1106.

24. "Extract from a letter from General [Richard] Butler, dated June 9, 1791," Duer Papers; J[ohn] Wilkins to Wm. Duer, Jul. 6, 1791, Duer Papers, BV II, NYHS; Prucha, *Sword of the Republic*, 22-27.

25. Harry M. Ward, *The Department of War, 1781-1795* (Pittsburgh, 1962), 139-40 for a summary of the report; the investigating committee was appointed on March 22, 1792, *Annals*, 2 Cong., 1 Sess., 493-94; the final report on which the following paragraphs are based is ibid., 2 Cong., 2 Sess., 1106-13, 1310-17.

26. *State Papers: Claims*, I, 259 for the report of a House Committee on a government claim on Fowler for a balance due on the 1790 contract; the committee dismissed the claim and found a balance owing the contractor, not the government; see also ibid., *Military Affairs*, I, 36-39, 41-44; "Sketch of the Account w. Wm. Duer . . .," Register of the Treasury, Estimates & Statements for 1792, Vol. 134-T, 80-82, RG 53, NA; Bills, Receipts & Notes, fol. IX, Duer Papers, NYHS; correspondence of Wm. Duer and Henry Knox, 1791, Knox Papers, XXVII, XXVIII, MHS; see above, 80, for "due bills."

27. "Agreement to apply . . .," Apr. 29, 1791, SUM Papers, Doc. # 7, Passaic County [NJ] Historical Society, Paterson, NJ; see the following by Jacob E. Cooke on the development of the plan for the Society, "Tench Coxe, Alexander Hamilton, and the Encouragement of American Manufactures," *William and Mary Quarterly*, 3 s., 32 (1975): 369-92; *Tench Coxe and the Early Republic* (Chapel Hill, 1978), Chap. 9; *Alexander Hamilton* (New York, 1982), Chap. 9; also John R. Nelson, Jr., "Alexander Hamilton and American Manufacturing: A Reexamination," *The Journal of American History*, 65 (1979): 971-95. The best treatment of the SEUM is still Joseph S. Davis, "The S.U.M.: The First New Jersey Corporation," *Essays in the Earlier History of American Corporations* (Cambridge, 1917), I, 349-518, hereafter cited as Davis, "SUM Essay." Thomas Lowery to Wm. Duer, Feb. 7, 1792, Duer Papers, BV II, NYHS; Wm. Duer to Walter Livingston, Nov. 6, 1791, Livingston Coll., NYHS.

28. Minute Book, SUM, Dec. 9, 17, 18, 19, 20, 21, 1791, Paterson (NJ) Public Library; Docs. # 14, 304, SUM Papers, PCHS; Davis, "SUM Essay," 371.

29. Walter Rutherfurd to John Rutherfurd, Sep. 30, 1791, Rutherfurd Coll., NYHS; Alexander Macomb to William Constable, Dec. 3, 1791, Jan. 1, 1792, Constable Papers, NYPL.

30. Davis, "SUM Essay," 410, 415, 418; although the Society never succeeded as an industrial enterprise, it later paid rich dividends from leaseholds and water rights when Paterson developed in the late nineteenth century; it survived into the 1940s; Nathan Schachner, *Alexander Hamilton* (New York, 1957), 281; see below, 176, for another misuse of the SEUM's funds.

31. Arch[ibald] Stewart to Wm. Duer, Jun. 12, 1788, Duer Papers; see also an undated

copyist's bill for work on leases, assignments of titles, etc., for the distillery, Duer Papers, Box IX, folder # 2, NYHS; "Agreement between Wm. Duer and Walter Livingston, Nov. 27, 1791," Livingston Coll., NYHS; William Constable to Robert Morris, Dec. 14, 1791, Constable Papers, NYPL.

32. Contract between M. Trennet and Wm. Duer, Nov. 29, 1790, Duer Papers, Box V, Deeds Folder # 2; Wm. Duer to Benjamin Walker, Nov. 30, 1790, Duer Papers, NYHS; Alexander Macomb to William Constable, Feb. 21, 1792, Constable Papers, NYPL.

33. Richard Platt to S. B. Webb, Mar. 4, 1792, W. C. Ford, ed., *Correspondence and Journals of Samuel Blachley Webb* (New York, 1894), III, 177; Wm. Duer to Alexander Hamilton, Jan. 19, 1791, Myers Coll., #402, NYPL; Joseph Tillery to Alexander Hamilton, Jan. 1791, cited in Mitchell, *Hamilton*, II, 136; see Young, *Republicans*, esp. Chaps. 8 and 9 for a good treatment of New York state politics at this time.

34. Andrew Craigie to Daniel Parker, May 8, 1790, Craigie Papers, AAS; see above, 165, for Craigie's earlier promise; Wm. Constable to Gouverneur Morris, Jun. 1, 1790, Constable Papers, NYPL; Andrew Craigie to Daniel Parker, Jul. 8, 1790, Craigie Papers, AAS. See Ferguson, *Purse*, Chap. 14; Dumas Malone, *Jefferson and the Rights of Man* (Boston, 1951), Chap. XVI, esp. 297-306; Mitchell, *Hamilton*, II, Chap. IV, for complementary treatments of congressional action on Hamilton's program.

35. Wm. Duer to George Reid, Apr. 4, 1790, Duer Papers; "List of Securities Owned by Wm. Duer and Walter Livingston, May 20, 1790," Duer Papers, Box V, folder # 1, NYHS; Davis, "Duer Essay," Appendix A, 340; Royal Flint to Walter Livingston, Jul. 28, 1791, Livingston Coll., Uncat., Duer-Flint Corr., NYHS; William Steele to Wm. Duer, Jul. 17, Oct. 1, 1790, Duer Papers, NYHS.

36. Edward Fox to Andrew Craigie, Nov. 30, Dec. 3, 1789, Craigie Papers, AAS.

37. William Constable to James Seagrave, Aug. 27, 1790, Constable Papers, NYPL; William North to Benjamin Walker, Jun. 3, 1790, cited in Palmer, *Steuben*, 379; Nicholas and John Roosevelt to Walter Livingston, Oct. 4, 1790, Livingston Coll., NYHS; from Aug. to Dec. 1790, the Treasury Department purchased $250,000 worth of stocks at a cost of $180,000 for the Sinking Fund, *State Papers: Finances*, I, 81-82; Nicholas Roosevelt later backed Robert Fulton in his construction of the Clermont and founded a family which gave the United States two presidents, Theodore and Franklin Delano. Nicholas Roosevelt to Wm. Duer, Apr. 15, 1791, John and Nicholas Roosevelt to Wm. Duer, Apr. 18, 1791, see also Nicholas Roosevelt to Wm. Duer, Mar. 23, 25, 31, 1791, Duer Papers, NYHS.

38. Walter Livingston to Wm. Duer, Mar. 19, 1791, "List of Endorsements for Wm. Duer, April [1792?]," Livingston Coll., NYHS; William Steele to Wm. Duer, Apr. 7, 1791, Catherine Duer to Wm. Duer, Apr. 13, 1791, [Apr. 1791?], Duer Papers, NYHS.

39. Joseph Hardy to Wm. Duer, Nov. 18, Dec. 9, 13, 14, 15, 1790, Jan. 13, 25, Feb. 3, 19, May 13, 1791, Wm. Duer to James Adams, Dec. 8, 1790, to Matt. McConnell, Dec. 9, 1790, Duer Papers, NYHS.

40. Receipt signed by Wm. Duer to Walter Livingston, Jun. 18, 1791, Livingston Coll., NYHS; Statement of Account, Wm. Duer with George Sutton, Dec. 1790 to Feb. 1791, Duer Papers, Box VIII, NYHS.

41. Mitchell, *Hamilton*, II, 104; Miller, *Hamilton*, 261-62, 267-69; Bray Hammond, *Banks and Politics in America* (Princeton, 1957), Chap. 5 is an authoritative account; L[aban] Bronson to Wm. Duer, Jun. 27, 1791, "List of bank scrip purchased through George Sutton on account Wm. Duer, Aug. 1, 1791," Duer Papers, Box V, NYHS: Davis, "Duer Essay," Appendix B, 341.

42. Ibid., Appendix A, 340; James Madison to Thomas Jefferson, Jul. 10, 1791, Robert A. Rutland, et al., eds, *The Papers of James Madison* (Charlottesville, VA, 1983), XIV, 42-43; hereafter cited as Rutland, *Madison Papers*; "A Real Friend to Public Credit," *The Gazette of the United States* (Phila.), Aug. 13, 1791; Alexander Hamilton to Rufus King, Aug. 7, [17?], 1791, Syrett, *Hamilton Papers*, IX, 75-76; Hamilton's suggested prices were: scrip, $195, 6 percents, twenty-two shillings, 3 percents,

twelve shillings, deferreds, twelve shillings, eight pence; Wm. Duer to Alexander Hamilton, Aug. 16, 1791, ibid., XXVI, 617-18; *The Daily Advertiser* (New York), Aug. 17, 1791; Alexander Hamilton to Wm. Duer, Aug. 17, 1791, Syrett, *Hamilton Papers*, IX, 74-75; see also, Robert Troup to Alexander Hamilton, Sep. 12, 1791, ibid, XXVI, 622-23.

43. Alexander Hamilton to William Seton, Aug. 15, 16, 1791, ibid., IX, 68-69; *State Papers: Finances*, I, 112.

44. Burton A. Konkle, *Thomas Willing* (Phila., 1937), 143; Wm. Duer to ?, Oct. 27, 1791, Duer Papers, NYHS.

45. Receipt of John Henry, Aug. 27, 1791, Wm. Duer to Hugh Peebles, Jun. 17, 1791, Duer Papers, NYHS; Gouverneur Morris to William Constable, Jan. 8, 1791, John Jay Papers, CUL; James Madison to Thomas Jefferson, Aug. 4, 1791, Rutland, *Madison Papers*, XIV, 65; William Constable to Robert Morris, Jul. 17, 1791, Constable Papers, NYPL; Statements of Account of Wm. Duer with George Sutton, with John Ireland, Jul.-Sep. 1791, Duer Papers, Box IV, NYHS.

46. Joseph S. Davis, "Eighteenth Century Business Corporations in the United States," *Essays in the Earlier History of American Corporations* (Cambridge, 1917), I, Chaps. I, II, esp. 80-91, Appendix B; see also Walter Rutherfurd to John Rutherfurd, Feb. 5, 1792, Rutherfurd Coll., NYHS for contemporary reaction to the banking craze; Henry Remsen to Thomas Jefferson, Apr. 23, 1792, Thomas Jefferson Papers LC, is an especially complete account of all the various forms of speculation which were going on in New York in the late winter and early spring of 1792.

47. Walter Rutherfurd to John Rutherfurd, Nov. 27 [letter of Nov. 25], 1791, Rutherfurd Coll., NYHS; Ruth L. Higgins, *Expansion in New York* (Columbus, OH, 1931), 141-42; Agreement between Wm. Duer and Alexander Macomb, Dec. 29, 1791, Duer Papers, BV II, NYHS; see "The several answers of Benjamin Seixas Defendant," Jul. 24, 1794, Livingston Coll., 26, NYHS for further details of the partnership.

48. Alexander Macomb to William Constable, Jan. 1, 1792, Constable Papers, NYPL: "Wm. Duer, Memorandum," Nov. 16, 1791, Livingston Coll., NYHS.

49. Alexander Macomb to Wm. Duer, Jan. 1, 1792, Duer Papers, BV II, NYHS; Mitchell, *Hamilton*, II, 171; Wm. Duer to Walter Livingston, Jan. 10, 179[2], Livingston Coll., NYHS; Alexander Macomb to William Constable, Jan. 1, 11, 1792, Constable Papers, NYPL; see also Seth Johnson to Andrew Craigie, Jan. 22, 1791, Craigie Papers, AAS, for evidence that Duer convinced New Yorkers he was buying heavily in Bank of New York stock; Wm. Duer, Alexander Macomb and Isaac Whippo to Benjamin Walker, Jan. 28, 1792, Simon Gratz Coll., HSP.

50. William Constable to Alexander Macomb, Feb. 12, 1792 (two letters), Constable Papers, NYPL.

51. Alexander Macomb to William Constable, Feb. 21, 1792, Daniel McCormick to William Constable, Mar. 7, 1792, Constable Papers, NYPL; Seth Johnson to Andrew Craigie, Apr. 15, 1792, Craigie Papers, AAS; "An Act to incorporate . . . [BUS]," Feb. 25, 1791, "An Act supplementary . . .," Mar. 2, 1791, *Annals*, 1 Cong., Appendix, 2375-82; Walter Livingston to Wm. Duer, Jan. 18, 1792, see also John Pintard to Walter Livingston, Jan. 19, 1792, Wm. Duer to Walter Livingston, Feb. 3, 1792, Articles of Agreement between Walter Livingston and Wm. Duer, Feb. 18, 1792, Wm. Duer to Walter Livingston, Feb. 27, [1792], Livingston Coll., NYHS.

52. Wm. Duer in account with John Dewhurst, Feb. 20, 1792, loc. cit. see above, 191; Minute Book, SUM, Jan. 17, 18, 19, 20, 21, 1792, Paterson (NJ) Public Library; Wm. Seton to Wm. Duer, Mar. 29, 1792, Livingston Coll., NYHS; *The Daily Advertiser* (New York), Jan. 31, 1792. Seth Johnson to Andrew Craigie, Mar. 25, 1792, Craigie Papers, AAS.

53. Henry Remsen to Thomas Jefferson, Apr. 23, 1792, Jefferson Papers, LC; Bank of New York, Minute Book, Mar. 8, 1792 (see Dec. 1791 through Mar. 1792 for the opinions of bank officers), Corporate Documentation, Bank of New York Archives; Wm. Duer to Jeremiah Wadsworth, Mar. 12, 1791 [1792?], Jeremiah Wadsworth

Papers, CHS; Clement Biddle to George Lewis, Mar. 11, 1792, Clement Biddle Letter Book, HSP.

54. Oliver Wolcott, Jr. to Richard Harrison, Mar. 12, 17, 1792, Oliver Wolcott Papers, CHS; Alexander Hamilton to Wm. Duer, Mar. 14, 1792, Syrett, *Hamilton Papers*, XI, 131-32; Wm. Duer to Alexander Hamilton, Mar. 18, 1792, in Allen M. Hamilton, *The Intimate Life of Alexander Hamilton* (London, 1910), 272; see the Hardy letters cited above, n. 39, for some of the Treasury's earlier efforts, see also, N. Eveliegh to Wm. Duer, Mar. 4, 1791, Duer Papers, NYHS; see "Explanation of Accounts, 1792-1794," Oliver Wolcott, Jr., Comptroller, RG 217, NA, for a statement of some of the monies owed by Duer.

55. Walter Livingston to Wm. Duer, Mar. 16, 23, 1792, Livingston Coll., NYHS; "Letter of a New York Gentleman to a Friend in Hartford, Mar. 20, 1792," *The Diary* (New York), Apr. 17, 1792; *The Daily Advertiser* (New York), Mar. 19, 20, 21, 23, 1792.

56. Wm. Duer to Walter Livingston, Mar. 22, 1792, Livingston Coll., NYHS; Seth Johnson to Andrew Craigie, Mar. 25, 1792, Craigie Papers, AAS.

Chapter VII

The Speculator Fallen: Debtors' Prison

March 1792–May 1799

From the sanctuary of his prison cell, Duer addressed his creditors with a public notice which was as significant for what it omitted as for what it included. It contained a promise to make a settlement within nine months by which the principal and legal interest of all debts would be paid. But the mode of settlement was not spelled out nor was it made clear how Duer would be able to pay in December what he was not able to pay in March, with the added burden of interest which had accumulated in the interval. He proposed to settle first with widows and orphans, the largest group to be hit by any financial setback, or so it would seem, and those "to whom any considerable delay would operate as a ruin," presumably the small lenders who had taken Pintard and others' offers of usurious interest. No distinction was made in the announcement between such notes and those bearing legal interest, other than specifying that only legal interest would be paid. He also promised to stay in prison until a complete settlement had been made, thus offering his body as a surety, where previously his word had been sufficient. In an excusing preface, he ascribed his imprisonment to "the malice of open enemies and the insinuations of supposed friends" which had "chilled the first glow of benevolence" by some of Duer's creditors. It was now up to him to guard his reputation and the interest of all his creditors—"A sacred trust!" On the 28th, he distributed a handbill advising "Widows, Trustees of Orphans, Mechanics or Tradesmen" holding his notes to show them to William S. Livingston, a preliminary step for settlement. Some of his creditors may have been reassured by this, although the categories listed—

185

conspicuously excluding Madame McCarty—make it look more
like window dressing than anything else. Duer's reference to
enemies cutting him down after the "first glow of benevolence"
was not, however, just another excuse put forward by someone
who had been brought down as much by the sheer scope of his
operations as any other circumstances. As noted, some of the
Livingstons, especially Brockholst and John, had been among
the major sellers in the time immediately before Duer's failure.
When that event appeared likely, some proposed that the various
speculators forget their different positions and aid Duer on the
assumption that the chain reaction his failure might set off would
cause deeper losses to more people than any reconciliation of
contracts and accounts. The Livingstons, whose cooperation was
essential, defeated the proposal, expecting to divide the spoils,
that is their creditor-shares of Duer's assets, while avoiding failure
themselves. As the panic set off by Duer's failure unfolded, Brockholst admitted he had never been so wrong as when he refused
to help the fallen speculator. Although Livingston did not fail,
there was little in the way of spoils to divide.[1] One major reason
for Duer entering prison was to guarantee his personal safety.
The usurious loans had been made by persons whose knowledge
of the operations of high finance was quite limited. Their resentment, however, at losing not only the absurdly high interest
promised, but their principal as well, was unlimited. As early as
26 March, Duer had asked Walter Livingston to enlist a few
acquaintances from the waterfront to take some unspecified "measures" which would prevent the jail from being mobbed. Several
visitors testified that the prospect of mob violence seemed to be
what most upset Duer. Seth Johnson pitied him for "the state
of mind he is in is dreadful & must if not changed wear him
down." His distress did not come from remorse, "for I fear he
has none,—but from expecting that attempts will be made to
take him out and massacre him." These fears were not foolish,
for on 9 April, a crowd gathered outside the jail and "Stoned
the Building a little." A thunderstorm cut short this display of
ill temper, but it convinced some New Yorkers that more was in
prospect. "Citizen" caused a broadside to be printed and distributed in the city, urging the creditors of Duer, Macomb, and
Livingston to form a committee and make definite plans of repayment; this might convince those who had been hurt that "mis-

fortune, and not guilt" had caused the present distress. Anyone interested in avoiding further disorder would have been well advised to follow "Citizen's" proposals, for on the 18th a large crowd again gathered outside the jail and "seemed to be in great earnest about taking Mr. D—r, and using him in the genteelest manner circumstances would admit of." The circumstances seemed to admit of no gentility at all to the sheriff, who had some difficulty dispersing the mob, which was reported to have been chanting the unlikely cry: "We will have Mr. D—r, he has gotten our money." On the 19th, the New York City Common Council referred to the "riotous assemblage" outside the prison and urged respectable citizens to stay away from the prison and keep those under their authority away also. Henry Remsen, Jefferson's former clerk at the State Department, offered a different perspective on these disorders when he reported to the secretary that someone had distributed handbills about the city "exciting the citizens to inflict punishment on the authors of their wrongs, since they could obtain no redress." He believed those about the jail were mainly "boys & servants, who went from a notion of curiosity rather than a design of doing mischief," and that most of the violence resulted from the sheriff's ham-handed efforts to disperse a largely good-natured crowd. Whatever its origins, the crowds and the violence about the jail spread a perception among respectable citizens that the peace of the city was seriously threatened by the repercussions of Duer's fall.[2]

Neither of the reported disturbances, and there may have been unreported ones, did more than frighten Duer. Nor, ultimately, did one disgruntled creditor go any further, but he certainly threatened more than verbal violence. Pierre DePeyster, a local merchant, managed to confront Duer and challenged him with the unpleasant alternative of paying or fighting a duel. DePeyster, "pulling out a pair of pistols, told him to take his choice.... The gallant Colonel thought it most prudent to pay the 1,500 dollars and get rid of the Tory." Duer was not the only one to suffer from such individual attempts to secure satisfaction. One local resident reported her dismay at the "Speculators" fighting in the streets—"Cursing & abusing each other like pick pockets & trying every fraud to prey on each other's distress." And such ungentle conduct was not confined to the lesser speculators; *The Diary* recorded a violent encounter between "the privateers W[hi]p[p]o and M[acom]b, two noted ships belonging to admiral D[ue]r's fleet, which lasted for some considerable time," only to be broken up by the personal intervention of Mayor Richard Varick. Duer's panic threatened not only the economic life of the city, but also seriously strained its social fabric.[3]

Just how much did it take to upset New York and New Yorkers so much, and how serious was the effect of Duer's failure? One place to start is an estimate of how much he owed when he went under. As Duer did his best to avoid a final settlement and his records, by his own admission, were incomplete and disordered even before he went to jail, no certain result is possible. Past estimates have varied from $3,000,000, which is probably too high, to $10,000, which is certainly too low. Shortly after his partner's failure, Walter Livingston put down Duer's total obligations as $750,000, of which Livingston believed himself responsible for one-half. Alexander Macomb thought he owed $1,000,000 on account of Duer and another contemporary estimate by an anonymous correspondent to *The Gazette of the United States* set Duer's liabilities down as $1,583,000. If contemporaries, interested contemporaries at that, could differ so widely, it is little wonder that later writers have differed almost as widely.[4]

Of the various estimates, Walter Livingston's should have been the most reliable; certainly his records were the most complete— owing to his concern over Duer's speculating, his basically good business habits, and his common sense. But his anxiety about being made to bear the major, if not the entire cost of settlement, compounded by Duer's behavior (to be treated presently), may also have led him to underestimate the total, so that he dismissed some claims before they were made. His figure then, may be too low. Alexander Macomb's figure of $1,000,000 is also suspect. Macomb, as should be obvious, was not fully aware of all that Duer was up to and his figure is too round to be based on records, which he admitted he did not possess. As his estimate included several amounts owed to institutions by way of co-signing Duer's notes, figures which were also counted separately, it can be cut to $600,000. The notes given to the small lenders, the ones bearing usurious rates of interest, were figured by Mrs. Duer's cousin, Walter Rutherfurd, to amount to $600,000, a figure Macomb acceded to. Duer owed the Bank of New York $79,000 plus an unknown sum to the Bank of the United States. But since the latter institution had helped to bring on the panic by severely restricting discounts late in February, it may have managed to get most of its loans back before Duer stopped payment. The claim of the Treasury of the United States, which had helped to bring the New Yorker down, consisted of $150,000 in indents of interest which Duer had not accounted for since his service to the Board of Treasury. To this was added whatever might be owing on his wartime contracts, a sum never finally calculated. Robert Troup had lent him $17,500, but had received deferred stocks as collateral. He owed George Sutton more than $100,000 in an account rendered in November 1792. The accounts of a number of other brokers associated with Duer in his final operations do not survive and they could easily have been as large. It is certain that George Knox, Royal Flint, Richard Platt, and Isaac Whippo were all seriously affected, if not brought down themselves, by their association with Duer. He had also taken $10,000 of the funds entrusted to him by SEUM to hire foreign mechanics and used it in his speculations. He had borrowed, through Alexander Macomb, $50,000 from SEUM, but gave collateral which was later sold. The direct losses to the Society were thus cut to $15,000. Melancton Smith, who frequently lent Duer small sums for short periods of time, was caught for $13,000 when he went to jail and Andrew Craigie, retired in Cambridge when the crash came, lost only $5,000 in securities and counted himself fortunate. Some of the Scioto bills were still out; David S. Franks could point to about $300 plus other undetermined amounts for which he was being sued and Benjamin Walker had never been paid, either expenses or salary, for his trip to Paris. Finally, Rufus Putnam was owed $2,861.42 for "cabbins" built for the emigrants at Gallipolis in 1790.[5] All this comes to a total of $2,002,860, a figure which should be treated with care, and certainly not accepted uncritically. Some debts are not included, others, especially the usurious notes, may be counted more than once, and some of the creditors or co-signers, as already noted, had their own reasons for over or underestimating the amounts in question. Also, some of these debts were covered by collateral which almost took care of the principal, as in the case of SEUM. While they have been counted in at the full amount, the actual loss to the creditor was substantially less or none at all. Some of

Duer's veteran creditors have also been excluded. John Holker, for example, never stopped trying to collect from Duer and Parker until his death reconciled the account, and figured a balance due him, in October 1795, of £11,935.17.11 (PA cy.) from Duer, or about $31,500.[6]

These losses, although no single person lost as heavily as Duer, were certainly substantial, if not ruinous, for others. Those immediately associated with Duer were among the first to go; John Pintard fled the city, Isaac Whippo, George Knox, and Royal Flint, all advertised for a meeting with their creditors before the end of March. In April, Richard Platt and Leonard Bleecker inserted the familiar advertisements.[7] Those most heavily involved with Duer, Walter Livingston and Alexander Macomb, survived the longest, the former by running away to his country home, the other because of his substantial resources, both financial and psychological. Before their experiences are covered, it would be good to make clear that the effects of the panic touched off by Duer's failure touched many more than just those immediately involved with him or who had lent him money. The speculation had been general enough to include merchants and others who had previously either stayed clear of the stocks or viewed them only as long-term investments. Henry Remsen believed that Duer's operations had been active enough to draw nine-tenths of the stock held for speculation to the city. There the steadily increasing prices early in 1792 tempted those who could borrow to buy at

> 22/, 23/ or 24 cash, and sold it to the company or Duer on credit, some payable for when delivered, and others payable for at a future day and deliverable immediately, for 25/, 26/ and 27/. There are others who bought for 22/ and sold for 24—the third purchaser sold for 25/—the fourth for 26/—the fifth for 27/ or 28—the last purchaser being the company [i.e., Duer's agents]. All these dealings were on credit. The company failing & the stock falling in value, much lower than the first price of 22/—every one of those persons lost, some their whole fortunes, others the greater part of it.

In this way, the shock to the artificial economy of the speculators spread throughout the city's real economy and produced a situation in which it seemed to Seth Johnson that "everything is afloat & confidence destroyed—this town has rec[eive]d a shock which it will not get over in many years—happy is the man who is far removed from the confusion & distress that prevails—Men look as if some general calamity had taken place." About the only false note Johnson hit was in the expected duration of the panic's effect on the city—it recovered in a matter of months, not years—but his overall impression seems valid.[8]

Since the Bank of the United States branch did not open until 1 April, the only bank in full operation before and after Duer's fall was the Bank of New York. Every six months, the Bank adjusted its accounts and declared a dividend (or not, as circumstances warranted). Contrasting its revenues in the six month periods before and after 1 May 1792 shows a drop of $19,438 in interest income (from $43,561), $2,449,192 in bills discounted (from $13,924,473), and $47,840,071 in cash received (from $73,633,224). When one recalls that the bank restricted discounts the previous fall and winter when the increasing speculation made its officers nervous and it had to defend itself against the plans for new banks, it is clear that these declines are from levels already affected badly by the frenzied trading in government bonds. Duer's panic obviously affected general economic activity and not just the speculators. His borrowing had so lowered the quantity of cash in circulation that, even before he entered jail, wheat had to be sold for a thirty day bill, rather than the cash which the seller preferred and expected. In early April, a citizen lamented the continued scarcity of cash "and as for confidence there is no such thing, not a grocer can get credit for a hogshead of sugar or a puncheon of rum." Although there was certainly some exaggeration in the reports of those making their way as best they could through the city's confused economy—"In point of public & private distress nothing can exceed the present – a plague, famine, or fire perhaps could not have done so much evil," Seth Johnson moaned in mid-April—the general economy of the city was affected for a time and persons who had nothing directly to do with either Duer or speculation suffered.[9]

Against his debts, Duer had substantial resources, some of which had already been pledged to specific creditors. The Bank of New York, in notifying Duer of the balance owed, also noted that the stocks deposited as collateral seemed adequate to discharge the debt and that the bank would simply wait for a more advantageous time to sell them and satisfy the obligation. Within a year, the bank was able to note that the obligations of both Duer and Livingston had been satisfied. The SEUM was in almost as fortunate a position. But few of Duer's other creditors were, especially the holders of the usurious notes. Deeds for extensive tracts of land in New York and some acreage in Vermont, plus a quantity of stocks, had been delivered to Walter Livingston as security for the notes he had co-signed. Before the end of the year, William Bingham of Philadelphia bought Duer's share of the Maine land speculation, ending some confused negotiations between Duer and Knox who wanted to take over the former's share. (Unfortunately, the money received from this sale was invested with James Greenleaf, who also went broke; his undoing was land speculation in the District of Columbia.) Duer's share of the *America* had already been signed away. He owned the land at Fort Miller, his residence in New York City, and some other city lots, as well as scattered tracts here and there, for example, a one-fifth share in a farm outside of Philadelphia which was sold in 1795, netting Duer $1,000. A measured, prudent liquidation of these assets could possibly have paid off the principal creditors, and while few, if any, of them would have been paid in full, he nevertheless might have been able to regain his freedom. Under the legislation that was in effect in New York State at that time, if creditors of three-quarters of the value of Duer's debts agreed to a settlement, the balance would have been discharged and he could have resumed normal life and attempted to re-enter the business world.[10] But, that would have been the prudent thing to do. When had Duer ever followed a prudent course of action?

With the possible exception of Macomb, Walter Livingston was the most extensive guarantor of Duer's notes and, recognizing his importance, Duer did not stint in giving him advice and encouragement, but little more. All that had to be done, Livingston was told and retold, was for the two of them to stand together. He was to make plans with no one but Duer and answer no one's questions but Duer's; enemies were lurking behind every IOU, or so it seemed, and if they were not careful, the security held by Livingston would be wasted, instead of satisfying all proper obligations, as could be done. Livingston announced his own insolvency on 26 March. In his announcement, he stated that he had been persuaded by Duer's apparent prosperity into guaranteeing notes which Duer could not now pay. Although the security Duer had given him was adequate, it consisted of land and stocks which, all reasonable persons would admit, could not be sold advantageously at that time. Any settlement would have to wait for a restoration of public confidence. In the meantime, creditors could confidently rely on the word of a man "whose personal pursuits have neither been imprudent or unprosperous." Hidden in this was Livingston's determination to postpone for as long as possible, perhaps avoid forever, honoring his obligations. He wanted to hold back because he feared the security would not be adequate and he would be forced to pay substantial sums from his own property. This holding back was also what Duer wanted. He had already thrown a cloud over all the notes co-signed by Livingston by asserting that some had been negotiated at usurious interest and would have to be taken care of by a general arrangement (a euphemism for paying only a portion of the principal). None of the security, Livingston was advised, could be used for them. First, Duer urged, they had to take care of public institutions; despite the money he owed to SEUM, Duer seemed to include only the Bank of New York in this category; "let us . . . unite our Exertions to make the Bank secure."

As soon as this was done, they could start on a plan, an infallible one Duer had devised to raise the value of the securities Livingston held. Because he relayed this marvelous plan to his unhappy co-signer orally, exactly what it was is not known. However, some idea of its value can perhaps be seen in Livingston's flight, despite what he said was a serious illness, to his country estate shortly after being told of it. This much more pleasant alternative to debtors' prison did not end the talk of effecting some kind of settlement; it just made it easier for Livingston (and Duer) to postpone any real effort to pay the creditors.[11]

Duer used the expected (or hoped-for) intervention of Secretary Hamilton to try and reassure Livingston. In mid-April, he advised him to publish a plan of repayment, any plan "by which we can gain Time till Hamilton arrives." Nor were the two speculators the only ones who looked for the secretary's arrival; Mrs. Henrietta Colden also believed that only his presence would calm the city's temper. But Hamilton, probably recognizing what a political liability Duer had become, found it impossible, perhaps conveniently so, to leave Philadelphia. The hapless speculator would have to be content, if he really wanted only the secretary's advice and not his interested intervention, with counsel by mail.

This he got in abundance. Hamilton believed that friends who depended only on Duer's good name when they lent should be first in line when he paid off his creditors. Next were public institutions; "on this point, the manufacturing society will claim peculiar regard. . . . The public interest and my own reputation are deeply concerned in the matter," he confided. The government should be third in line. The secretary then went on to make several nice distinctions between people who sold stock to Duer or who had lent him money at usurious interest, making the conventional division between widows and orphans and the "mere veteran usurers." But, then, as if to make unnecessary his previous advice, he counseled Duer to pay off the first two categories of creditors and give the remainder of his property to a court. "The law will do the rest." He closed by urging Duer to be "honorable, calm, and firm." This unexceptionable advice was all the help Duer received from Hamilton, whose department allowed no further laxity in its claims against him.[12] Although Hamilton would assist him later, especially in the last year of his life, with small loans (really gifts), as long as he was secretary, he kept a discreet distance from the imprisoned speculator.

None of this, of course, helped Duer and Livingston, but it is doubtful that anything except scandalous intervention by federal and state authorities could have helped Duer. A week after he went to prison, Seth Johnson predicted correctly that Duer would do all he could to avoid a settlement: "I am fearful he can not, or means not, to do well. . . . I doubt his ever doing anything of consequence." Johnson's prediction (and Livingston's apprehension) was borne out by what followed between the speculator and his unhappy guarantor. Livingston justified his flight from the city by a well-founded fear of physical harm, the demands of creditors for twenty shillings to the pound and full interest for a year, and the call of the Bank of New York for $7,000 immediately. According to Livingston, this meant the loss of his share of the family estates, plus all personal property, thus leaving his family with no means of support. No one could expect this. To satisfy his obligations on behalf of Duer, he offered land valued by him at $330,000 plus his interest in the *America*, counted in at $120,000, for a total of $450,000. Duer showed how he meant to deal with Livingston by placing an advertisement in a New York paper promising, in Livingston's name, that he would soon make definite propositions to his creditors. Livingston knew nothing of it until he read it in the paper. He whimpered to his cousin, William Schuyler Livingston, that Duer had answered none of his letters and that William must see to it that Walter got a copy of anything Duer proposed in his name before it was published. If this was not done, "I shall cut a very sorrowful figure in the Eyes of the Public." The best face that can be put on this is that Duer was assuming his advice to Livingston to leave things to him was being followed. But Livingston, although distraught, was not so foolish as to do that, especially since Duer's ideas sometimes backfired. He once suggested they take advantage of the usury law to cancel some of the outstanding notes and Livingston allowed his son-in-law, Philip H. Livingston, to mention this around the city; "the idea of your intending to take advantage of a quirk of the law exasperated" some hitherto friendly creditors so much that the plan was immediately dropped. What Livingston mainly seemed to fear was that he would sell Duer's security, satisfy all of what appeared to be the outstanding claims, and then be presented with additional claims he would have to pay out of his own pocket. Since Duer never provided a comprehensive listing of accounts, balances due and the like, Livingston never did know where he stood and may have had cause to fear.[13]

Duer's advice to Livingston followed a fairly constant pattern. He urged him to make no general arrangements, do everything together with him, let him direct things and, above all, keep what he held as security and its value, a secret. If this was done, both would come out well; if this was not done, both could be ruined. Livingston's reaction to this also followed a fairly constant pattern. If all was going to be well, he asked, why did Duer not let him know just where he stood. All the lists of creditors supplied so far had been incomplete or had listed incorrect amounts. He pointed to several steps which Duer could take which would relieve the pressure on him, but which for unknown reasons, Duer refused to take. The reasons were unknown because, as usual, Duer often failed to answer letters. The delay was costing them money. In August 1792, some of the usurious notes were selling around the city for pennies on the pound; Duer's refusal to buy them risked their later validation by a court for principal and legal interest. The answer to Livingston's complaints and queries could only be that Duer was not really interested in reaching any settlement with his creditors, for it would probably deprive him of just about all his fortune. Still a speculator, a gambler, Duer was betting his own (and Livingston's) wealth on the possibility of keeping back a sizeable portion of his assets from any settlement of his affairs.[14]

In October 1792, Henry Livingston tried to negotiate a settlement on behalf of his brother. For a while, all went well, but then Duer began to raise objection after objection. He doubted Walter was committing all the security he had been given. Then he took umbrage at Walter's intention to seek release from the debts by way of the state bankruptcy law. An exasperated Henry finally declared that "as far as the propositions [of] Duer be assured he never meant (in my opinion) to take them into effect." Almost a year later, Duer proposed another general settlement, one which put a 1769 mortgage on his Fort Miller property, held by his married sister, first on the list of obligations to be paid; this effort collapsed when he was not satisfied that the mortgage would indeed be the first obligation paid.[15] In 1794, Livingston lost patience with Duer and transferred his interest in the family estate to Henry and Philip Henry Livingston, his brother and son-in-law respectively. He then moved to sell lands in Tioga and Herkimer Counties which Duer had given him as security. Duer managed to block the sale temporarily with an injunction which was dissolved by Walter's cooperative cousin, Robert R. Livingston, Chancellor of the State of New York, the state's highest judicial official. Although the dissolution was quite proper and in order, Walter urged the sheriff of Herkimer County to execute the sale with as little publicity as possible, probably because he feared more delaying moves by Duer. With the proceeds of the sale, Livingston was able to satisfy most of the judgments against him and get largely free of Duer.[16]

Daniel McCormick, an officer of the Bank of New York, on hearing of Duer's imprisonment, noted that "Numbers of people will be ruined." He was very likely thinking of Duer's speculating associates, not those removed from the new mania, and, of course, he was correct. John Pintard, who had been principally responsible for securing the usurious notes from the grocers and working people, found it expedient to leave the state. Some, believing Pintard's claims when he solicited the loans that Duer had lodged sufficient security with him, condemned him for not paying up out of that security, while others assumed he was lying all along. Either way, Seth Johnson's verdict that he was "a perfect swindler" was shared by many. Pintard handed over what he said was all the property Duer had left with him and fled to New Jersey where he worked as a commissioner on bridge and surveying projects. Even there, he was not beyond the reach of angry creditors and spent thirteen months in debtors' prison in Newark. He finally put the Duer episode behind him by taking advantage of the federal bankruptcy law of 1800 and returned, becoming an influential merchant and public figure in New York. Richard Platt tried to take advantage of New York's bankruptcy law in 1796, but failed, only to succeed with the federal law in 1800. Isaac Whippo also fled the city in April, reputedly carrying a sum of money with him; brought back to town, he never recovered solvency and was said to have crept away to Holland in 1794. John Dewhurst used Pennsylvania's liberal bankruptcy law to re-establish himself in Philadelphia in 1794. Some, although seriously affected, managed to make it through without either prison or bankruptcy. George Knox was operating in the city again by August 1792. In April, Seth Johnson listed five big speculators hurt badly by the panic, but all five made it through, with "nothing lost save honor," as a later Wall Street operator would put it.[17]

Just as it took some of Duer's associates years to re-establish themselves (if they made it at all), it also took New Yorkers a long time to forget the accusations of bad dealing made in 1792. Four years later, when an attempt was made to lighten New York's laws concerning debt and bankruptcy, the developing Republican interest refused to support it. Their refusal was owing partly to a conviction that men like Duer and Alexander Macomb should not be allowed to escape debtors' prison, a possible consequence of the proposed revisions. New Yorkers would seem to have had good reason for their anger, even if it did take on a political color later. As Duer was entering prison, Macomb was smilingly reassuring acquaintances that he was "perfectly safe in whatsoever he put his name to and that he had nothing to do with the Bills or Notes after he signed them. The holders had a right to do what they pleased with them." However, this blithe disregard for legal and moral obligations did not tell the whole story. Macomb confided to William Constable his fears as to the repercussions of Duer's wild, usurious borrowing, of which he claimed to be unaware. "I lament my having ever had to do with this damned Duer . . . if this business should bring me to distress. . . . Indeed, it will be hard." So, rather like the unjust steward in the New Testament parable, he went about collecting what he could, receiving, for example, quantities of stocks on 2 April, promising to pay on the 13th, in the meantime, sending the stocks off to Great Britain on a packet to fulfill a contract there. He sent other property beyond the reach of New York creditors. On the 11th, Macomb stopped payment, facing a number of contracts payable on the 15th, in addition to the promises to pay on the 13th, which he had made on the 2nd. Later, it came out that he had secured some British correspondents, Phynn, Ellice & Co. and others for near £90,000. In place of his private estate, he blithely offered "£4,000 in Hyson & Souchong Teas @9/2d/ lb. . . . The Creditors, & indeed the whole Town are much exasperated against him," for good reason, it would seem. He entered debtors' prison on 18 April, where he had time to ponder his foolishness and formulate new and precise moral distinctions: "This damn'd Speculative concern appears more like gambling than anything else, and as I never made any of the Engagements or negotiated any of the accursed business myself I do not feel the same obligation morally on account of it as I do to that business which I transacted myself – and yet many suffer greatly by this same unfortunate concern." One wonders how he would have felt if his speculative gamble had turned out well instead of badly. Whatever state his conscience might have been in, he was able to draw on temporal as well as spiritual resources and in February 1793, Seth Johnson noted that a Mr. Clason had bought up enough of Macomb's notes to set the repentant free. The purchases were made at about 25 percent of face value and payable in six, nine, or twelve months.[18]

New Yorkers were not the only ones to suffer in Duer's panic. Johnson commented blandly that a number of the "Connecticut group" lost as a result of Duer's operations and speculators in Boston and Philadelphia also felt the tremors. But, perhaps as a sign that even speculators still worked within local or regional economies, the effects in the other northern cities were not nearly as severe as in New York City. For example, in Philadelphia, while operators feared repercussions as soon as they heard of Duer's reverses, the first reference to tangible effects was not until mid-April when Ebenezer Hazard noted that "the evil had reached this city: some bankruptcies have taken, more are expected, and *many* [orig. emph.] people will be hurt." Within three weeks, however, the experienced speculator, Narlbro Frazier rejoiced that "things in general wear a much better aspect than they did 10 days or a fortnight past," and stocks had recovered nicely with 6 percents bringing twenty one shillings. All along, William Bingham had seen that the troubles would pass quickly and he advised a friend in New York that "Great Speculations might now successfully be made by those who have the Command of Money," a condition few New Yorkers enjoyed at that time.[19]

One "person" affected by the fall in the price of government bonds, yet not suffering a lack of ready cash, was the government itself. As in the previous August, Hamilton decided to enter the market in an attempt to raise prices. This could not aid Duer, who was past redemption, nor was it done in a manner designed to aid any particular speculator; rather, the secretary's purpose was to cut short the panic and restore public confidence as soon as possible. He feared just what many were starting to write, both privately and publicly, that the events in New York City showed the basic unsoundness of Hamilton's policies, their unsuitability for a people bent on the bold experiment of republican government.[20] Such feelings or opinions could not be completely routed, but a return of prosperity and stable prices for government bonds would give them less credibility. Fears were running so strongly that just the rumor of Treasury purchases in Philadelphia gave prices a slight boost in New York, prompting Robert Troup to suggest that government purchases would be of "good Consequence here." Hamilton instructed William Seton, Cashier of the Bank of New York, the government's agent in the city, to purchase up to $50,000 of 6 percents if the price dropped below par. A meeting of the Commissioners of the Sinking Fund on 26 March authorized a further $100,000 with the same stipulation. (This was later extended to 3 percents and deferreds.) With later authorizations and extensions, Seton purchased almost $192,000, face value, of certificates for a little more than $151,000 in cash. Duer's panic, thus, profited the people of the United States collectively, almost $41,000. One purchase of $20,000, was made from a single, unnamed individual, but the rest were in amounts around $1,000. Thus no one in particular benefitted from the government's intervention. Rather, speculators in general and market prices were assisted. It might be pointed out that the purpose of the Sinking Fund, for which the purchases were being made, was to retire the public debt, not aid speculators or hold up prices. Yet Hamilton's total purchases for the year were for a little more that $364,000 (face value); thus, more than one-half of the Sinking Fund purchases for 1792 went to manage the market and only incidentally to retire the debt.[21]

Hamilton's concern for the political damage Duer's panic could do was well advised. During the height of the troubles, the newspapers were filled with moralistic essays denouncing the reckless and unjust plundering of the innocent carried on by the now deservedly fallen speculators. Earnest advice to reverse the funding operation so recently carried on, even to repeal the charter of the Bank of the United States appeared. Suggestions that dealing in government bonds and the like be forbidden appeared moderate alongside some of the more frenetic essays. James Madison, who had led congressional opposition to Hamilton's fiscal program, viewed all of this with alarm, a stance which had become almost second nature to him by now. His statements, along with those who supported him in Congress, were discounted as only to be expected. But Secretary of State Jefferson chose the spring of 1792 to renew his threats of resigning, mainly because of what he viewed as Hamilton's interference in his own department. He was also very concerned about the course of national policy and dwelt on his objections in a long letter to President Washington in May 1792. The recent troubles in New York City, still working their way through the city's economy, were attributed to "a corrupt squadron of paper dealers," some of whom had helped to push the funding and assumption through Congress. It is impossible to isolate these objections from the other areas touched on by Jefferson, but the major intent of the letter was to convince Washington to accept election for a second term. It is also impossible to say why Washington decided to stay for another term; as he had on other occasions, he simply let events take their course until his acceptance could be assumed. Thus it is possible that Duer's panic and the public feelings it aroused were among the factors which influenced the president to accept re-election, a decision few near him would have bet on in the spring of 1792.[22]

The New York State elections for assembly and governor were held in the spring of 1792, just as the panic's repercussions were being felt. It became a contest between George Clinton, governor since 1777, and Philip Schuyler, leader of the Federalists in the assembly. Clinton's opponent was actually John Jay, then serving as Chief Justice of the United States Supreme Court, who, in the best eighteenth-century tradition, sat out the election in his library lest he appear to be seeking votes. Nevertheless, one of the more talked about questions was the extent to which Jay was associated with Hamilton and, consequently, with his financial system to which Duer's failure, the subsequent disturbances, and panic were attributed. Duer's panic was thus used to try and stun Hamilton, who was not running for any office, in order to injure Jay. Clinton won a narrow victory after the ballots for three western counties were thrown out because they had been transported to the capital in an improper manner. The counties, whose votes were never tallied, were expected to be Jay's and could easily have swung the election to him. Despite Federalist and even some Republican cries of foul, Clinton remained in office. Duer's panic certainly had worked against Jay, but the election's result turned much more on the disputed counties than on any significant issues. After the election, Duer used his leisure in debtors' prison to argue against the discarding of the uncounted votes. Using the pseudonym "Gracchus," he went on for four essays, railing about Clintonian sins in an unsurprising and pedestrian manner. His political essays were no more successful than his financial speculations had been.[23]

Not all of Duer's financial operations while in debtors' prison were confined to fending off his creditors. Walter Rutherfurd believed he had received as much as $80,000 from various sources and frittered it away in various speculations with James Greenleaf. A large portion of that sum would have been the money received from Bingham for the Maine land contract. This was used to buy a cotton mill along the Bronx River in lower Westchester County; shortly thereafter the mill, along with a tract of land in Vermont, was sold to Greenleaf, a speculator whose career and end were similar to Duer's. The latter's services as a manager, both of the mill and of some of Greenleaf's speculations, were apparently included in the price. He was to receive $3,000 a year for seven years as well as one-quarter of the profits of any successful speculations. Seth Johnson reported the rumor of Duer having been allowed $18,000 commission on the first two operations he planned for Greenleaf. However well he may have handled Greenleaf's affairs, Duer could not rescue them from a debacle caused by speculation in land in the District of Columbia conducted jointly with Robert Morris. These brought Greenleaf (and Morris) down in 1796 and closed off that possible source of income. Duer apparently also thought of another try at western land speculation and sent an agent down into Kentucky to spy out the prospects. He reported that the confusion of titles and claims and counter-claims brought about by the Southern system of individual location and surveying made it almost impossible to guarantee a good title and the project was dropped.[24]

Further business reverses aside, Duer's life in prison was not too harsh. He had two rooms allotted to him, one of which he used as a kind of office in which two clerks worked. Food and clothing were purchased by the debtors, so he did not have to eat prison fare. Nor were the debtors confined with those imprisoned for criminal offenses, but instead occupied a separate wing. In their section, they allotted cells and settled quarrels among themselves in a kangaroo court for which Duer served as judge. While he was presiding, the most serious penalty the court imposed was to sentence one debtor to sleep in the stairwell for calling another's wife a whore. However, the culprit appealed to the sheriff and the sentence was set aside as unduly severe. Even in debtors' prison, there was a kangaroo appellate court.[25]

While Duer may have been released from prison for a time in 1797, it was only temporary, for he required a parole signed by Oliver Wolcott, Jr., then Secretary of the Treasury, in order to be released during a yellow fever epidemic in 1798. Although Wolcott may have intended this to be indefinite, it was interpreted strictly by the federal marshal and Duer was returned to prison. From there, early in 1799, he pleaded both his ill health and the needs of his family in asking for Alexander Hamilton's intercession. About the end of February or the beginning of March, he was released, a $45,000 bond signed by Robert Troup and William Hill guaranteeing his presence in the city. The illness, the major symptoms of which were an inability to urinate and extreme pain, grew worse in April when a relative noted he was experiencing a "putrid Fever." On 7 May 1799, he died.[26]

Shortly after his death, James Greenleaf discovered that Vermont law did not guarantee dower rights to widows and he ceased making some small payments based on such rights which he had been paying to Mrs. Duer. She asked him to resume in a series of artful letters in which she pleaded the "cruel Poignancy" of her situation, being reduced from a life of ease to being dunned herself by her late husband's creditors. She was no more successful with Greenleaf than her husband's creditors had been with him. Robert R. Livingston began a subscription within a month of Duer's death to help the widow and her eight children, but her cousin wondered if it was really needed. She had moved to a nice house on Chambers Street where she had two boarders at eighty pounds a year each, while the rent for the house was only eighty pounds a year. General Alexander's widow, "Lady Stirling," had the income from twenty shares of bank stock and lived with them. Walter Rutherfurd worried that the girls would be "brought up in Splendid [*sic*] and in Idleness." Whatever her true financial situation might have been, she improved it by marrying William Neilson, a quietly successful merchant, with whom she spent the balance of her years.[27] They were certainly a sober contrast to her life with Duer.

References

1. "Colonel Duer's proposition to his Creditors, March 24, 1792," *The Diary* (New York), Mar. 26, 1792; *Dunlap's Daily American Advertiser* (Phila.), Mar. 29, 1792; Henrietta Maria Colden to John Laurance, Apr. 11, 1792, John Laurance Papers, NYHS, hereafter cited as Laurance Papers; Seth Johnson to Andrew Craigie, Apr. 8, 1792, Craigie Papers, AAS. See Edwin R. Purple, *Genealogical Notes of the Colden Family in America* (New York, 1873), 11, 13 for identification of Mrs. Colden as the widow of Richard N. Colden (d. 1777), grandson of Cadwallader Colden, the colonial New York politician and scientist.
2. Wm. Duer to Walter Livingston, Mar. 26, 1792, William S. Livingston to Walter Livingston, Apr. 10, 1792, Livingston Coll., NYHS; Seth Johnson to Andrew Craigie, Apr. 15, 1792, Craigie Papers, AAS; *Dunlap's American Daily Advertiser* (Phila.), Apr. 16, 1792; *The Diary* (New York), Apr. 19, 20, 1792; Henry Remsen to Thomas Jefferson, Apr. 23, 1792, Jefferson Papers, LC; Benjamin Tallmadge to Jeremiah Wadsworth, Apr. 19, 1792, Wadsworth Papers, CHS. See Paul A. Gilje, *The Road to Mobocracy: Popular Disorder in New York City, 1763-1834* (Chapel Hill, NC, 1987), 83-85, for a broader treatment of these disturbances; there are some inaccuracies in Gilje's account.
3. "Written by an intimate friend of the author's, living near the city and personally acquainted with the people involved," to Thomas Jones, Apr. 3, 1792, in Thomas Jones, *History of New York During the Revolutionary War*, ed. E. F. DeLancey (New

York, 1879), II, 584; Henrietta Maria Colden to John Laurance, Apr. 11, 1792, Laurance Papers, NYHS; The Diary (New York), Apr. 11, 1792.

4. *Appleton's Cyclopedia of Biography* (New York, 1887), II, 245; "Colonel William Duer," *The Knickerbocker Magazine*, 40 (Aug. 1852): 101; Walter Livingston to Henry W. Livingston, Mar. 26, 1792, Livingston Coll., NYHS; Alexander Macomb to William Constable, Jun. 9, 1792, Constable Papers, NYPL; *The Gazette of the United States* (Phila.), Apr. 21, 1792; see also an anonymous writer's guess of $3,000,000 made to Thomas Jones, op. cit., III, 589.

5. Walter Rutherfurd to John Rutherfurd, Mar. 14, 1792, Rutherfurd Coll., NYHS; Wm. Seton to Wm. Duer, Mar. 26, 1792, Livingston Coll., NYHS; "Account 3508," Misc. Treas. Accounts, 1790-1894, Account Registered, Apr. 15, 1793, Blotter #15, 8411-12, "Explanation of Accounts, 1792-1794," Oliver Wolcott, Jr., Mar. 12, 1792, RG 217, NA; see "United States v. Wm. Duer, Daniel Parker, and John Holker," Aug. 1792 to Apr. 1799, Records of the Federal District Court, Eastern District of Pennsylvania, RG 21, NA for the government's unsuccessful case against Duer and friends; Wm. Duer—Robert Troup account, Mar. 16, 1792, Livingston Coll., 27, NYHS; Statement of Account with George Sutton, Nov. 2, 1792, Duer Papers, Box IX:, NYHS; SUM Minute Book, Apr. 20, 1792, Paterson (NJ) Pub. Lib.; Robin Brooks, "Melancton Smith: New York Anti-Federalist, 1744-1798," unpub. Ph.D. diss., Univ. of Rochester, 1964, 61-64; Entry, Wm. Duer, Jul. 13, 1796, Ledger "A," 1788-1798, 146, David S. Franks to Andrew Craigie, Apr. 20, 1792, Benjamin Walker to Andrew Craigie, Jul. 8, 1792, Craigie Papers, AAS; Rowena Buell, *The Memoirs of Rufus Putnam* (Boston, 1903), 116.

6. Account of Wm. Duer with John Holker, Oct. 31, 1795; see also John Holker to US Minister to France, Sep. 12, 1817, Dept. of St. Misc. Letters Calendar, RG 59, NA, for an attempt to enlist the minister's aid in collecting judgments on Daniel Parker.

7. Seth Johnson to Andrew Craigie, Mar. 25, 1792, Royal Flint to ___, Mar. 28, 1792, Craigie Papers, AAS; *The Daily Advertiser* (New York), Mar. 27, 29, 31, 1792; *The Diary* (New York), Apr. 17, 19, 1792.

8. Henry Remsen to Thomas Jefferson, Apr. 23, 1792, Jefferson Papers, LC; Seth Johnson to Andrew Craigie, Mar. 25, 1792, Craigie Papers, AAS.

9. "Settlement of the Books for the Dividend of May 1792, . . . for the Dividend of November 1792," Bank of New York, Financial Records, Bank of New York Archives; see "Prospectus for the Dividend of May 1793, . . ." loc. cit. for comment as to securing "the Debt of Duer & Livingston"; Benjamin Strong to Sebah Strong, Mar. 19, 1792, Strong Family Papers, NYHS; "A Friend" to Thomas Jones, Apr. 3, 1792, Thomas Jones, op. cit., II, 589-90; Seth Johnson to Andrew Craigie, Apr. 11, 1792, Craigie Papers, AAS.

10. William Seton to Wm. Duer, Mar. 26, 1792, Livingston Coll., NYHS; "Prospectus for the Dividend of May 1793," Bank of New York Financial Records, Bank of New York Archives; Henry Knox to Wm. Duer, Dec. 21, 1792, Knox Papers, XXXIII, MHS; Seth Johnson to Andrew Craigie, Mar. 25, 1795, Craigie Papers, AAS; Peter Coleman, *Debtors and Creditors in America* (Madison, WI, 1974), 123-24, see also 116-18 for New York State law concerning imprisonment for debt.

11. Wm. Duer to Walter Livingston, Mar. 23, 1792, Livingston Coll, NYHS; (11, cont.) *Dunlap's American Daily Advertiser* (Phila.), Mar. 29, 1792; see also "Public Statement by Walter Livingston of His Relations with William Duer, March 24, 1792," James Duane to Walter Livingston, Mar. 24, 1792; Duane seems to have composed the "Statement" and then declined to act for Livingston by pointing out his inexperience in cases of this sort; Wm. Duer to Walter Livingston, Mar. 24, 1792, Walter Livingston to Henry W. Livingston, Mar. 26, 1792, Wm. Duer to Walter Livingston, Apr. 9, 1792; see also Mar. 27-28, Apr. 1, 2, 1792, Livingston Coll., NYHS.

12. Wm. Duer to Walter Livingston, Apr. 14, 1792, Livingston Coll, NYHS; Henrietta Maria Colden to John Laurance, Apr. 11, 1792, Laurance Papers, NYHS; Alexander Hamilton to Wm. Duer, Apr. 22, May 23, 1792, Syrett, *Hamilton Papers*, XI, 325-26, 170-72.

13. [Seth Johnson] to Andrew Craigie, Apr. 1, 1792, Craigie Papers, AAS; Walter Livingston to Philip S. Livingston, Apr. 17, 1792, ___to William Schuyler Livingston, Apr. 17, 1792, Robert Troup to Walter Livingston, May 7, 1792, Walter Livingston to Wm. Duer, May 16, 1791, Livingston Coll., NYHS.

14. Wm. Duer to Walter Livingston, [May 19, 1792], Walter Livingston to Wm. Duer, May 20, Jun. 20, Aug. 8, 1792, Livingston Coll., NYHS.

15. Henry Livingston to Walter Livingston, Oct. 16, 1792, see also Oct. 11, 14, 28, 31, Nov. 4, 1792, Wm. Duer to Walter Livingston, Sep. 18, Dec. 2, 1793, Livingston Coll., NYHS; see above, 3, for the original mortgage. In 1788, 1789, Duer had attempted through Craigie and Parker to reach an agreement with George Rose, his sister's husband, about exchanging the mortgage for some American debt certificates. The attempt apparently failed because of Parker's inattention, see Andrew Craigie to Daniel Parker, Nov. 19, 1788, [Mar.—Apr. 1789], Craigie Papers, AAS. On Jun. 24, 1796, the mortgage was transferred to Hugh Peebles, Duer Papers, Box V, NYHS; earlier that year, Peebles had purchased the Fort Miller land for £3,200 NY ($8,127), see New York (State) Courts, Supreme Court of Judicature, Papers Relating to Wm. Duer, Jan. 30, 1796 (7), Feb. 24, 1796 (9), Mar. 23, 1796, (10), #10828, NYSL; also, William Hill to Hugh Peebles, Oct. 31, 1796, Misc. Ms., NYHS.

16. George Dangerfield, *Chancellor Robert R. Livingston* (New York, 1960), 280-81; Walter Livingston to William Calbrath, Apr. 17, Oct. 20, 1794, Livingston Coll., NYHS; note that Livingston was not totally free and that there were continuing quarrels over small balances, see his Letter Book and his "Memo & Acct. Book" for these transactions.

17. Daniel McCormick to William Constable, Mar. 24, 1792, Constable Papers, NYPL; Seth Johnson to Andrew Craigie, Mar. 25, 1792, Craigie Papers, AAS; Henry Remsen to Thomas Jefferson, Apr. 23, 1792, Jefferson Papers, LC; John G. Wilson, *John Pintard* (New York, 1902), 21-22; see also, David Sterling, "New York Patriarch: A Life of John Pintard, 1759-1844," unpub. Ph.D. diss., New York Univ., 1958; Richard Platt to Walter Livingston, Jul. 7, 1796, Livingston Coll., NYHS; Davis, "Duer Essay," 316; *The Diary* (New York), Apr. 17, 1792; Philip S. Livingston to Walter Livingston, Dec. 18, 1794, Livingston Coll., NYHS; Syrett, *Hamilton Papers*, XII, 31, n. 7; Seth Johnson to Andrew Craigie, Apr. 22, 1792, Craigie Papers, AAS; in 1797, a Savannah, Georgia, newspaper reported Whippo as in command of a Spanish privateer, active off the southern coast, still robbing his fellow citizens, *Columbian Museum*, Jun. 6, 1797, in Donald Stewart, *The Opposition Press of the Federalist Period* (Albany, NY, 1969), 64, hereafter cited as Stewart, *Opposition Press*.

18. Young, *Republicans*, 533; Daniel McCormick to William Constable, Mar. 24, 1792, Alexander Macomb to William Constable, Mar. 28, 1792, (see also, Apr. 7, 1792), Constable Papers, NYPL; Henry Remsen to Thomas Jefferson, Apr. 23, 1792, Jefferson Papers, LC; Seth Johnson to Andrew Craigie, Apr. 11, 1792, Craigie Papers, AAS; William Seton to Alexander Hamilton, Apr. 11, 1792, Syrett, *Hamilton Papers*, XI, 263-64; Seth Johnson to Andrew Craigie, Apr. 18, 1792, Craigie Papers, AAS; Alexander Macomb to William Constable, Jun. 6, 1792, Constable Papers, NYPL; Seth Johnson to Andrew Craigie, Feb. 25, 1793, Craigie Papers, AAS; others had even longer memories; in January 1800, while Congress was considering the federal bankruptcy law of that year, the Worcester, MA, *Independent Gazetteer* prayed: "May the laws ever prove mild and lenient to the unfortunate, but a scourge to Evil-DUERS." Stewart, *Opposition Press*, 64.

19. Seth Johnson to Andrew Craigie, Apr. 22, 1792, Craigie Papers, AAS; Philip Key to Matthew Blair, Mar. 28, 1798, Misc. Ms., NYHS; Ebenezer Hazard to Jeremy Belknap, Apr. 13, 1792, "Correspondence of Jeremy Belknap and Ebenezer Hazard," *Collections* of the Massachusetts Historical Society, 5 s., III (1877), 290; Narlbro Frazier to Andrew Craigie, May 9, 1792, Craigie Papers, AAS; Margaret L. Brown, "William Bingham, Eighteenth Century Magnate," *Pennsylvania Magazine of History & Biography*, 61 (1938): 405-406.

20. Seth Johnson to Andrew Craigie, Apr. 15, 1792, Craigie Papers, AAS; *The Weekly Museum* (New York), May 19, 1792 has a particularly virulent letter blaming Congress entirely for the recent speculative panic; James Madison to Edmund Pendleton, Mar. 15, Apr. 9, 1792, ___to Henry Lee, Apr. 15, 1792, Rutland, *Madison Papers*, XIV, 262-63, 280-81, 287-88; Thomas Jefferson to Henry Remsen, Apr. 14, 1792, Jefferson Papers, LC.

21. Robert Troup to Alexander Hamilton, Mar. 21, 1792, Syrett, *Hamilton Papers*, XI, 164 (following references are all to this vol.); Alexander Hamilton to William Seton, Mar. 25, 1792, 190-91; Meeting of the Commissioners of the Sinking Fund, Mar. 26, 1792, 193, Apr. 4, 1792, 224; William Seton to Alexander Hamilton, Mar. 26, 1792, 194-95; Alexander Hamilton to William Seton, Apr. 4, 1792, 225-26; William Seton to Alexander Hamilton, Apr. 9, 1792, 257-58; Alexander Hamilton to President & Directors of the Bank of New York, Apr. 12, 1792; Meeting of the Commissioners of the Sinking Fund, Apr. 12, 1792, 272; Alexander Hamilton to William Seton, Apr. 12, 1792, 272-73; William Seton to Alexander Hamilton, Apr. 16, 1792, 288-90; "Sinking Fund Purchases," Nov. 1792, *State Papers: Finance*, I, 166; see *Dunlap's American Daily Advertiser* (Phila.), Apr. 18, 1792 for the effect of these purchases: 6 percents went from 19/6d to 20/, 6 percents from 10/ to 12/, deferreds from 10/6 to 12/6.

22. The newspaper commentary is treated in Stewart, *Opposition Press*, Chap. II, *passim*; Thomas Jefferson to George Washington, May 23, 1792, Paul Leicester Ford, ed., *The Writings of Thomas Jefferson* (New York, 1895), VI, 1-6.

23. Young, *Republicans*, Chaps. 13, 14, 15, esp. 198 ff. for a reliable account of both elections; Alexander Macomb to William Constable, Jun. 15, 1792, Constable Papers, NYPL; see *The Weekly Museum* (New York), Apr. 7, 1792 for an example of the political advice given to "all honest mechanics and tradesmen"; the "Gracchus" essays were in *The Daily Advertiser* (New York), Jun. 15, 22, Jul. 3, 17, 1792; see "a Friend to Order," Jun. 19, 1792 for an identification of Duer as "Gracchus." Duer probably chose the name for the presumed association of the Gracchi with the cause of the people in late republican Rome.

24. [Walter Rutherfurd] to John Rutherfurd, May 20, 1794, Rutherfurd Coll., NYHS; Wm. Duer to James Greenleaf, Aug. 21–Dec. 8, 1794, seventeen letters, Etting Coll., HSP; Wm. Duer to James Greenleaf, Dec. 17, 29, 1794, Simon Gratz Coll., HSP; John Daniel to Wm. Duer, Nov. 31, 1794, Duer Papers, Box VI, "Contracts"; Wm. Duer to James Greenleaf, Dec. 12, 1794, Duer Papers, Misc. Papers, NYHS; Seth Johnson to Andrew Craigie, Apr. 18, 1795, Craigie Papers, AAS; M[edad?] Mitchell to Wm. Duer, Jan. 25, 1795, Duer Papers, NYHS.

25. Walter Rutherfurd to John Rutherfurd, Mar. 28, 1792, Rutherfurd Coll., NYHS; Duer Papers, Box IV, Debtors' Prison Papers, Box III, Bills, Receipts, Notes, 1791-97, NYHS.

26. Wm. Duer to Alexander Hamilton, Jan. 13, 17, Feb. 16, 1799, Syrett, *Hamilton Papers*, XXVI, 761-65; Walter Rutherfurd to John Rutherfurd, Jan. 14, Feb. 7, 24, Apr. 9, 18, 22, May 3, 1799, Rutherfurd Coll., NYHS.

27. Catherine Duer to James Greenleaf, Dec. 29, 1799, Jul. 11, Aug. 22, Sep. 29, 1800, Etting Coll., HSP; William Hill to Hugh Peebles, Oct. 31, 1796, Misc. Ms., William Hill, NYHS; William Barrett [John Scoville], *The Old Merchants of New York* (New York, 1885), III, 143.

Chapter VIII

Conclusion

William Duer's death while on parole from debtor's prison was an ignoble end to what could have been a career of service to his country which would have placed him alongside such men as John Jay, James Duane, and Robert R. Livingston. Certainly, his work in the New York State Convention and his service in the Continental Congress when the fortunes of that body and of America were at a very low point entitle him to respect. While he served the public, he served it well. Even the shortness of his public career should not be allowed to detract from its merit. Many civilians, even soldiers, drifted in and out of public service during the war for American independence, according to fluctuations in either their country's fortunes or their own. Until 1779, Duer was constant.

But early in his career, even while he was in the Convention, he showed his enduring tendencies to mix public business with private profit, and to take on more than either his energy or his other duties allowed, as when he undertook to purchase grain for Quartermaster-General Thomas Mifflin, while charged with several other tasks by the Convention. Duer was not unique; many others in public life mixed their private business with official duties. Few however, did it as consistently, on as grand a scale, or for as long a period of time as Duer. His seat in the Continental Congress was the only public office he held during which he did not engage in outside commercial activity. While in Congress, he was, for a time, among men completely strange to him and located far from where he had previously done business. While Congress was in York, little except public business could be done.

Although he may have concentrated on public business while in Congress, his service there set the stage for his attempt, in partnership with several public officials, to supply naval timber to allied countries. And his Army contracts would probably not have been awarded except for his friendship with Robert Morris or, at least, not awarded so easily. His service in Congress did not hurt his later economic activity. His next term of government service, that of Secretary to the Board of Treasury, was marked by flagrant misuse of his office for private, even illegal, gain. The Jarvis contract, the French debt syndicate, and the Scioto Company, all gained their original impetus from Duer's position. These, however, were slight transgressions when contrasted with his theft of the Treasury warrants and their conversion to his private use. No considerations of different ethical codes prevailing at the time or other factors can excuse that act. The organization of the federal government in 1789 and his appointment to the Treasury Department gave him the chance to continue his combination of speculation and public service. The fact that federal law forbade such trading while employed by the Treasury Department did not seem to deter him at all, but it may have been a cause of his early resignation in March 1790. From then until his financial collapse in March 1792, as an entirely private person, he could no longer blend his private business with public service, but there can be little doubt that people listened to Duer or joined with him partly because of his past association with Hamilton and the conduct of the government's finances.

Possibly more helpful to Duer's economic activities than his government service was his closeness with those government officials who administered his contracts. Robert Morris's eagerness to see Duer get a contract when the system was begun in 1781, his sacrificing of Sands, Livingston & Company when he did not have enough money to pay both New York contractors, and his general laxity in holding Duer to the exact terms of the contract (although Duer's performance probably did not fall scandalously short of what could reasonably be expected) were examples of this. Such aid was often given to Duer. Hamilton's ready granting of leave to Benjamin Walker when it appeared the Scioto Company's Paris agent was in trouble comes to mind, as does the apparent toleration of Duer's slipshod execution of the western Army contracts in 1791. A final example was the purchase of stock which William Seton made for the Treasury Department during the August 1791 fall in prices. Such aid helped Duer at several points in his career, particularly in his re-establishment in commercial life after serving in Congress, and his first serious check in stock speculating.

It is difficult to see that Duer's career had any permanent effect on the development of the American economy or changed in any way the relationship between government and business. He was not really an innovator, in that his major effort was given to land and stock speculation, the two common ways to quick and easy wealth for operators of his generation, or so they thought. Where he did differ from his contemporaries was in the audacity, the size and number of his speculations, not their kind.

His activity on behalf of the Society for Establishing Useful Manufactures was one path few of his generation followed; his motivation here was to do a favor for Hamilton and, most important, to see what speculative gains could be gotten out of it, not to blaze a path as a pioneer industrialist. Duer's fall did not permanently injure the Society's chances for prosperity. His theft of $10,000 and the loss of about $55,000 more caused by the panic itself, certainly checked the Society's early growth. But the United States of the 1790s lacked the markets, means of transportation, capital facilities, and myriad other components which make up the foundation of a modern industrial economy. Once these were supplied, American industry grew. The supplying, however, was the work of decades, not months. The Society was a hothouse flower that tried to grow outside; it was the chill winds of America's agrarian economy that stunted its growth, not Duer's speculations. Indirectly, those speculations did help provide the United States with a vital accessory to finance capitalism, an organized securities market. Appalled at the damage done to their own interests as well as the general economy of the city, a group of brokers devised in the "Buttonwood Tree Agreement" of April 1792, a primitive version of the modern "put and call" system of stock transactions. This would lead, eventually, to the organization of the New York Stock Exchange in the 1830s but, in the short run, it helped to calm down the market's swings and made more difficult the kind of collusive bidding which Duer had used to drive up stock prices during stock auctions.

The relationship between government and businessmen was not changed by Duer and his panic. The aid he received, the special favors expected by businessmen allied with the party in power, and the mixing of business and public service by office-holders remained common. Even the formulation of a code of ethics forbidding such special use of the government's powers and resources had to wait until the present century, and its development and application are still far from complete. Duer's career simply furnished the most spectacular example of the use of public office for private profit during the Confederation and early national periods of our history.

What remains to be examined is Duer's personal failure to redeem the bright promise that was apparent in 1776 and 1777. His career in elective office was short but effective. He left both the Convention and the congress with the apparent approbation of most of his colleagues. Yet from 1780 on, even when he served the public in an administrative capacity, he devoted himself almost completely to making money, sometimes abusing his official position to do so. Duer's service in the Assembly of New York in 1786 is no exception to this, as he concentrated almost exclusively on two bills affecting the economic interests of his class. The only plausible explanation for this failure to pursue further his political career is his desire to make money. There can be little doubt that he wanted to receive popular acclaim for public service, witness the effort given to composing the "Philo-Publius" essays. But Duer could never, as Alexander Hamilton could, forget his personal fortune in favor of the fortunes of his country.

Other patriots served in Congress or in their state legislatures and departed, enjoying a good reputation, to give themselves over to private business. What damned Duer in the eyes of his contemporaries was his failure. This was brought about, as most of his unsuccessful projects were, by his inability to concentrate on one thing and only one thing at a time, by his propensity to have too many hares in the chase as Holker aptly put it. He never lacked confidence in his own ability, but no man could hope to manage, as Duer was attempting in early 1792, the SEUM, the Maine land company, the remnants of the Scioto, an Army contract, a mercantile business, and his stock speculations. No one had to conspire to bring Duer down; the flaw was in his failure to recognize that he had limitations. He could have survived avarice or rashness, taken singly, but, combined in one temperament, they proved fatal.

Bibliography

PRIMARY SOURCES

Books

Adams, Charles Francis, ed. *Familiar Letters of John Adams and His Wife Abigail Adams During the Revolution*. New York: Hurd and Houghton, 1876.

Alvord, Clarence W. , ed. *Kaskaskia Records, 1778-1790*. Collections of the Illinois State Library, Vol. V; Virginia Series, Vol. II. Springfield, IL: Illinois State Historical Society, 1909.

Barnum, H. L. *The Spy Unmasked; or, Memoirs of Enoch Crosby, The Hero of Mr. Cooper's Tale of the Neutral Ground*. New York: J.& J. Harper, 1828.

[Boucher, Jonathan]. *The American Times, A Satire in Three Parts. In Which Are Delineated the Characters of the American Rebellion. Amongst the Principal Are. . . Duer. . . etc.* By Camillo Querno, Poet Laureate to the Congress. New York: James Rivington, 1780.

Bowling, Kenneth R., and Veit, Helen E., eds. *The Diary of William Maclay and Other Notes on Senate Debates*. Documentary History of the First Federal Congress of the United States of America. Baltimore: Johns Hopkins University Press, 1988. Vol. 9.

Boyd, Julian P., et al., eds., *The Papers of Thomas Jefferson*. 22 vols. Princeton, NJ: Princeton University Press, 1950-.

Brissot deWarville, J. P. and Etienne Claviere. *The Commerce of America with Europe; particularly with France and Great Britain . . . and Pointing out the Actual Situation of the United States of North America in regard to Trade, Manufactures, and Population*. London: J. S. Jordan, 1794.

Brissot deWarville, J. P. *New Travels in the United States of America*. 2nd ed., corrected. London: J. S. Jordan, 1794.

Buell, Rowena, ed. *The Memoirs of Rufus Putnam*. New York: Houghton Mifflin, 1903.

Burnett, Edmund C., ed. *Letters of Members of the Continental Congress*. 8 vols. Washington: Carnegie Institution of Washington, 1921-36.

Callendar, James Thompson. *Sketches of the History of America*. Philadelphia: Snowden and McCorkle, 1798.

———. *Sedgewick & Co. or A Key to the Six Per Cent Cabinet*. Philadelphia: The Author, 1798.

Cappon, Lester, ed. *The Adams-Jefferson Letters*. 2 vols. Chapel Hill: University of North Carolina Press, 1959.

Clarke, Matthew St. Clair and D. A. Hall, comps. *Legislative and Documentary History of the Bank of the United States*. Washington: Gales and Seaton, 1832.

The Public Papers of George Clinton, first governor of the State of New York, 1777-1795, 1801-1804. Introduction by Hugh Hastings, State Historian. 10 vols. New York: Wynkoop, Hallenbeck, Crawford Co., 1899-1904.

Cobbett, William. *Porcupine's Works; Containing Various Writings and Selections*. 12 vols. London: Cobbett and Morgan, 1801. Vol. I.

"Correspondence of Jeremy Belknap and Ebenezer Hazard." *Collections* of the Massachusetts Historical Society, 5 s., III (1877).

Cutler, William P., ed. *The Life, Journals and Correspondence of the Reverend Manasseh Cutler*. 2 vols. Cincinnati: R. Clarke and Co., 1888.

Dann, John C., ed. *The Revolution Remembered: Eyewitness Accounts of the War for Independence*. Chicago: University of Chicago Press, 1980.

Davenport, Beatrix Cary, ed. *A Diary of the French Revolution by Gouverneur Morris*. 2 vols. Boston: Houghton Mifflin, 1939.

Deas, Anne I., ed. *Correspondence of Mr. Ralph Izard*. New York: Charles S. Francis, 1844.

Duer, William Alexander. *Memoirs, Correspondence and Manuscripts of General Lafayette*. New York: Saunders and Otley, 1837.

———. *New York As It Was During the Latter Part of the Last Century*. An Anniversary Address delivered before the St. Nicholas Society. New York: Stanford & Swords, 1849.

_____. *Reminiscences of an Old New Yorker*. New York: W. L. Andrews, 1867.

Ezell, John S., ed. *The New Democracy in America: Travels of Francisco deMiranda in the United States, 1783-1784*. Translated by Judson P. Wood. Norman: University of Oklahoma Press, 1963.

The Federalist: A Collection of Essays Written in Favor of the New Constitution as Agreed Upon by the Federal Convention, September 17, 1787. 2 vols. New York: J. and A. M'Lean, 1788.

Fernow, Berthold, ed. *Documents Relating to the Colonial History of the State of New York*. Albany: Weed, Parsons & Co., 1887.

Fitzpatrick, John C., ed. *The Writings of George Washington*. 39 vols. Washington: Government Printing Office, 1931-38.

_____, ed. *The Diaries of George Washington*. 4 vols. Boston: Houghton Mifflin Co., 1925.

Foner, Philip S., ed. *The Complete Writings of Thomas Paine*. 2 vols. New York: The Citadel Press, 1945.

Force, Peter A., comp. *American Archives: A Documentary History of the United States of America*. 4th ser. 6 vols. Washington: M. St. Clair Clarke and Peter Force, 1837-1846. 5th ser. 3 vols. Washington: St. Clair Clarke and Peter Force, 1848-1853.

Ford, Paul Leicester, ed. *The Writings of Thomas Jefferson*. 10 vols. New York: G. P. Putnam's Sons, 1892-99.

Ford, Worthington C., ed. *Correspondence and Journals of Samuel Blachley Webb*. 3 vols. New York: no printer, 1894.

Gibbs, George, ed. *Memoirs of the Administrations of Washington and John Adams Edited from the Papers of Oliver Wolcott, Secretary of the Treasury*. 2 vols. New York: Printed for the Subscribers, 1846.

Graydon, Alexander. *Memoirs of His Own Time with Reminiscences of the Men and Events of the Revolution*. Edited by John Stockton Littell. Philadelphia: Lindsay L. Blakiston, 1846.

Hamilton, James A. *Reminiscences or, Men and Events At Home and Abroad During Three Quarters of a Century*. New York: Charles Scribner and Co., 1869.

Hamilton, John C. *History of the Republic of the United States of America as Traced in the Writings of Alexander Hamilton and His Contemporaries*. 2 vols. New York: D. Appleton and Co., 1857-1858.

_____, ed. *The Federalist*. 2 vols. Philadelphia: J. B. Lippincott & Co., 1865.

Hamilton, Stanislaus M., ed. *The Writings of James Monroe*. 7 vols. New York: G. P. Putnam's Sons, 1898-1903.

Henkels, Stanislaus V., ed. *The Confidential Correspondence of Robert Morris*. Philadelphia: The Editor, 1917.

Hill, William H., ed. *The Gibson Papers*. Washington County (N.Y.) Historical Society *Collections*, Nos. 1 (1954), 2 (1955), 3 (1956).

Hulbert, Archer B., ed. "Records of the Original Proceedings of the Ohio Company," *Marietta College Historical Collections*, Vols. 1, 2 (1917).

Institution of the Society of the Cincinnati . . . at the Cantonment on the Banks of the Hudson River, May, 1783 . . . A List of Officers and Members of the New York State Society. New York: J. M. Elliott, 1851.

Isham, Charles, ed. *The Deane Papers*. 5 vols. Collections of the New-York Historical Society. New York: Printed for the Society, 1886-1890.

Jones, Thomas. *History of New York During the Revolutionary War*. Edited by Edward Floyd DeLancey. 2 vols. New York: The New-York Historical Society, 1879.

King, Charles R., ed. *The Life and Correspondence of Rufus King*. 6 vols. New York: G. P. Putnam's Sons, 1894-1900.

The Lee Papers. 4 vols. New-York Historical Society Collections. New York: Printed for the Society, 1871-1874.

Letters and Other Writings of James Madison. 4 vols. New York: R. Worthington, 1884.

[Logan, George]. *Five Letters Addressed to the Yeomanry of the United States: On the Dangerous Scheme of Governor Duer and Mr. Secretary Hamilton to Establish National Manufactures*. By a Farmer. Philadelphia: Eleazer Oswald, 1792.

O'Callaghan, Edmund Bailey, ed. *The Documentary History of the State of New York*. 4 vols. Albany: Weed, Parsons & Co., 1850-1851.

_____, ed. *Calendar of Historical Manuscripts in the Office of the Secretary of State, Albany, New York*. 2 vols. Albany: Weed, Parsons & Co., 1865-1866.

Perroud, Cl., ed. *J.–P. Brissot, Correspondance et Papiers*. Paris: Librarie Alphonse Picard & Fils, 1912.

Phelps-Stokes, Isaac Newton, comp. *The Iconography of Man-hattan Island, 1498-1909*. 6 vols. New York: Robert H. Dodd, 1915-1928.

Rutland, Robert A., et al., eds. *The Papers of James Madison*. Charlottesville: University Press of Virginia, 1983. Vol. XIV.

Sabine, William H. W., ed. *Historical Memoirs of William Smith, 12 July 1776 to 25 July 1778*. New York: The Author, 1958.

_____, ed. *Historical Memoirs of William Smith, 16 March 1763 to 9 July 1776*. New York: The Author, 1956.

Shy, John, ed. *Winding Down: The Revolutionary War Letters of Lieutenant Benjamin Gilbert of Massachusetts, 1780-1783*. Ann Arbor: University of Michigan Press, William L. Clements Library, 1989.

Smith, William Henry, ed. *The Life and Public Services of Arthur St. Clair*. 2 vols. Cincinnati: Robert Clarke & Co., 1882.

Stevens, B[enjamin] F[ranklin], ed. *Facsimilies of Manuscripts in European Archives Relating to America, 1773-1783*. 25 Vols. London: Malby and Sons, 1889-1898.

Syrett, Harold C., ed. *The Papers of Alexander Hamilton*. 27 vols. New York: Columbia University Press, 1961-1987.

Wilkinson, James. *Memoirs of My Own Times*. 3 vols. Philadelphia: Abraham Small, 1816.

Articles and Pamphlets

"Correspondence between the Honorable Henry Laurens and His Son, John, 1777-1780," *The South Carolina Historical and Genealogical Magazine*, 6 (1905): 3-11, 47-52, 103-10, 137-60.

"[Marquis Phillippe] DuCoudray's Observations on the Forts Intended for the Defense of the Two Passages of the River Delaware, 1777," *Pennsylvania Magazine of History and Biography*, 24 (1900): 343-47.

[Duer, William]. "Address to the Inhabitants of Alexandria and other Sea Ports in the United States of America, from a Proprietor of Lands on the Scioto." no place, no printer, 1790.

Jordan, John W., ed. "Narrative of John Heckewelder's Journey to the Wabash in 1792," *Pennsylvania Magazine of History and Biography*, 12 (1888): 34-54, 165-84.

"Letters from the Marquis deLafayette to Honorable Henry Lau-

rens," *The South Carolina Historical and Genealogical Magazine*,
7 (1906): 3-11, 53-68, 115-29, 179-93; 8 (1907): 3-18, 57-
68, 123-31, 181-88; 9: (1908): 3-8, 59-68, 109-14, 173-80.

Government Documents

*American State Papers, Legislative and Executive, of the Congress of
   the United States.* 38 vols. Washington: Gales and Seaton, 1832-
   1861.

*Annals of Congress: The Debates and Proceedings in the Congress of
   the United States.* 42 vols. Washington: Gales and Seaton, 1834-
   1852.

Barck, Dorothy C., ed. *Minutes of the Committee and of the First
   Commission for Detecting and Defeating Conspiracies in the State
   of New York, December 11, 1776 – September 23, 1778.* Collections of the New-York Historical Society. New York: Printed
   for the Society, 1924-1925.

*Calendar of Historical Manuscripts Relating to the War of the Rev-
   olution in the Office of the Secretary of State, Albany, New York.*
   2 vols. Albany: Weed, Parsons and Co., 1868.

Ford, Worthington C., et al., eds. *Journals of the Continental
   Congress.* 34 vols. Washington: Government Printing Office,
   1904-1937.

*Journal of the Assembly of the State of New York, Ninth Session,
   January-May 1786.* New York: Samuel and John Loudon, 1786.

*Journals of the Provincial Congress, Provincial Convention, Com-
   mittee of Safety and Council of Safety of the State of New York,
   1775-1776-1777.* 2 vols. Albany: Thurlow Weed, 1842.

*Minutes of the Council of Appointment, State of New York, April 2,
   1778 - May 3, 1779.* Collections of the New-York Historical
   Society. New York: Printed for the Society, 1925.

The Public Statutes at Large of the United States of America. Edited
   by Richard Peters. Vol. I. Boston: Charles C. Little and James
   Brown, 1850.

Sullivan, James, ed. *Minutes of the Albany Committee of Correspondence, 1775-1778.* 2 vols. Albany: The University of the
   State of New York, 1923-1925.

Manuscript Collections

American Antiquarian Society, Worcester, Massachusetts - AAS
    Andrew Craigie Papers
Baker Memorial Library, Harvard University, Graduate School
    of Business Administration, Cambridge, Massachusetts
    Daniel Parker Letter Book
Bank of New York Archives, New York City
    Financial Records, 1792, 1793, Office of Corporate Docu-
    mentation
William L. Clements Library, Ann Arbor, Michigan
    Nathanael Greene Papers
    Josiah Harmar Papers
    John Holker Papers
Columbia University Library, Special Collections, New York City
    - CUL
    John Jay Papers
    Gouverneur Morris Papers
Connecticut Historical Society, Hartford - CHS
    Jeremiah Wadsworth Papers
Historic Hudson Valley, Tarrytown, NY
    Philip VanCortlandt Memorandum Book [typescript]
Historical Society of Pennsylvania, Philadelphia - HSP
    Clement Biddle Letter Book
    Dreer Collections: Robert Morris Letters, Members of the Old
        Congress
    Etting Collection
    Gibson Papers
    Gratz Collection
    Hutchins Papers
    C. F. Jenkins Collection, Old Congress
    Irvine Papers
    Provincial Delegates Letters, 1754-1829
    Society Collection
Library of Congress, Washington, DC - LC
    Alexander Hamilton Papers
    John Holker Papers
    Thomas Jefferson Papers
    James Madison Papers
    Gouverneur Morris Papers

Robert Morris Papers
George Washington Papers
Massachusetts Historical Society, Boston - MHS
  William Heath Papers
  Thomas Jefferson Papers, Jefferson Coolidge Collection
  Henry Knox Papers
  Timothy Pickering Papers
  Washburn Collection
  Winthrop Sargent Papers
National Archives, Washington, DC - NA
  Records of the Federal Circuit Court, Eastern District of Pennsylvania, RG 21
  Records of the Loan of 1790 (Subscription Register of the Funded Debt) Vol. 548, New York, RG 53
  Register of the Treasury, Estimates and Statements for 1792, Vol. 134-T, RG 53
  Department of State, Miscellaneous Letters, 1790-99, RG 59
  Revolutionary War Records, War Department Collection, RG 93
  Miscellaneous Treasury Accounts, 1790-1894, Account 3508, RG 217
  Oliver Wolcott's Explanation of Accounts, 1792-1794, RG 217
  Ledger B, 1776-1789, Register's Office, RG 217
New-York Historical Society, New York City - NYHS
  William Alexander (Lord Stirling) Papers
  James Duane Papers
  William Duer Papers
  Hugh Hughes Papers
  John Laurance Papers
  Jonathan Lawrence and Melancton Smith Papers
  Robert Cambridge Livingston Letterbooks
  Robert R. Livingston Collection
  Alexander McDougall Papers
  Rutherfurd Collection
  Scioto and Ohio Land Company Papers
New York Public Library, New York City - NYPL
  Constable-Pierrepont Papers
  Emmett Collection
  Myers Collection

Philip Schuyler Papers
New York State Library, Albany - NYSL
New York (State) Courts, Supreme Court of Judicature
Washington [Charlotte] County, Records of the Court of
Common Pleas, Vol. I
John Williams Papers
Passaic County Historical Society, Paterson, NJ - PCHS
Society for Useful Manufactures Collection
Paterson Public Library, Paterson, NJ
Minutes of the Directors of the Society for
Establishing Useful Manufactures, Vol. I, 1791-1928
Pierpont Morgan Library, New York City
Marquis de Lafayette Papers

Newspapers

The Daily Advertiser (New York), 1786-1792.
The Daily Gazette (New York), January-March 1792
The Diary (New York), February-April 1792
Dunlap's American Daily Advertiser (Philadelphia), July 1778-
March 1779
Gazette of the United States (Philadelphia), January-May 1792
The Gentleman's Magazine and Historical Chronicle (London),
January-June 1823
The Independent Journal (New York), October-December 1787
The Journal (New York), January-August 1792
The New York Journal (New York, Kingston, Poughkeepsie),
1776-1779
The Pennsylvania Gazette (Philadelphia), January-March 1779,
January-March 1792
The Weekly Museum (New York), April 1791-May 1792

SECONDARY SOURCES

Unpublished Material

Baker, LeGrand Liston, "The Board of Treasury, 1784-1789:
Responsibility Without Power," Ph. D. diss., University of
Wisconsin, 1972.

Bowers, Paul Chadwick, Jr., "Richard Henry Lee and the Continental Congress, 1774-1779," Ph. D. diss., Duke University, 1965.

Brooks, Robin, "Melancton Smith: New York Anti-Federalist, 1744-1798," Ph. D. diss., University of Rochester, 1964.

Chase, Philander Dean, "Baron Von Steuben in the War of Independence," Ph. D. diss., Duke University, 1972.

Chernow, Barbara Ann, "Robert Morris: Land Speculator, 1790-1801," Ph. D. diss., Columbia University, 1974.

Davis, William, "William Constable, New York Merchant and Land Speculator, 1772-1803," Ph. D. diss., Harvard University, 1957.

DeLorenzo, Dominic D., "The New York Federalists: Forces of Order," Ph. D. diss., Columbia University, 1979.

Dolan, Graham Philip, "Major General William Heath and the First Years of the American Revolution," Ph. D. diss., Boston University, 1966.

Egan, Clifford, "Daniel Parker: An Exploratory Sketch," paper presented at the July 1981 meeting of the Society for Historians of the Early American Republic, Siena College, Loudonville, NY.

Fitch, Keith William, "American Nationalism and the Revolution, 1763-1776: A Case Study of the Movement in the Colony of New York," Ph. D. diss., Purdue University, 1972.

Jenks, Major B., "George Clinton and New York State Politics, 1775 to 1801," Ph. D. diss., Cornell University, 1936.

Jones, Robert F., "Stock Speculation and the Revolutionary Debt: Andrew Craigie, 1787-1792," paper presented at the July 1981 meeting of the Society for Historians of the Early American Republic, Siena College, Loudonville, NY.

Kline, Mary-Jo, "Gouverneur Morris and the New Nation, 1775-1788," Ph. D. diss., Columbia University, 1970.

Nuxoll, Elizabeth M., "Congress and the Munitions Merchants: the Secret Committee of Trade During the American Revolution, 1775-1777," Ph. D. diss., City University of New York, 1979.

Platt, John D., Jr., "Jeremiah Wadsworth: Federalist Entrepreneur," Ph. D. diss., Columbia University, 1966.

Rolater, Frederic Strickland, "The Continental Congress: A Study in the Origin of American Public Administration, 1774-1781," Ph. D. diss., University of Southern California, 1970.

Rommel, John George, Jr., "Richard Varick: New York Aristocrat," Ph. D. diss., Columbia University, 1966.

Sterling, David L., "New York Patriarch: A Life of John Pintard, 1759-1844," Ph. D. diss., New York University, 1958.

Taylor, Clifton James, "John Watts of Colonial and Revolutionary New York," Ph. D. diss., University of Tennessee, 1981.

Articles and Essays

Abernethy, Thomas P. "Commercial Activities of Silas Deane in France," *The American Historical Review*, 39 (1934): 477-85.

Bates, Whitney K. "Northern Speculators and Southern State Debts: 1790," *The William and Mary Quarterly*, 3 s., 19 (1962): 30-48.

Boyd, Julian P. "The First Conflict in the Cabinet," Appendix to Julian P. Boyd, ed., *The Papers of Thomas Jefferson* (Princeton, 1971), 18: 611-88.

_____. "Silas Deane: Death by a Kindly Teacher of Treason?" *The William and Mary Quarterly*, 3 s., 16 (1959): 165-87, 319-42, 515-50.

Brown, Margaret L. "William Bingham, Eighteenth Century Magnate," *The Pennsylvania Magazine of History and Biography*, 61 (1937): 387-434.

Carp, E. Wayne. "The Origins of the Nationalist Movement of 1780-1783," *The Pennsylvania Magazine of History and Biography*, 108 (1983): 363-92.

Collier, Christopher. "Continental Bonds in Connecticut," *The William and Mary Quarterly*, 3 s., 22 (1965): 646-51.

Cooke, Jacob E. "Tench Coxe, Alexander Hamilton, and the Encouragement of American Manufactures," *The William and Mary Quarterly*, 3 s., 32 (1975): 369-92.

Davis, R. E. "The Circulating Medium of the Period of the Confederation," *The Numismatic Scrapbook Magazine*, 4 (1938): 1-6.

Dawes, Ephraim Cutler. "The Scioto Purchase in 1787," *Magazine of American History*, 22 (1889): 470-82.

Ferguson, E. James. "Business, Government and Congressional

Investigation in the Revolution," *The William and Quarterly*, 3 s., 16 (1959): 293-318.

Fleming, R. H. "Phynn, Ellice and Company," *Toronto University Contributions to Canadian Economics*, 4 (1932): 7-42.

Glaser, Lynn. "Continental Currency," *The Numismatic Scrapbook Magazine*, 29 (1963): 3454-64.

Haskett, Richard C. "William Paterson, Attorney-General of New Jersey: Public Office and Private Profit in the American Revolution," *The William and Mary Quarterly*, 3 s., 7 (1950): 26-38.

Hulburt, Archer B. "Andrew Craigie and the Scioto Associates," *Proceedings, American Antiquarian Society*, n.s., 23 (1913): 222-36.

———. "The Methods and Operations of the Scioto Group of Speculators," *Mississippi Valley Historical Review*, 1 (1914-15): 502-15; 2 (1915-16): 56-73.

Johnston, Henry P. "New York After the Revolution," *Magazine of American History*, 29 (1893): 305-31.

Jones, Robert F. "Economic Opportunism and the Constitution in New York State: The Example of William Duer," *New York History*, 68 (1987): 357-72.

Jordan, John W. "Bethlehem During the Revolution," *Pennsylvania Magazine of History and Biography*, 12 (1888): 385-406; 13 (1889): 71-89.

———. "The Military Hospitals at Bethlehem and Lititz during the Revolution," *Pennsylvania Magazine of History and Biography*, 20 (1896): 137-57.

Livermore, Shaw. "The Advent of Corporations in New York," *New York History*, 16 (1935): 286-98.

Morgan, A. Wayne. "The Origins and the Establishment of the first BUS," *Business History Review*, 30 (1956): 472-92.

Nelson, John R., Jr. "Alexander Hamilton and American Manufacturing: A Reexamination," *Journal of American History*, 65 (1978-79): 971-95.

Riley, James C. "Foreign Credit and Fiscal Stability: Dutch Investment in the United States, 1781-1794," *Journal of American History*, 65 (1978-79): 654-78.

Simpson, Sarah H. J. "The Federal Procession in the City of New York," The New-York Historical Society *Quarterly Bulletin*, 9 (1925): 39-56.

Tailby, Donald G. "Foreign Interest Remittances by the United

States, 1785-1787: A Story of Malfeasance," *Business History Review*, 41 (1967): 161-76.

Tuttle, J. F. "Hibernia Furnace and the Surrounding Country in the Revolutionary War," *Proceedings of the New Jersey Historical Society*, 2 s., 6 (1880): 148-73.

Wettereau, James. "Branches of the First Bank of the United States," *Journal of Economic History*, Suppl. (Dec. 1942), 66-100.

Books

Abbott, Wilbur C. *New York in the American Revolution*. New York: Macmillan, 1929.

Abernethy, Thomas Perkins. *Western Lands and the American Revolution*. New York: Appleton-Century, 1937.

Alden, John Richard. *General Charles Lee: Traitor or Patriot?* Baton Rouge: Louisiana State University Press, 1951.

——. *Stephen Sayre: American Revolutionary Adventurer*. Baton Rouge: Louisiana State University Press, 1983.

Alexander, DeAlva Stanwood. *A Political History of the State of New York*. 3 vols. New York: Henry Holt, 1906-1909.

Alexander, Edward P. *A Revolutionary Conservative: James Duane of New York*. New York: Columbia University Press, 1938.

Anderson, William G. *The Price of Liberty: The Public Debt of the American Revolution*. Charlottesville: University Press of Virginia, 1983.

Barck, Oscar Theodore, Jr. *New York City During the War for Independence with Special Reference to the Period of British Occupation*. New York: Columbia University Press, 1938.

Barrett, Walter [Joseph A. Scoville]. *The Old Merchants of New York City*. 5 vols. New York: Thomas R. Knox & Company, 1885.

Becker, Carl L. *The History of Political Parties in the Province of New York*. Madison: University of Wisconsin Press, 1960.

Belote, Thomas T. "The Scioto Speculation and the French Settlement at Gallipolis," *University Studies*, University of Cincinnati, 2 s., Vol. III (1907).

Bonomi, Patricia U. *A Factious People: Politics and Society in Colonial New York*. New York: Columbia University Press, 1971.

Brant, Irving. *James Madison: Father of the Constitution, 1787-1800*. New York: Bobbs-Merrill, 1950.

Breck, Samuel. *Historical Sketch of Continental Paper Money*. Philadelphia: A. C. Kline, 1863.

Brunhouse, Robert L. *The Counter Revolution in Pennsylvania, 1776-1790*. Harrisburg: Pennsylvania Historical and Museum Commission, 1942.

Buell, Rowena. *The Memoirs of Rufus Putnam*. Boston: Houghton, Mifflin, 1903.

Burnett, Edmund Cody. *The Continental Congress*. New York: Macmillan, 1941.

Callahan, North. *Henry Knox, General Washington's General*. New York: Rinehart, 1958.

Carp, E. Wayne. *To Starve the Army at Pleasure: Continental Army Administration and American Political Culture, 1775-1783*. Chapel Hill: University of North Carolina Press, 1984.

Champagne, Roger J. *Alexander McDougall and the American Revolution in New York*. Schenectady, NY: Union College Press, 1975.

Cochran, Thomas C. *New York in the Confederation: An Economic Study*. Philadelphia: University of Pennsylvania Press, 1932.

Coleman, Peter J. *Debtors and Creditors in America: Insolvency, Imprisonment for Debt and Bankruptcy, 1606-1900*. Madison: State Historical Society of Wisconsin, 1974.

Cooke, Jacob E. *Alexander Hamilton*. New York: Charles Scribner's Sons, 1982.

_____ . *Tench Coxe and the Early Republic*. Chapel Hill: University of North Carolina Press, 1978.

Dangerfield, George R. *Chancellor Robert R. Livingston of New York, 1746-1813*. New York: Harcourt, Brace, 1960.

Davis, Joseph Stancliffe. *Essays in the Earlier History of American Corporations*. 2 vols. Cambridge, MA: Harvard University Press, 1917.

DelMar, Alexander. *The History of Money in America From the Earliest Times to the Establishment of the Constitution*. New York: Cambridge Encyclopedia Company, 1917.

DePauw, Linda Grant. *The Eleventh Pillar: New York State and the Federal Constitution*. Ithaca, NY: Cornell University Press, 1966.

Dillon, Dorothy R. *The New York Triumvirate: A Study of the Legal and Political Careers of William Livingston, John Morin*

Scott, William Smith, Jr. New York: Columbia University Press, 1949.

Downes, Randolph C. *Council Fires on the Upper Ohio.* Pittsburgh: University of Pittsburgh Press, 1940, repr., 1968.

Duer, William Alexander. *A Course of Lectures on the Constitutional Jurisprudence of the United States.* New York: Harper & Bros., 1874.

———. *The Life of William Alexander, Earl of Stirling.* Collections of the New Jersey Historical Society, Vol. II. New York: Wiley & Putnam, 1847.

Dunlap, William. *History of the New Netherlands, Province of New York, and State of New York to the Adoption of the Federal Constitution.* 2 vols. New York: Printed for the Author, 1839-1840. Vol. II.

East, Robert A. *Business Enterprise in the American Revolutionary Era.* New York: Columbia University Press, 1938, repr., 1964.

Ellery, Eloise. *Brissot de Warville.* Boston: Houghton Mifflin, 1915.

Ferguson, E. James. *The Power of the Purse: A History of American Public Finance, 1776-1790.* Chapel Hill: University of North Carolina Press, 1961.

Fitzpatrick, John C. *George Washington Himself.* Indianapolis: Bobbs, Merrill, 1933.

Flexner, James T. *The Traitor and the Spy: Benedict Arnold and John André.* New York: Harcourt, Brace, 1953, repr. as *The Benedict Arnold Case.* New York: Collier, 1962.

Flick, Alexander C., ed. *History of the State of New York.* 10 vols. New York State Historical Association. New York: Columbia University Press, 1933-1937.

———. *Loyalism in New York During the American Revolution.* New York: Columbia University Press, 1901.

———. *The American Revolution in New York: Its Political, Social, and Economic Significance.* Albany: University of the State of New York, 1926.

Foner, Eric. *Tom Paine and Revolutionary America.* New York: Oxford University Press, 1976.

Fox, Dixon Ryan. *Yankees and Yorkers.* New York: New York University Press, 1940.

Freeman, Douglass Southall. *George Washington, Leader of the Revolution, 1776-1778.* New York: Charles Scribner's Sons, 1951.

Gerlach, Don R. *Philip Schuyler and the American Revolution in*

New York, 1733-1777. Lincoln: University of Nebraska Press, 1964.

Gilje, Paul A. *The Road to Mobocracy: Popular Disorder in New York City, 1763-1834*. Chapel Hill: University of North Carolina Press, 1987.

Gottschalk, Louis. *Lafayette Joins the American Army*. Chicago: University of Chicago Press, 1937.

Greene, Francis Vinton. *The Revolutionary War and the Military Policy of the United States*. New York: Charles Scribner's Sons, 1911.

Hamilton, Allen McLane. *The Intimate Life of Alexander Hamilton*. New York: Charles Scribner's Sons, 1911.

Hamm, Margherita Arlina. *Famous Families of New York*. 2 vols. New York: G. P. Putnam's Sons, 1902.

Hammond, Bray. *Banks and Politics in America from the Revolution to the Civil War*. Princeton: Princeton University Press, 1957.

Hammond, Jabez D. *The History of Political Parties in the State of New York from the Ratification of the Federal Constitution to December, 1840*. Albany: C. Van Benthuysen, 1842.

Harrington, Virginia D. *The New York Merchant on the Eve of the Revolution*. New York: Columbia University Press, 1935.

Hatch, Louis Clinton. *The Administration of the American Revolutionary Army*. New York: Longmans, Green, 1904.

Henderson, H. James. *Party Politics in the Continental Congress*. New York: McGraw-Hill, 1974.

Higgins, Ruth L. *Expansion in New York with Especial Reference to the Eighteenth Century*. Columbus: Ohio State University, 1931.

Hill, William H. *History of Washington County, New York*. Fort Edward, NY: Honeywood Press, 1932.

_____ . *A Brief History of the Printing Press in Washington, Saratoga, and Warren Counties, State of New York*. Fort Edward, NY: Privately Printed, 1930.

History and Biography of Washington County and the Town of Queensbury, New York. Richmond, IN: Gresham Publishing, 1894.

History of Washington County, New York. Philadelphia: Everts & Ensign, 1878.

Holdsworth, John Thomas, Davis R. Dewey. *The First and Second Banks of the United States*. 61 Cong., 2 Sess., Senate Doc. 571. Washington: Government Printing Office, 1910.

Hufeland, Otto. *Westchester County During the American Revolution, 1775-1783*. White Plains: Westchester County Historical Society, 1926.

Hughes, Rupert. *George Washington*. 3 vols. New York: Morrow, 1926-1930.

Jacobs, James R. *The Beginning of the U. S. Army, 1783-1812*. Princeton: Princeton University Press, 1947.

Johnson, Victor Leroy. *The Administration of the American Commissariat during the Revolutionary War*. Philadelphia: Privately Printed, 1941.

Jones, Robert F. *George Washington*. Boston: G. K. Hall for Twayne, 1979, rev. ed., Fordham University Press, 1986.

Knollenberg, Bernhard. *George Washington and the American Revolution*. New York: Macmillan, 1940.

Kohn, Richard H. *The Eagle and the Sword: The Beginning of the Military Establishment in America*. New York: Free Press, 1975.

Konkle, Burton Alva. *Thomas Willing and the first American Financial System*. Philadelphia: University of Pennsylvania Press, 1937.

Lossing, Benson J. *The Life and Times of Philip Schuyler*. 2 vols. New York: Sheldon, 1872-1873.

Main, Jackson Turner. *The Sovereign States, 1775-1783*. New York: Franklin Watts, 1973.

Malone, Dumas. *Jefferson and the Rights of Man*. Boston: Little, Brown, 1951.

Mason, Bernard. *The Road to Independence: The Revolutionary Movement in New York, 1773-1777*. Lexington: University of Kentucky Press, 1966.

McCoy, Drew. *The Elusive Republic: Political Economy in Jeffersonian America*. Chapel Hill: University of North Carolina Press, 1980, Norton pb. repr.

Miller, John C. *Alexander Hamilton: Portrait in Paradox*. New York: Harper, 1961.

Miner, Clarence E. *The Ratification of the Federal Constitution by the State of New York*. New York: Columbia University Press, 1921.

Mitchell, Broadus. *Alexander Hamilton*. 2 vols. New York: Macmillan, 1957-1962.

Monaghan, Frank. *John Jay: Defender of Liberty*. New York: Bobbs-Merrill, 1935.

Morris, Richard B. *The Peacemakers: The Great Powers & American Independence.* New York: Harper & Row, 1965.

Nelson, Paul. *General Horatio Gates.* Baton Rouge: Louisiana State University Press, 1976.

———. *William Alexander, Lord Stirling.* University, AL: University of Alabama Press, 1987.

Onuf, Peter S. *The Origins of the Federal Republic: Jurisdictional Controversies in the United States, 1775-1787.* Philadelphia: University of Pennsylvania Press, 1983.

Palmer, John McAuley. *General Von Steuben.* New Haven, CN: Yale University Press, 1937.

Palmer, R. R. *The Age of the Democratic Revolution: The Challenge.* Princeton: Princeton University Press, 1959.

Pickering, Octavius. *The Life of Timothy Pickering.* 4 vols. Vols. II-IV written by Charles Wentworth Upham. Boston: Little, Brown, 1867-1873.

Pomerantz, Sydney I. *New York: An American City, 1783-1803; A Study of Urban Life.* New York: Columbia University Press, 1938.

Prucha, Francis Paul. *The Sword of the Republic: The United States Army on the Frontier, 1783-1846.* New York: Macmillan, 1969.

Rakove, Jack N. *The Beginnings of National Politics: An Interpretative History of the Continental Congress.* New York: Knopf, 1979.

Rossie, Jonathan Gregory. *The Politics of Command in the American Revolution.* Syracuse: University of Syracuse Press, 1974.

Rossman, Kenneth R. *Thomas Mifflin and the Politics of the American Revolution.* Chapel Hill: University of North Carolina Press, 1952.

Sanders, Jenning Bryan. *Evolution of the Executive Departments of the Continental Congress, 1774-1789.* Chapel Hill: University of North Carolina Press, 1935.

Smith, Page. *John Adams.* 2 vols. Garden City, NY: Doubleday, 1962.

Smith, Philip C. F. *The Empress of China.* Philadelphia: Philadelphia Maritime Museum, 1984.

Smith, Thomas E. V. *The City of New York in the Year of Washington's Inauguration, 1789.* New York: Anson D. F. Randolph, 1889.

Spaulding, Ernest Wilder. *New York in the Critical Period, 1783-1789.* New York: Columbia University Press, 1932.

_____ . *His Excellency George Clinton: Critic of the Constitution*. New York: Macmillan, 1938.

Stewart, Donald H. *The Opposition Press of the Federalist Period*. Albany: State University of New York Press, 1969.

Stone, William L. *Washington County, New York, Its History to the Close of the Nineteenth Century*. New York: New York History Company, 1901.

Thach, Charles C., Jr. *The Creation of the Presidency, 1775-1789: A Study in Constitutional History*. Baltimore: Johns Hopkins University Press, 1923.

Tilghman, Oswald. *Memoir of Colonel Tench Tilghman*. Albany: Munsell, 1876.

Todd, Charles Burr. *Life and Letters of Joel Barlow*. New York: G. P. Putnam's Sons, 1886.

Van Doren, Carl. *Secret History of the American Revolution*. New York: Viking, 1941.

Vattel, Emmerich de. *The Law of Nations; or, Principles of the Law of nature . . . Tr. from the French*. London: J. Newbury, 1760, '59.

VerSteeg, Clarence L. *Robert Morris: Revolutionary Financier*. Philadelphia: University of Pennsylvania Press, 1954.

Walters, Raymond, Jr. *Albert Gallatin: Jeffersonian Financier and Diplomat*. New York: Macmillan, 1957.

Ward, Harry M. *The Department of War, 1781-1795*. Pittsburgh: University of Pittsburgh Press, 1962.

Werner, Edgar A. *Civil List and Constitutional History of the Colony and State of New York*. Albany: Weed, Parsons, 1888.

White, Leonard D. *The Federalists: A Study in Administrative History*. New York: Macmillan, 1948

Wilson, James Grant. *John Pintard, Founder of the New-York Historical Society*. New York: Printed for the Society, 1902.

Woodress, James. *A Yankee's Odyssey: the Life of Joel Barlow*. Philadelphia: Lippincott, 1958.

Young, Alfred F. *The Democratic-Republicans of New York: The Origins, 1763-1797*. Chapel Hill: University of North Carolina Press, 1967.

Miscellaneous

Gaines, Pierce Welch. *Political Works of Concealed Authorship During the Administrations of Washington, Adams, and Jefferson,*

1789-1809, with Attributions. New Haven: Yale University Library, 1959.

McCusker, John J. *Money and Exchange in Europe and America, 1600-1775.* Chapel Hill: University of North Carolina Press, 1967.

Purple, Edwin R. *Genealogical Notes of the Colden Family in America.* New York: Privately Printed, 1873.

Roseboom, Joseph R., comp. *A Biographical Dictionary of Early American Jews . . . through 1800.* Lexington: University of Kentucky Press, 1960.

Vail, R. W. G., ed. *The Voice of the Old Frontier.* Philadelphia: University of Pennsylvania Press, 1949.

Wilson, James Grant, and John Fiske, eds. *Appleton's Cyclopedia of American Biography.* 6 vols. New York: Appleton, 1886-1889.

Yeoman, R. S. *A Guide Book of United States Coins.* 19th ed. Racine, WI: Whitman Publishing Co., 1966.

INDEX

Note: All locations are given according to modern boundaries.

www.ingramcontent.com/pod-product-compliance
Lightning Source LLC
Chambersburg PA
CBHW080923100426

42812CB00007B/2353